M000159764

TAKE THIS WAR AND SHOVE IT!

"Mah fellow Americans, though it makes mah heart heavy, I cain't say I'm surprised to see another book painting me as a garldanged villain. I ask you to consider my plight: that prick Kennedy painted me into a tight-ass corner. And let's get this out of the damned way: I had nothing, nothing to do with the hit put on that boy in Dallas that November day in '63. Now it's true—and I'm gonna show you that a politician is capable of telling the truth occasionally—that while representing the Lone Star State in the Senate I did make remarks to the effect that if Ho Chi Minh wasn't knocked on his ass soon, any yellow dwarf with a pocketknife could threaten the power of the United States. But I guar-an-damn-tee you this: had I been given just a few minutes alone in a confined space with that little bastard Ho, you'd be living in a whole different world now, a world where absolutely no one would dare challenge US power. I was famed for mah powers of persuasion, remember. I would've grabbed that little bastard by his testicles and squeezed the Communism right out of him, every last drop! See, where I come from, we call that holding a rational discussion to settle our differences. As for this book I was asked to comment on, I can only say I wish this little Commie bastard's activities had been brought to mah personal attention at the time he was demonstrating against the war in his Army uniform—what a disgrace!—so I could've seen to it he got the punishment he deserved. The impudence! Defying his Commander-in-Chief publicly! Is this guy colored? I didn't get the full lowdown on that. You know, colored people—black, brown, red, yellow—they were the bane of my life! And buh-leeve you me, they were really gettin' uppity back there in the 1960s. It's a goddamn pity! Anyhow, I could've set this fellow straight as quick as I would've done with Ho Chi Minh. I would've whipped out mah big boy—it's true what they say, 'Everything is bigger in Texas'—and I woulda beat that little shit about the head and shoulders with mah pecker until he woulda begged to be sent to duty in Veetnam pronto-like, I shit you not! A good ol' Texas ass-whuppin' is all that boy needed. Now, have I ever told you about the time, down by the banks of the Perdenales River, that I … blah, blah, blah."

—the ghost of President Lyndon Baines Johnson

"Despite the intense heat where I reside nowadays, which affects one's ability to concentrate, Nixon did read this revolting anti-American screed. He's your real-McCoy hardcore little Commie bastard, this writer. Trust me, I know. I built my whole political career on combatting the Red Menace, you know. And let me just say, at this point, that you really should read my Six Crises and other brilliant literary works. Anyhow, Nixon, unlike certain other US presidents, was/is a reader. And what I read in this fellow's memoir is unabashed hatred of our great nation. A nation I always strove to make greater, no matter the personal cost to me. And what was my reward for this? Why, those goddamn radic-libs, that McGovern and his whole crowd, and that lousy kike, Daniel Ellsberg—oh, don't get me started, the list would be too long!—they all conspired against me constantly. The whole Watergate thing was a frame-up, I tell you. Nixon was and is an innocent man. A true blue Patriot—make sure that comes through with a capital 'p,' whoever's editing this— laid low. They never liked me, the goddamn liberal Jew Establishment, with their lying liberal Jew media. I'll bet the guy who wrote this despicable memoir is a Jew, too. Always, always blabbing about my five-o'clock shadow and the sweaty upper lip thing! And sneering at my beautiful wife, Pat, and her good Republican cloth coat; my beautiful daughters, Julie and Tricia; even our little dog, Checkers. Nixon the villain! Dastardly Nixon! Impeach him, drive him from office. That was their game. Well, it's time to go dig up Agnew for our daily game of Canasta. Gotta watch him like a hawk, though, the cheating prick! So let me just say in closing: I can't understand why the Army didn't throw the book at this Commie bastard dissident soldier and put him away for a long, long time. I'm glad I served my country in a *Navy* uniform! Oh, and let me say one last thing: you don't have Nixon to kick around anymore, do you, you liberal media bastards?!"

—the ghost of President Richard M. Nixon

"I'm sorry, but I seem to have misplaced the book I was asked to comment on. You know, I played football in college before proper helmets were invented. Something about Vietnam, wasn't it? That was a hell of a fight, but the good old USA won in the end. Uh, that's correct, isn't it?"

—the ghost of President Gerald R. Ford

"Given a million more ground troops, a few trillion dollars and about 30 more years, I have no doubt I would have defeated General Giap and his minions. 'People's War' indeed! But those wimps in the US Congress tied the military's hands behind our backs and wouldn't let us *really* fight to win! I mean, everybody knows that, right? So hundreds of thousands of additional US troops would have died or been maimed for life, so what? You lousy civilian types, who don't know the meaning of service to your country—do you think war is a picnic? I was a soldier, I did my best in the quest for total victory. Don't blame me for the sabotage done by the diplomats. I hold my head high, and I'm still wearing my dress uniform. Here in Hell. It's a little uncomfortable, what with the heat down here, but I can take it. I will take it. Because I'm a man. Not a little faggot Pinko like the author of this pack of lies memoir you're holding in your hands for some reason."

—the ghost of General William Westmoreland, Commander of all US forces in Vietnam, 1964-1968

"What can I add to what these incredible patriots have already said about this atrocity of a book, this endless stream of libelous lies? The author even has the audacity to question the accuracy of the intel gathered by my Special Agents in the field! Had this Pinko's actions against our great country been brought more closely to my attention at the time, I would certainly have pushed the Army to prosecute him to the full extent of the law. His acts of dissent, which he thinks were protected as free speech, surely crossed the line into the realms of sedition, treason and lending aid to the enemy! He should have been consigned to the deepest dungeon available in a Federal penitentiary for the rest of his life. And I bet he's a queer, too! Most of your lousy Commies are, you know. Still a virgin when he was 21! Give me a break. Well, you must excuse me now, I have a nice new pair of high heels to try on. Oh, are you surprised I have special privileges down here? Heck, I made my first deal with the Prince of Darkness when I signed on with Attorney General Palmer to ferret out those filthy anarchist European immigrants who were coming into our great nation and contaminating our pure American blood. Decade after decade I served our nation selflessly, and all these little Commie creeps do is to keep carping about stuff like COINTELPRO! Get over it!"

—the ghost of John Edgar Hoover, Director of the FBI, 1924-1972

"I haven't read the book in question and I don't wish to. However, I am sure I am criticized in it. Anti-semitism! And let me just say that you shouldn't take my good friend Mr. Nixon's use of the term 'kike' seriously. We had a very warm personal relationship during my time in Dick's White House. He even invited me to pray with him when the Watergate thing was at peak crisis stage. Other than that, I have no comment. So go away!"

—**Henry Kissinger**, inexplicably still alive at time of publication

"As you should be aware, I'm not really a keen reader. Unless it's something praising me to the skies, as I deserve. But I had some of my people look into this book I was asked to comment on, and The Donald is not a happy camper! See, I really get pissed off by these liberal losers who are always whining about our Great Nation without contributing anything positive. Always trying to tear America down! Me, I'm a builder. But you know, the Politically Correct crowd, they were out for my blood from the first day of my presidency. And they stole my sacred landslide victory in the 2020 election! You've probably heard that enough times, but it still sticks in my craw. So, they tell me the guy who wrote this book demonstrated publicly against the Vietnam War while wearing his Army uniform. I wish I'd been Commander-in-Chief back then! I'd've shown this dirtbag how traitors were treated in the good old days! And let me say, for the record, that the pain of not being able to personally go whip Ho Chi Minh's ass was even greater for me than the physical pain from the bone spurs in my heels. You know, that condition that, unfortunately, kept me out of the military in my own youth. And that's all I'm gonna say about that. My bone spurs are killing me right now. I guess it's going to rain soon."

—**Donald J. Trump**, 45th President of the United States of America

＊ ＊ ＊

AUTHOR'S NOTE: The preceding is my personal expression of irritation at the trend in traditional publishing of printing pages of "advance praise" in the front of a book. I have attempted to inject some humor, but I am also making serious political commentary. Re-read the above if you doubt that. What follows in this book contains some incidents from real life that I hope you find amusing, but the tone is more somber. The subjects—war and peace, life and death, right versus wrong—could not be more serious, after all.

TAKE THIS WAR AND SHOVE IT!

To know what is right, and not to do it, is cowardice.

—attributed to Confucius, Chinese philosopher, c. 500 BC

Ex hoc militare imperatoribus vestris desisto. **(From this moment I no longer serve your emperors.)**

—Marcellus, Roman centurion who converted to Christianity, addressing his superiors before the assembled legions. Marcellus was promptly executed. (Quoted in Volume III of <u>The History of the Decline and Fall of the Roman Empire</u>, by Edward Gibbon)

. . . They said "Suppose the country is entering upon a war—where do you stand then? Do you arrogate to yourself the privilege of going your own way in the matter, in the face of the nation?"
"Yes," I said, "that is my position. If I thought it an unrighteous war I would say so. If I were invited to shoulder a musket in that cause and march under that flag, I would decline. I would not voluntarily march under this country's flag, nor any other, when it was my private judgment that the country was in the wrong."

—<u>Autobiography of Mark Twain, Volume 1</u>

[I]t is the considered belief of the writer . . . that wars are fought by the finest people that there are . . . but they are made, provoked and initiated by straight economic rivalries and by swine that stand to profit from them. I believe that all the people who stand to profit by a war and help provoke it should be shot on the first day it starts . . .

—Ernest Hemingway, in his Introduction to
1948 edition of <u>A Farewell to Arms</u>

Of nature the ancients loved to sing the beauty:
Moon and flowers, snow and wind, mist, hills and streams.
But in our days poems should contain verses steely,
And poets should form assault teams.

—Ho Chi Minh, <u>Prison Diary</u>; Foreign Languages
Publishing House; Hanoi, 1972

The bankers and the diplomats are going in the army,
We're going to make things easy cause it's all so new and strange;
We'll give them silver shovels when they have to dig a hole,
And they can sing in harmony when answering the roll,
They'll eat their old K-rations from a hand-embroidered box,
And when they die, we'll bring them home, and bury them in
Fort Knox.
(Chorus):
Oh, oh, we hate to see them go,
The gentlemen of distinction in the army.

—We Hate to See Them Go, *by Malvina Reynolds*
(Copyright 1958, Schroder Music Co.; renewed
1987. Used with permission.)

[I]t takes a certain amount of courage to go to war, but not as much as
to refuse to go to war.

—Joseph Heller, World War II veteran, author of <u>Catch-22</u>; interviewed in Paul Krassner's 'The Realist,' 1962

The only glory in war is in the imagination of those who were never
there.

—Mike Hastie, Army Medic, Vietnam

TAKE THIS WAR AND SHOVE IT!

A Most Unwilling Soldier 1967-1971

by

Gregory Laxer

Unbearable Truth Publications

Front cover photo credits Main image: the author's actual Army dress jacket with two authorized decorations, plus two decidedly not authorized/Fyr Drak Fabrications; upper left: napalm explosion, Michael Zysman/shutterstock.com; upper right: veterans' cemetery, Nadia Yong/shutterstock.com. *Cover design* Fyr Drak Fabrications (www.fyrdrak.com)

For permission requests, or to negotiate purchase
of bulk quantities of this book at a discount,
contact the author at www.gregorylaxer.com

Library of Congress Cataloging-in-
Publication Data has been applied for.

Print ISBN: 978-1-09839-391-5
eBook ISBN: 978-1-09839-392-2

Printed in the United States of America

DEDICATIONS

*To the peoples of Vietnam, Cambodia and Laos who still bear the scars—physical, emotional, and upon their countrysides—of my country's crimes against you: Were I invested with magical powers, I would erase all those scars in an instant. And to **Chuck Searcy**, US Navy veteran of the war who co-chairs Project RENEW, working to disarm the unexploded ordnance that continues to plague Vietnam a half-century after it was scattered.*

To the everyday citizens who found the courage to participate in the American Anti-War Movement, despite jaundiced glances from relatives, friends, neighbors, co-workers or employers.

Finally, to all who have been persecuted, prosecuted, imprisoned and worse for the "crime" of opposing unjust wars, or being "whistleblowers" against governmental wrongdoing.

* * *

In Memoriam, **Andrew Stapp** (1944-2014), founder and Chairman of the American Servicemen's Union

CONTENTS

PREFACE

The peculiar truth about truth is this: there are about seven billion versions of it at large, one for every human being on the planet. I am about to tell you the truth of the Vietnam War as I absorbed it, what I did to try to sabotage it from within the US military, and why. You will reach your own conclusions as to my actions having been admirable or "treasonous." Taking my anti-war stance public was not a quest for martyrdom or personal attention, but done in obedience to my conscience, in the hope of spreading the idea that unjust, <u>unjustified</u> war **can** be resisted. My simple wish is that I persuade someone, somewhere, to think very deeply before accepting the government's invitation to participate in or support war. Taking that idea one step further, if you know a young person thinking about enlisting in the US military today, you might offer them a copy of this book. The potential enlistee will find here the unvarnished reality of the military and its actions, which I argue have changed very little in the past half-century.

I am a member of "the baby boom" generation, conceived in the wave of hope and optimism that followed the defeat of the Fascist Axis Powers in World War II. But I have come to realize that mine should really be called **the Vietnam Generation**. No young male citizen in the United States was not touched, in one way or another, by the war. Some found ways to avoid it, but the existence of the draft hung over us all. And the mothers, sisters, lovers and spouses of young men were likewise affected. By no means did all young Americans oppose or try to resist the War Machine, but it was well-nigh impossible to pretend one could ignore it. Millions of us were sucked into the military and over 58,000 did not emerge alive. Those of us who survived physically are starting to die off from various causes. We who feel compelled to speak out about those years, those events, and the roles we played therein, hear the clock ticking loudly.

This being the memoir of a member of that generation, you will find herein tales of illicit drugs and a lot of Rock 'n' Roll. I am deeply passionate about music. I am something of a Musicology PhD. (music lover with Permanent hearing Damage). What about sex? You know, "sex and drugs and Rock 'n' Roll"? You'll find precious little. Whatever it is women want, I seem to lack it in spades, to coin a phrase. I tell you this upfront as a demonstration of my honesty.

At the time of my writing, the Vietnam Era remains a very divisive chapter in US history. During the Obama presidency the US Government launched a multi-year propaganda effort to "commemorate" the 50th anniversary of major events in the Vietnam War by revising history, painting its murderous activities as a "noble" undertaking, trying to show the military in the best possible light. This effort is scheduled to continue until 2025, which will mark a half-century since the United States suffered its ignominious but richly deserved defeat. In September 2017, the Public Broadcasting Service presented an 18-hour documentary film on the war, produced and directed by "America's Storyteller," Ken Burns, with his longtime associate Lynn Novick. I have some choice words for this project in **APPENDIX 8**.

The structure and language of this book

As I did not spring fully-formed from the head of Zeus to be subjected to the tender ministrations of the US Army, in **CHAPTER I** I tell you how I came into existence and found myself in the predicament of opposing the war, yet volunteering for military service. The ensuing chapters chronologically trace the course of my military "career." I conclude with an **EPILOGUE** titled "The Ghosts of Vietnam are Marching Still," summarizing my post-active-duty anti-war activity up to the final defeat of the invading US forces. In this segment I propose a three-pronged program to finally lay to rest the ghosts of the war. My necessary criticism of certain works of other authors on the subject of the war also appears here. This is followed by a lengthy, philosophically wide-ranging **ESSAY**, wherein I have the audacity to address the human condition, and finally several Appendixes of supplemental material.

During my time on active duty, I mailed 65 letters and postcards home to my parents. The salutation was almost always "Dear Folks," but the main aim was to try to assure my mother—possibly "the most Jewish non-Jewish mother on Earth"—that I was okay. My mother scrupulously preserved these missives and thought they might be worth publishing some day. I contemplated that idea over the years, but didn't pursue it for the longest time. The letters provide the chronological skeleton on which to hang my story. I had originally planned to publish all of them intact. Ultimately, I eliminated some letters entirely if they didn't discuss significant new developments. From the letters that do appear, I edited out discussion of most petty matters. But nothing has been edited out to try to avoid personal embarrassment. Thus, you will see in my earliest letters I used phrases like "colored people" and "negroes," before my consciousness became elevated on matters of race in American society.

In terms of the "mechanics" of my writing, I often enclose in quotation marks words whose authenticity I question or wish to mock. For example, I do not recognize that there was ever a legitimate entity called The Republic of South Vietnam, since outside powers artificially divided a nation. So you will see "south Vietnam" in this book. Ditto for "Viet Cong," since the Vietnamese guerrillas in the south of the country did not call themselves that. And speaking of Vietnam, the country's proper designation rendered in English is "Viet Nam," but in print media during the war years it was often rendered as a single word, and that's what I became accustomed to. I am well aware that there are multiple Americas, but I accede here at times to the common practice among US citizens of using "America" as synonymous with "the United States." The phrase "the Vietnam War," or "the American War in Vietnam," must be understood to encompass US military actions against the peoples of Cambodia and Laos as well. And you definitely will <u>not</u> see a phrase like "We [the USA] sent 50,000 additional troops" or "We killed X number of civilians." I was decidedly and militantly **not** a part of any such "we"!

Words from foreign languages that have not been incorporated into common English usage will appear in Italics. Terms from "hippie" lingo that have connotations differing from everyday meanings will first appear in quotation marks; once they've been explained they'll appear unadorned. Titles of books referenced will be underlined; titles of record albums and motion pictures will appear in Italics. With rare exceptions, I have disguised, to protect privacy, the names of all persons I encountered in the Army not openly engaged in opposing the war.

No incident in this book has been manufactured or exaggerated for effect, and no dialogue invented or spiced up with colorful language. When I say a statement is essentially verbatim, I would pretty well bet my life on its accuracy. I am blessed (cursed?) with an excellent memory—not infallible, but excellent.

Hereupon, then, follows the story of my personal response to being sucked into the insane vortex of an utterly unjustified war, how an individual of conscience interacted with the larger social forces of the era, and how all this molded the person I am today.

July 6, 2021

50th Anniversary of my "official" exit from the Army

CHAPTER I
"Little Boxes"

New York State 1948-1967

Little boxes on the hillside,
Little boxes made of ticky-tacky
Little boxes on the hillside,
Little boxes all the same . . .
And the people in the houses
All went to the university
Where they were put in boxes
And they came out all the same . . .

—Little Boxes, *by Malvina Reynolds*

The preparations for my arrival had been meticulously put in place. My mother had given up smoking during my gestation, and was taking protein supplements as well. Mom was about four months past her fortieth birthday that January day in 1948 when the labor pangs made themselves felt.

New York City was on the receiving end of one of its roughest winters since the Great Blizzard of 1888. In the Borough of Queens, passage on the roads was difficult. Somewhere the stars shone down, but not on Jackson Heights that night that stretched into day and finally saw me delivered. It was a long, painful ordeal for my mother. She would suffer lower back problems the rest of her life.

The foreshadows of coming events were falling across the world in far-off places. Masses of people were seeking their independence from domination by their former self-appointed "masters." In a relatively small nation called Vietnam, whose name let alone geographical location hardly anyone in America knew, France was reasserting itself. I was but two years old when war erupted in Korea. Nary a voice was raised here questioning the "need" for that conflict. As a male of the species born in the USA, I would eventually come to grips with the Vietnam War, for I would reach age 18 in 1966. Don't conclude that I am a fatalist—I merely have laid out historical facts. [See **APPENDIX 1:** A Condensed History of the Vietnam War.]

I was born to George W. and Hetty (Dawes) Laxer, having been preceded by a little over five years by my sister, Linda. On my father's side of our genealogy, Linda and I constituted only the second generation born in the United States. On my mother's side, the Dawes clan had supposedly been in New England since before the events that broke out in 1775. In terms of ancestry/ethnicity, you may mark me down as a true mongrel and I'll not be the least bit insulted.

My parents met after Hetty Dawes moved to Brooklyn, New York— quite a change from Ellsworth, Maine. After completing high school, she was working office jobs. George Laxer was working as a bank teller; the Market Crash of 1929 meant no college education for him. Money was too scarce for such a luxury. They found a shared interest in horseback riding, renting them by the hour in Cunningham Park in Queens County. Despite being 31 years of age, my father was called up for possible military service when the US entered World War II. A suspicious shadow on his lung X-ray (a touch of tuberculosis?) kept him from harm's way.

When I was still quite small, the family moved to the Flushing neighborhood of Queens. I couldn't have been more than three years of age when I first expressed my great interest in and love for Science. To learn how electricity works, I inserted the tips of the blades of a pair of all-metal scissors into a wall outlet. Lesson learned. I was told in later years I fairly flew backwards, sustaining a nasty gash on the back of my noggin when same encountered an iron radiator. An object in motion tends to remain in motion until acted upon by an external force. Point proved, Sir Isaac Newton!

Around this time, George was selling insurance policies for a company with a regional office in Trenton, New Jersey. He seized an opportunity to work for G.D. Searle, an up-and-coming pharmaceutical company head-quartered near Chicago. Dad was the last guy without a college degree this company ever hired as a "pharmaceutical detail man" (salesman in plain English) for the Metropolitan New York region. He managed to orga-nize his route efficiently enough that he sometimes snuck in a matinee movie or spent an afternoon hanging out at a stockbroker's office in swank Great Neck (Long Island), where he occasionally encountered 'Professor' Irwin Corey, the comedian who billed himself as 'The World's Foremost Authority.' Meanwhile, once there were children to raise, Hetty had become a classic stay-at-home housewife.

"All made of ticky-tacky": Pioneering suburbanites, 1952

Having come of age in the Great Depression, my parents were not profli-gate spenders. The frugality learned from his German Protestant mother allowed my father to move us into a freshly-constructed 3-bedroom single-level ranch house in the town of Syosset. Former potato fields on Long Island were sprouting Levittown-style developments such as this like weeds or, well, potatoes. Syosset is in northeastern Nassau County, inland from shoreline towns like Oyster Bay. Mom and Dad each had their own car. For a couple of summers Hetty commuted to the public beach at Oyster Bay to staff a watchtower, scanning the skies from dusk until midnight for possible sneak attacks by the Soviet Union. She was armed with Civil Defense Ground Observer Corps binoculars and a guidebook pointing out the "salient features" of Soviet aircraft as seen in silhouette. She occa-sionally reported unusual lights in the sky, but we never did fall victim to marauding Russkies.

A "walking encyclopedia"

Having been born early in the year, I started Kindergarten a bit later than most of my peers. By 6th Grade I was tied for title of tallest boy, approaching six feet. In South Grove Elementary School my grades were consistently good. As soon as I learned to read, I was hooked on that activity. Eyeglasses soon followed. I excelled in spelling bees, and you could be sure the last two students standing at the end would be myself and my arch-nemesis in this arena, Becky Williams. After I incurred a major laceration near my knee playing stickball out on the street, then managed to reopen the wound multiple times taking additional spills on the asphalt, I became a bit of a bookworm. Unquestionably, my brain was better at processing written words and ideas than coordinating my limbs. Science very quickly became my favorite subject. Any time the Sunday night Walt Disney TV program topic was a nature documentary, my parents and I were glued to the tube.

Even at that young age, my reading skewed heavily toward nonfiction. I wanted to know what made the world—nay, the Universe—tick. In school I acquired a reputation as a "walking encyclopedia." I pretty much had a photographic memory and didn't need to study much to do well on tests. Writing came pretty naturally to me. I attribute this to my habit of reading at every opportunity. Or perhaps it was a mutation that took place in my brain as it nearly boiled in its own juices when I was around age 11. Until I had my tonsils removed the following year, any kind of common cold or flu would trigger very high fevers. On this occasion, my temperature spiked to nearly 106 degrees, which is life-threatening. An alcohol bath was necessary to pull me back from the brink.

Early studies of sociological issues

I was but 12 years old, with perhaps still febrile brain—or 13, at the oldest— when I discovered the works of Henry David Thoreau. The "Essay on Civil Disobedience" grabbed me immediately. It was eye-opening to discover that Thoreau protested the US's seizure by force of a goodly chunk of what had been Mexico (the War of 1847-49) by refusing to pay his taxes, which led to his imprisonment, if only for one night. And then, of course, there were the Walden essays. My fascination with the natural world and what makes it tick was sufficient for me to take Thoreau profoundly to heart.

I was keenly following the struggle for civil rights for black Americans and other minority groups. The Reverend Dr. Martin Luther King, Jr. was already a well-known figure in 1960, when I entered junior high school. Surpassing as an educational tool all the fine lectures in our school system about "liberty and justice for all" and "democracy" was the reality brought every evening into our living rooms, courtesy of the national TV newscasts. But this ugliness was not confined to the Deep South. It wasn't until the early '60s that a black family managed to purchase a home in Syosset. The house was promptly firebombed. My own admiration for the courage of those fighting for civil rights was unbounded. I started to expand my reading from hard Science to societal issues, pushed on by Dr. King's contemporary writings. Also, John Howard Griffin's <u>Black Like Me</u> (published 1961) made a big impression on me. Having found a way to chemically darken his skin, the white author passed himself off as a black man in the American South. The book recounted the hostility and discrimination he experienced as a result.

From Thoreau I moved on to Gandhi, essays on non-violence by Count Leo Tolstoy, and spiritual works by Thomas Merton and Pierre Teilhard de Chardin. I was sufficiently open-minded to wade into books by philosophers like these who dabbled in poetry and mysticism. I saw Earth's first artificial satellite, the USSR's famous Sputnik, pass right over our yard in Syosset in 1957, just where and when The NY Times had indicated. Humans had started to reach for the Cosmos, though not for entirely the right reasons. I very much wanted there to be intelligent life elsewhere, and I was ready to greet its ambassadors any time they might condescend to visit.

Behold the 12-year-old misanthrope

Looking at the state of the world—the world Man had produced, not Nature—made me more than a little unfond of the human race. Before Americans started hearing the name of the country called Vietnam, there were plenty of conflicts raging on planet Earth. Any perceived difference between people—racial, religious, cultural—would be seized as an excuse for mutual slaughter. Great swaths of the world still suffered from tropical diseases and malnutrition. The "advanced nations" seemed to only be paying lip service to their woes. My feelings of malaise were certainly not unique. The young are inherently skeptical of the status quo in any society that allows a modicum of independent thought. No one will ever know if it was the feeling of despair about the future, with the prospect of nuclear war constantly hanging over our heads, that drove a member of our Syosset High Class of '66 to hang himself in our sophomore year. But I certainly wouldn't rule it out.

I had close friends growing up, certainly. One of them, Mark Rosenstein, turned me on to Joseph Heller's brilliant semi-autobiographical war novel, Catch-22. The social satire displayed in the early years of MAD Magazine influenced my sensibilities as well. In junior and senior high school, I retained a small band of good friends but I was never part of any clique. I had friends among the jocks and friends among the eggheads (the term "nerd" had yet to appear). I had friends who accompanied me to drag strips, and friends who wrote poetry. Occasionally I contributed a humorous work to the Syosset High School newspaper, The Pulse. I enrolled in Creative Writing and my short story about racial injustice was published in the school literary journal. Other elective classes I gravitated to were Journalism and Photography.

I dodged being labeled an egghead by starting to work out with weights at age 14. I weighed 210 pounds by age 16, with upper arms among the biggest in school. My bodybuilding led to my being recruited for the Track & Field team for the Shot Put and Discus Throw, though I wasn't much more than mediocre in my events. But the camaraderie of being part of a team chipped away at my icy feelings toward the human race. I emerged somewhat from my shell. I appointed myself an honorary cheerleader (from the bleachers) at our football and basketball games. Syosset was a contender for top spot in quite a few sports within Nassau County in those years.

I developed crushes on various schoolmates, but was too shy to pursue them. I was one of the weirdos who skipped both Junior and Senior Proms. Scorning the conventional wisdom that these were must-attend events also allowed escaping the pain of rejection in seeking dates. For that matter, I felt no compulsion to participate in our senior Graduation ceremony, but my parents insisted I do so.

As the years went by, my enthusiasm for school had waned. I could have been pretty well a straight-A student had I applied myself. I pursued with relish, on my own time, what truly interested me: Paleontology, Anthropology, Sociology. I read Robert Ardrey's speculations on human evolution, <u>African Genesis</u>, and later his <u>The Territorial Imperative</u>. I read <u>On Aggression</u> by Konrad Lorenz, seeking answers to Man's apparent innate love of violence. I had a solid 'B' average overall by senior year, good enough for acceptance at the three universities to which I applied: Ohio State, Penn State and Syracuse University. I had chosen Journalism for my Major.

Far more importantly, I had made this determination while still in my junior year at Syosset High: I would **not** participate in the US war against the people of Vietnam in any way, shape or manner. I had made it through my school years without engaging in any real physical altercation with anyone. Though I'd yet to encounter the term *machismo*, I found fighting pretty damned stupid. I had embraced pacifism as a way of life, in the spirit of Gandhi and Dr. King.

Realities of "The Great Society": Violence abroad, violence at home

Violence is as American as cherry pie.

—H. 'Rap' Brown, militant civil rights activist, c. 1967

The evening newscasts were still bringing into our American living rooms images of human beings being brutally suppressed as they struggled for the most elementary rights all our citizens supposedly were entitled to. President Lyndon B. Johnson, having succeeded the assassinated John F. Kennedy, was in a bind. Nations around the globe—particularly on the African continent—that had formerly been ruled directly by "the Great Powers" were achieving a measure of independence. Was it possible to "win their hearts and minds" for the Western model of "democracy" and steer them away from aligning with the Soviet Bloc or Chairman Mao's People's Republic of China? Kennedy had sent the first significant number of troops into Vietnam, in the guise of "advisers"; turning back from this "holy" mission to "contain the spread of Communism" was not an option for an American president.

The TV coverage of what was happening on the home front was being seen around the world and Sheriff 'Bull' Connor, leading the attacks on Dr. King's civil rights crusaders in Alabama, did not make an appealing ambassador to the developing world. So Johnson's brain trust hatched the concept of "The Great Society." We would have "guns and butter" both: the guns in Southeast Asia or wherever Communism supposedly threatened to make gains; the butter spread domestically with programs to alleviate poverty and ensure a modicum of civil rights for all. The Civil Rights and Voting Rights Acts of 1964/65, despite much opposition, did pass in the US Congress. Nina Simone issued her powerful recording of her original song, "Mississippi Goddam," with an underlying message: "You may say I'm 'uppity,' but you had best treat me equally under the law!" I was in total sympathy for and support of the struggles of Dr. King, the other leaders in The Movement, and their foot soldiers. Here were people who literally put their own lives on the line day in and day out to fight on matters of principle, matters of elementary morality. No editorializing was necessary to guide my sympathies: the stark images of reality were more than adequate. To support the status quo, for me, was unthinkable.

On the same newscasts were American soldiers caught on camera committing atrocities and directing ARVNs (Army of the Republic of Viet Nam: troops of the puppet regimes in "south" Vietnam) to do the same. Beatings, torture, summary execution, rape, torching of whole villages and slaughter of livestock; and from the air, napalm and white phosphorous bombs (in blatant violation of international law), plus Agent Orange. This highly toxic herbicide would kill all vegetation in a "hostile area," including food crops. These were the methods employed in prosecuting the war. These were the methods apparently deemed necessary to stop a "domino" from falling. Something stunk here, stunk to high heaven. These were my high school years, 1964-66. I was aware that public protests of the Vietnam War had begun, but there were none near me I was aware of.

In Vietnam, a Buddhist monk was captured on film immolating himself in a public protest of the southern regime's suppression of religious freedoms. Then on November 2, 1965 a Quaker from Baltimore, Maryland in his early thirties—Norman Morrison, a father of three—calmly seated himself in a Pentagon parking lot, doused his clothes with gasoline and put lighted match to himself. The written statement he left made it clear this was an act of political protest against US violence being perpetrated abroad, in our name. In my eyes, Norman Morrison is an American hero. His act of self-sacrifice did not impress those in the offices inside the Pentagon, though "Defense" Secretary McNamara later acknowledged he'd been aware of it. I was under no imminent threat of conscription into the military—in theory, I'd have Student Deferments until 1970—but my personal determination to **not** put my stamp of approval on this terrible undertaking in Vietnam was firmly planted.

A truncated college career

At the conclusion of summer 1966 I was Joe College, off to upstate New York to start the next phase of life. "Good Vibrations," courtesy of The Beach Boys, were in the air. [For a discussion of the societal impact of the music of my generation, see **APPENDIX 2: Music with a Social Conscience.**] We freshmen arrived on campus at Syracuse in late August for orientation. There I made a stunning discovery: a student could not choose a subject in which to major until the junior year! I had seen no reference to this in the university's brochures. So, one was forced to undertake general Liberal Arts studies the first two years on campus. Ergo, no Journalism class for me before autumn of 1968. Despite my love of Science, I'd flunked out of Chemistry in high school—it, and the teacher, bored me to tears. I also hadn't pursued higher Math. Thus, I would have to seek credits in other areas. My having been placed in Sophomore English on the strength of the admission essay I'd penned (subject: war's appeal to little boys playing with toy guns versus its reality) proved little consolation. The dour Professor Mortenson did not grasp my sense of humor.

One early Monday morning, as I peered through a microscope sketching a portrait of a *paramecium*, I felt like I was in a time warp—I had met this little critter years before. And it hit me: the next two years would be like repeating high school! My visceral reaction: I ceased attending all classes about six weeks into the semester. This led to a collection of Incomplete grades except for Philosophy, where I scored a B+, earning three whole credits. The instructor there didn't mind if your body wasn't seated in his classroom as long as you turned in your essays on time.

Since my dad had paid my tuition and room and board for the whole semester, I may as well hang around and "do my own thing," I decided. The university presented a lecture series and I heard Norman Thomas, the noted humanist, and a very young Julian Bond give presentations. Both spoke against the ongoing war in Vietnam. Bond had been forced to go to the US Supreme Court to persuade the Georgia State Legislature to seat him there after his successful election. There was also a film series, with war as its theme. This was the first time I got to see Stanley Kubrick's *Paths Of Glory* (1957), which recounted a true incident of gross miscarriage of justice in the French Army during World War I.

My dorm, Booth Hall, was not co-ed. My floor, the fourth, was integrated. I was on cordial terms with everyone, but there wasn't a lot of socializing between white and black. The guys I spent most time with were basically all from the Eastern Seaboard. The most interesting acquaintance I made was Dan Weber, who came from a moneyed background. Dan was about 6-foot-2, with a mop of Beatles-style brown hair. He had mastered the art of keeping a cigarette drooping casually from the corner of his mouth. This guy was Jean-Paul Belmondo- cool! Dan turned me on to the poetry of Dylan Thomas, and the two-LP album *Blonde on Blonde* by another Dylan, a certain Bob. But there was a definite philosophical rift between Dan and myself on one topic: his avowed goal was to die before age 30!

There was a well-stocked bookstore a little way off campus, and that became my favorite haunt. The joy of studying what I wanted to returned. Hal Holbrook came to town with his remarkable "Mark Twain Tonight!"

stage show, which I attended with Charly Coleman, a kindred anti-Establishment soul. And I saw James Brown & The Famous Flames perform at the War Memorial Auditorium downtown. 'The Hardest Working Man In Show Business' was at the height of his powers. That was really the first Pop Music concert I ever attended.

Typically for a teen, I had introduced myself to alcohol while in high school. But I wasn't up to the challenge I took on one cold November night. In a public park across from our dorm, Coleman and I polished off several bottles of Colt 45 apiece, then headed for the popular off-campus bar, The Orange. I downed a Screwdriver and . . . details of what transpired the rest of that night were utterly lost to me until the point of our return to the dorm. It was a total memory blackout. I couldn't eat for the next 48 hours as I suffered the "dry heaves."

As my time on campus dwindled, I was keenly aware that the Vietnam War showed no sign of ebbing. But I did not fret about how that would affect me personally. What would come would come, and I would "cross that bridge when I came to it."

Officially a drop-out, rejected by the Peace Corps

When I came home for Thanksgiving break and announced that I was through with school, my father pretty well went through the roof. How could I throw his hard-earned money away like that? It was quickly agreed that I would go out and find a job until my draft status was resolved. But first I applied to join the Peace Corps, which would have exempted me from induction, at least temporarily. Alas, I got caught in a kind of collegiate Catch-22: here I was, a fugitive from college, but the Peace Corps was only looking for college graduates or people with skills in specialized areas. My application was promptly rejected.

Landing a job was no problem in early 1967. I went to work in the first factory that accepted me. I wasn't fussy because I knew Selective Service would soon learn of my departure from school and reclassify me 1-A, a prime candidate for being called to active duty. Amperex Electronics had a facility in Hicksville, not far from Syosset. My job was to seal vacuum tubes as they went by on a big, rotating drum. The factory was a union shop, so I actually became a card-carrying Teamster for a few weeks. Never got to meet Jimmy Hoffa, though.

The draft: a young man's options, 1967

My father was satisfied with my employment, though I didn't earn much. But great tension was building at home as my inescapable showdown with Uncle Sam approached. Let's look at the options for young men facing induction at that time:

- You could surrender to "fate" and take your chances, hoping to do your two years and emerge physically and psychologically intact;
- You could find some kind of exemption. This option was already gone for me;
- You could apply for official recognition as a Conscientious Objector to war; this might lead to alternative public service in the civilian arena, or service as a medic in the military. Nothing was guaranteed at the outset of the application process;
- You could flee US territory, not knowing when, if ever, you could legally return;
- You could commit the overt political act of refusing to be inducted, as did boxing legend Muhammad Ali, and be sentenced to a term in Federal Prison;
- You could deliberately attempt to fail the physical and/or psychological tests, a tale told in Arlo Guthrie's legendary "Alice's Restaurant";
- Finally, you could "beat the draft" by . . . **enlisting!!**

My mother had become quite emotionally unstable by this time. She loved her son very much, but she certainly didn't make any easier the decision process I had to now cope with. My inclination was to, in fact, refuse to be inducted. Because of my pacific nature—remember, I'd never even been in a real fight—Mom concluded I would be abused, sexually and physically, by hardened inmates in prison. She exercised a veto of this option by threatening to take her own life if I followed that road. The other options were not viable for me. I wasn't willing to flee the country of my birth, and I wasn't a faker who could convince Selective Service that I wasn't fit to serve. Why didn't I apply for official recognition as a Conscientious Objector, since clearly I was one? I didn't see any hope of success, due to my lack of anything resembling conventional religious beliefs.

I chose to enlist in the Army as soon as my reclassification to 1-A status arrived in the mail. This meant committing to three years in the military, versus the two a draftee must serve. However, the military did have a program whereby an enlistee could state a preference for the capacity in which he or she would serve, and I selected Medical. The not so fine print in the contract made it clear that how one would actually be employed would be determined by the needs of the military. You would be surprised how many of my peers enlisted precisely for this reason, to try to avoid the total crapshoot of being a draftee. To be sure, there was no shortage of citizens who believed it was their "patriotic duty" to voluntarily serve in the military. Don't believe for a moment that everybody in the 1960s and '70s was a "longhaired, pot-smoking, war-protesting hippie."

Should I trust the Army? Well, surely they needed medics. I signed on the dotted line. Perhaps by sheer chance I could make it through three years without being ordered to Vietnam. But I made it very clear to my parents that I drew the line at direct participation in US operations in a war I considered illegal and utterly immoral. Under these tense conditions, I was scheduled to report to Fort Hamilton in Brooklyn, NY on May 12, 1967 to begin my Army adventure.

Following Dr. King—April 15, 1967

Before I had to report for active duty, I had a chance to participate in the largest anti-war demonstration held in New York City up to that point. Martin Luther King, Jr. was the most prominent figure heading the march, and he was joined on the speaker's podium by many others, including Stokely Carmichael and H. 'Rap' Brown. I duly fell in, just another foot soldier for peace, among the multitude parading through the streets of Manhattan. It felt good to finally join with like-minded Americans in the common cause of peace and justice.

There was a very clear theme to this demonstration: It is no coincidence that folks are living in poverty and being treated as less than citizens here at home while the nation's resources are being squandered halfway around the planet to kill civilians . . . for what reason, exactly? How could America claim to be a beacon of light to the world while it sets these twin examples of irrefutably anti-human policies? The country desperately needed to change course.

It was earlier in the month, April 4 to be precise, that Dr. King had delivered a very important speech at Riverside Church on the Upper West Side of Manhattan. Some historians have surmised that it was this speech that sealed King's fate, as he made plain that henceforth he would not confine his activities to the Civil Rights Movement and poverty here at home, but would speak firmly his concerns over US foreign policy as well. He was assassinated one year to the day after this speech.

It was back to the subway and Long Island Railroad for me, back to sleepy little Syosset. I would put in my final weeks sealing vacuum tubes in Hicksville, counting down the days to May 12. I was committed to peacefully co-existing with the US Army . . . to the extent possible.

CHAPTER II

"Welcome to the Army, maggots!"

Fort Jackson, South Carolina
May 13-July 14, 1967

War is good business. Invest your son.

—*popular anti-war slogan of Vietnam Era*

Up bright and early on May 12, 1967 was I, my last (partial, at least) day as a civilian. Fort Hamilton, in Brooklyn, was pretty minor as military installations go, but played a significant role in the lives of many young men from the Greater Metropolitan Area. In short order we were sworn to uphold and defend the Constitution of the United States of America and defend the nation against "all enemies, foreign and domestic." So far, so good. Me, I didn't have any enemies, and I believed the Constitution, despite its shortcomings, was a generally pretty worthy document.

We former civilians all had written orders awaiting us, detailing our destinations for Basic Combat Training (BCT). The military's policy is to ship people far from their homes. This isolates you from familiar surroundings, making it easier to break down your sense of individuality, and rendering it a bit more complicated to declare "Screw this!" and just walk away from it all. Of course, this didn't stop GIs by the hundreds of thousands from doing precisely that. The statistics for guys going AWOL (Absent Without Official Leave) during the Vietnam Era were something the US military did not wish to boast about.

I was herded into a group of a couple dozen guys bound for Fort Jackson, South Carolina. Another fellow who gave the appearance of being rather intelligent and myself were made Co-Group Leaders, put in charge of seeing that everyone got to the destination. Wow, I'd been in the Army about a half hour and already I was "a leader of men"! Well, a co-leader at least. We were given a thick sheath of documents for all the guys in our group and then it was back to the subway for the ride to Pennsylvania Station in Manhattan.

Ft. Jackson is near Columbia, the capital of South Carolina. The train dear Uncle Sam had booked us on was not exactly an express; we wouldn't arrive at our destination until early the following morning. I never could sleep on moving conveyances, so this night above all would be a sleepless one for me. I had never been farther south than Washington, D.C., for the high school Senior Trip. We passed a lot of ramshackle houses and other decaying buildings as soon as we neared the rural South, but beyond that details are fuzzy. Our group arrived intact; no one had jumped train. We bleary-eyed city slickers were met at the station by Drill Instructors in their heavily starched khakis and "Smokey Bear hats." They wasted no time applying that ol' charming Army hospitality: we were herded onto an olive drab bus—and we better move our sorry asses in a "smart [meaning crisp, not intelligent] military manner!"—and off to the base we went.

"Off the bus! Move it, move it, move it!" We were squished into a rudimentary formation, along with groups of guys who'd arrived from other geographical starting points, in front of a long, single level building—the Reception Station. Here we would receive orientation speeches, along with tongue-lashings and sundry verbal insults. And given a psychological buildup for the famous first haircut: Army Haircut Style Number One, i.e. "the baldie." But we had arrived on a Saturday, so that would wait until Monday. We got to keep our hair and civilian clothes through the weekend, cooped up in a confined set of barracks.

Our initial processing consisted of far more than the famous haircut. There was a whole battery of written exams, not unlike SAT tests but lacking an essay component; testing of blood type and manufacture of our dog tags to indicate same (also "Religious Preference"—the only option offered that

I could choose was "No Preference"); putting our civvies (civilian clothing and shoes we'd arrived with) into storage; and finally the issuance of a ton of olive drab uniform and combat equipment items. After a few days I was able to steal enough time to write my first real letter home. My happy home for the next two months was to be:

CO. D, 6th BATTALION
2nd TRAINING BRIGADE
2nd PLATOON
FORT JACKSON, SOUTH CAROLINA

May 22, 1967

Dear Folks,

We have 30 minutes to ourselves prior to dinner, so I'm starting this letter now. I shall have to write bits and pieces at a time, whenever I'm not shining boots or belt buckles, etc. At that rate, it could take several days to complete this, but *c'est la vie.*

This Army's motto is "Hurry Up And Wait." For example, the issuing of our clothes ($250 worth!) was a matter of waiting on lines for 7 hours! Likewise for shots, chow, pay (so far I've received $21—more about that later), combat equipment, you name it, goddamnit!!

Today, Monday, it has poured all day, and it's <u>COLD</u>!! The previous nine days, it has averaged approx. 93 degrees. Two guys have collapsed from the heat before my very eyes—and they weren't even exercising, just standing there in the sun. (The officers have a cute habit of leaving us in the sun for long stretches, while they drink cold soda in the shade—believe me, they do it deliberately: all the guys agree on that, it's not just the conclusion of an anti-war protester.)

We are continuously harassed by the cadre—corporals and sergeants, as opposed to lieutenants, captains, etc., with whom we rarely come in contact. <u>They</u> call <u>us</u> every name in the book, every day. But <u>we</u> get in trouble for saying something as mild as "Hell." I've been personally pinpointed only three times: a Negro corporal swore because I didn't follow his mumbled instructions properly; then there was the drill sergeant, whose favorite expression is "you goddamned dickheads," who referred to me personally as a "damned dud" because I was striving to straighten out the column of soldiers I was standing in; and finally, there's the matter of conflicting orders: you follow the orders of one officer, and another one bawls you out for it! When we were issued our combat equipment, the master sergeant in charge of issuing it said, "If your helmet is scratched, place it on the ground in front of you; it it's okay, put it in your duffel bag with the rest of your equipment." Well now, mine was scratched all over the place, so I put it down. Meanwhile, a regular (as opposed to master) sgt. comes through the ranks, looking for a scapegoat. He spies my helmet, asks why it's on the ground; I point to the scratches. He glowers and screams, "Put that in your bag before I beat your goddamned head with it!!!"

NOTE: Mom, do not call Lyndon. There's nothing physical in the abuse heaped on us; it's all verbal. They can make us do extra running, sit-ups, KP, etc., but they know they can't hit us. (I have <u>not</u> received any such punishments as yet.) When they chew me out, I stare straight into their eyes and try not to laugh. And it's not easy to keep from laughing when you realize they're just acting: they're all decent enough men behind their masks. My analysis is this: the purpose behind the harassment is to condition us to obey all orders, so that when they get us to Vietnam, and order us to go wipe out a "Viet Cong" machine gun nest, we will snap to it instantly, unquestioningly. Naturally, they will fail dismally to get <u>me</u> in such a state of mind. I have signed over to them only my body for three years; they will never get my mind. Naturally, I do my best to conceal that fact from them, for in this army, "individual" is a dirty word.

On Monday, the 15th, we were all scalped, and <u>we</u> had to pay the stinking barber! And as if we had anything left to be cut, we have to continue to get haircuts at our own expense, weekly, for 5-8 weeks! Fortunately, it's only 85 cents a shot. The gym bag I brought? No good. I had to buy one for $3.40 that says U.S. ARMY on it! But you ain't heard nothin' yet. So many of our clothing and toilet articles have to be neatly displayed in our footlockers (subject to daily inspection) that we had to buy underwear to wear, toothbrushes to actually use on our teeth, etc. And we have to display a comb! As if we had something to use it on!

Propaganda has so far been surprisingly light. When we're supposed to be marching and singing or shouting at the tops of our voices such slogans as "When I get to Vietnam, I'm gonna kill me a Vietcong!!" or "Infantry, Infantry, all the way!" I mumble under my breath Stokely Carmichael's phrase, "Hell no! I won't go!" Believe it or not, today a colonel told us: "Actually, I think 'Don't make war, make love' is a pretty good slogan. Only, sometimes, we just <u>have</u> to make war. We can't help it." *Oy vey.*

The food is okay, I must admit; however, we have to eat it in 10 to 15 minutes, no matter how voluminous the meal. Somehow, I've avoided heartburn so far.

The Negroes are hard enough to understand, but there's worse to tell: our drill instructor is a Jap!! There are so many dialects and accents around here, you'd never guess it was the American Army! And speaking of accents, Puerto Ricans who speak little or no English at all are being drafted by the hundreds! It's disgraceful how Uncle Sam is getting cannon fodder.

Well, I think I've covered the important stuff. Will write again when I have time.

Love,
Greg

P.S.: The harassment usually stops after the first 3 weeks, and I have retained my sense of humor, so don't worry about me.

A Basic Training unit was a mix of men from four different components of the Army: the draftees; those of us who'd enlisted "voluntarily" (as if there was no draft hanging over our heads!); National Guardsmen; and, Enlisted Reserves. Guys in the latter two categories had to go through Basic Combat Training just like everyone else. After this, plus training in some specialized field, they got to go home, regrow their hair and resume their civilian lives, with occasional weekend exercises—pitch the tent, put the beer on ice! These guys tended to be from the more economically privileged strata of society, and had close to zero risk of being mobilized for actual combat. It was probably from a Guardsman or Reservist that I heard harassment by cadre "usually stops after the first 3 weeks." Reality would prove this claim not exactly accurate.

"Hommagonnakickayouindoss!!"

Though I had great sympathy for victims of race-based oppression in our society, I was raised in a virtually lily-white environment and thus hadn't had the opportunity to interact with members of racial minorities. Staff Sgt. Sampaga was our principal Drill Instructor, the member of the training cadre with whom we were most in contact. Some of us secretly referred to him as "Sgt. Sakamoto." Not until quite a while later would I learn that Sarge actually bore a Filipino surname.

There was a senior sergeant of Puerto Rican origin whom we only encountered occasionally. He was attached to Quartermaster Corps but if one of our regular DIs was not available on a given day, this guy would fill in for him. He cracked me up every time he unleashed his favorite phrase, "Hommagonnakickayouindoss!" As in: "You got 60 seconds to get outta dat barracks and in formation or hommagonnakickayouindoss!"

My assurance to my mom that the cadre weren't allowed to get physical with trainees also proved a little off the mark. The helmet liner is a fiberglass structure over which one places the "steel pot," or actual combat helmet. On several occasions members of the cadre removed their own helmet liners and used them to smack recruits on top of theirs. It was loud and it stung temporarily but that was the extent of the damage. Occasionally a sergeant would get so angry he'd give a trainee a good shove. One would hear stories that so-and-so "from that training company over there" had challenged his DI to a fight behind the barracks . . . and gotten a good whuppin'. "Officially" these events never happened. It was part of cadre's job to strut about with *machismo*, but beneath the show they were tough for real. It would have been a very rare event, I thought, for the trainee to emerge the victor in such a confrontation.

A forced integration

Jackie Robinson broke "the color barrier" in professional baseball a year before the nation's Armed Forces ceased being **officially segregated**. This resulted in a kind of forced integration in living arrangements, because beds were assigned on a strict alphabetical-by-surname basis. So it was that Ed 'Fat' Lewis, a big-city white guy, and 'Skinny' Lewis, a black guy from Chattanooga, Tennessee came to share a bunk bed in our World War II barracks—intended as strictly "temporary housing" in the 1940s. My immediate alphabetical neighbors were Ed Larsen and William Lester, plus the Lewis "brothers." Larsen was tall and skinny and pretty damned dyspeptic. Bill Lester had some college under his belt. He was soft-spoken, with a hint of a lisp. Most of the guys believed he was gay. Me? I had no opinion and couldn't care less. He was an intelligent kid, certainly not gung-ho. We had a good understanding from the outset. Here was a person with whom I could discuss philosophy and books in our rare opportunities to relax.

Added to the mix in my barracks was a contingent of draftees from Kentucky. They were living proof of the still prevalent poverty among rural white people. Most had apparently never been to a dentist in their lives. The Army's efficacious approach to their condition was to simply yank most of the teeth they brought with them, deemed too far gone to salvage, and fit them with dentures. I have to say these country boys took it quite well, all things considered.

Without a doubt there were racial tensions. But, in my unit, racial epithets were confined to whispers among one clique or another, not bandied about in a confrontational manner. We were all in deep shit together, trying to make it through day by day. Neutrality toward all, animosity toward none was my policy. I was already making it known that I was firmly opposed to the war, albeit not loudly. But I was marking myself as "different."

Never call your weapon a "gun"!!

May 28, 1967

Dear Folks,

Well, it's milestone time! Here I've been in the Army two whole weeks and I haven't seen the inside of a guardhouse yet! It is so goddamned hot that the ink is more liquid than it should be, so please excuse any smudges that might crop up.

On the positive side, two situations: 1.) My faith in humanity has been upheld by the guys here. They are just as fine a collection of people as the group I got to know at Syracuse; naturally, they come from lower income families, but economics is irrelevant and immaterial; 2.) Uncle Sam has given me glasses, to try to strengthen that weak right eye.

The harassment I spoke of last week subsided for a while, but is going stronger than ever now. Sometimes it takes quite an amusing form: a trainee committed the unpardonable sin of calling his rifle a "gun" and so had to run around for three minutes with weapon overhead, pointing to the appropriate object while yelling, "This is my rifle! These are my balls!"

Some observations on officers: power complexes aplenty! Most are young; they drink beer, brag about their sexual exploits, and leave rubber with their expensive cars. We have to run errands for them, clean their rooms, polish their cars. An immature lot, indeed, like little boys playing soldier.

There hasn't been too much propaganda yet. Thursday, we did see a film on Army history. I found these facts worth reporting: 1.) The campaign which destroyed the American Indian is painted as having brought "glory" to the Army!; 2.) The South is praised for having fought valiantly in the Civil War; 3.) The term "hero" is constantly applied to the U.S.; 4.) In the summary of WW II, there is no mention of Hiroshima or Nagasaki; 5.) There is no mention of Vietnam, presumably because it's not yet a war, since Congress has yet to declare war.

Well, that's about all to tell this week. Will write again next Sunday, theoretically (you can never tell when they'll find something new and absurd for us to do, even on the Sabbath). 'Bye.

Love,
Greg

P.S.: You should receive notice soon of my purchase of a Savings Bond. We were literally blackmailed into this: it was flatly stated that men who don't buy bonds don't get promoted! DON'T CALL THE PRESIDENT! You'll get me in a lot of trouble.

It should be noted that when I wrote "officer" in these letters, it usually referred to Non-Commissioned Officers—NCOs—not Commissioned Officers (lieutenants, captains, etc.). Many Army training commands insisted that only the Commissioned were to be addressed as "Sir"—which is, in fact, proper etiquette—but in our unit we had to apply this address to everyone above our own rank. This was to remind us of just how "low" we ourselves were.

Physical Training (PT) should not have been that big a deal for a guy who'd run off 40 pounds of bodyweight the previous summer. After my final Track & Field season in high school, I stopped consuming massive amounts of ice cream and milk and started running about five miles most days. The problem was that the hassle of the actual physical work, in the heat and humidity, was compounded by the stress of harassment. Being out of synchronicity, using improper form for an exercise, or talking or laughing with his mates would bring instant "heat" on a trainee. Extra loving attention from the DIs. "What's your favorite Army exercise, maggot?!" "The push-up, Drill Sergeant!" "I CAN'T HEAR YOU, PRIVATE!!" "I said the push-up, Sir!!" "I **STILL** CAN'T HEAR YOU, SON! SOUND OFF LIKE YOU GOT A PAIR!!" "THE PUSH-UP, SIR!" "The push-up!" was the mandatory reply, and the reward for remembering that was to be assigned 10 or 20 additional ones.

The training regimen was broken into one-hour blocs, 50 minutes of actual work followed by a 10-minute break. More than half the guys would use this break to smoke, even if they were still winded from doing PT. This unhealthy habit was totally condoned, if not encouraged, by the military. Yours truly would simply look for some shade, drink water and chat about the day's activities. Our overseers were careful about supplying adequate water, I give them credit for that. We were also encouraged to swallow plenty of salt tablets. A dubious practice, medically.

The Army could have written the book on high-pressure salesmanship when it came to US Savings Bonds. We were literally **coerced** into signing up after being in the military two weeks. You may well wonder why a dissident soldier would be concerned about being promoted. Simple: for the next three years, the Army was to be my **job**, my only source of income. No bond purchase, no promotion. The sooner I could boost my pay beyond the $98 a month we were getting initially, the better! Yes, we were earning about three bucks a day under the withering sun, and the withering insults from Cadre.

Pots & Pans!

June 8, 1967

Dear Folks,

I am starting this letter now, Thursday night, but won't have time to finish it until Sunday, no doubt. I have a bit of spare time tonight because today wasn't a regular training day; it was work detail day. Some guys get lousy jobs (lugging sandbags out in the hot sun, for example); for once I had good luck: I found myself doing landscape work on the front lawn of, believe it or not, the Catholic Chapel!!! What a fate for an agnostic! There was no supervision, so that made it a good job.

(continued on June 10)

On the way to and from my work detail at the Church Thursday, and again this morning, on a pre-breakfast run, I passed the Stockade, getting a good look at it. It's surrounded by barbed wire, complete with watch-towers, guards, etc. The actual buildings which house the inmates, however, are just like the barracks <u>we</u> live in. All were built in 1940, intended for temporary housing only. They were condemned in 1959, but, needless to say, are still in use. Therefore I don't think spending a few years in the stockade to assuage my conscience would be such a terrible experience. (No, I'm not in any kind of trouble; I'm just mentioning the stockade as an interesting observation.)

Another marvelous experience was, and will be, KP. I had it May 31, and I have it again June 12. This does not have to be miserable; it depends on the job you get. Well, needless to say, old "Lucky Laxer" got the absolutely worst job: washing out everything they cook with in the goddamn Mess Hall. These aren't just little pots and pans; some hold 40 gallons; then there are the cooking trays--tons of grease baked on; the bowl from the king-size Mixmaster; immense spoons, ladles. In other words, it was my job, from 5:15 AM to 7:00 PM to wash literally <u>everything</u>, except the stoves them-selves, that they use to cook for 240 men. Incidentally, I saw a rather fat, i.e. well-nourished cockroach in the kitchen, but being a pacifist, did not step on it. I wish I could say that we trainees are equally well-nourished. We're only allowed one glass of milk per meal; the main course is almost 100% carbohydrate, and we get fresh fruit but once a week. *Feh!*

The past two weeks we took up bayonet training. With each movement, we are supposed to growl loudly and aggressively. When the Drill Instructor shouts, "What's the Spirit of the Bayonet?" we are to reply thunderously, "TO KILL!!!" And to, "What are you?" we reply: "KILLERS!!!" This I find quite hilarious, but with good acting, I've been able to stay out of trouble (i.e. no one chews me out for not sounding like a killer). The company as a whole was chewed out by the DI for not sounding aggressive enough; he ended the little speech with this brilliant statement: "You are a goddamned disgrace to fuckin' humanity!" So we're a disgrace because we ("we" here refers to the men in general, not just we "peaceniks") don't particularly relish the thought of disemboweling someone with a bayonet!

My glasses are okay; they noticeably help me. Next week, we go to the rifle range. I hope my eyes don't fail me, because if you fail the rifle accuracy test, you fail Basic Training.

The harassment is still going, but the officers are concentrating their wrath on the fat men, making them do extra road work. Our (my platoon's) sergeant has loosened up, and occasionally we all have a jolly hilarious time. I've rarely laughed harder.

As of this coming Monday (my KP day), I'll be a one-month man in the Army and I haven't been locked up yet! Will wonders never cease? 'Bye till next weekend.

Love,
Greg

Me, an Officer? No, thanks!

According to that battery of written tests administered in our first days at the Reception Station, yours truly had a high IQ and would be most suitable for an MOS (Military Occupational Specialty) in medical, Military Police (!) or food preparation (!!). I had requested assignment to medical at the time of my enlistment, so this was encouraging—the Army agreed I was suitable for that pursuit.

A new wrinkle appeared just before I'd completed my first month of service. An officer I'd never seen before showed up at morning formation. He called several of us aside and informed us we would be welcome to apply for Officer Candidate School (OCS). This is a means of becoming a Commissioned Officer without attending West Point. The invitation took me completely by surprise. Of course I said "No, thanks" without hesitation. As a "lowly EM" (Enlisted Man), I looked at the officer caste with very jaundiced eye. The Army wanted to turn me into an oppressor of other GIs? Nice try, Uncle Sam, but my answer was the only one I could possibly give.

(Technically, it's not a) gas, gas, gas . . .

June 18, 1967

Dear Folks,

Well, this week was really interesting, with an interesting climax last night (Saturday). Here are the highlights:

On Tuesday, we went through gas training. By the time we were through, I felt like I'd been on a civil rights march to Selma, Alabama. Phase one: we enter a gas chamber filled with tear gas, with our gas masks on. But once inside, we remove the masks (one man at a time) and after a minute of exposure, must state loudly and clearly our name, rank and serial number. Besides the expected effect on the eyes, the gas causes a burning sensation on the skin. Phase 2: We enter a chlorine gas chamber without masks on, holding our breaths, then put them on. No ill effects suffered. Phase 3: They stand us in formation, in a field, masks off. They inform us that we are not to mask until we feel the effects of the gas (riot control gas). Anyone who masks early will have his mask confiscated (while the gas is still in the air, of course). As soon as the gas hit me, I had to close my eyes, and by the time I got the damned mask on, I'd swallowed enough to choke and feel nauseous. But the worst effect was on all skin exposed; it felt like it was on fire for three minutes. So now I know what to expect next time I'm in a riot.

Friday, we finally went to the rifle range. I deliberately left my glasses home. Let's get one thing straight: you sight with the right eye unless you're left-handed. The target was 25 meters distant. Now get this—the target was only 3 inches by 1 1/2 inches. My eyes coordinated okay, but things got blurry after awhile. Despite all these handicaps, this beginner put 5 out of 18 shots in the target. If I'm not careful, they'll send me to Vietnam tomorrow!!

Our Platoon Sergeant gets more hilarious every day. He's developing nicknames for us. He can't pronounce, due to his Japanese accent, Jacobowski, so he calls him "Polak." A 25-year-old draftee who makes no effort at all, and blames it on his left-handedness, he calls, appropriately, "Left-Handed." A guy named Haas becomes "Hasshole." Me? I'm "Bighead," and frequently "Goddamn Bighead." Apparently, the Sarge isn't used to brainy people; he's certainly convinced that my head is disproportionately large for my body. The other day, he called me "the dumbest guy in the Company"; I couldn't keep from laughing right in his face at that comment.

Tomorrow, we go back to the range. I will take my glasses and see if I can get 18 of 18 shots in there.

Wow!! I almost forgot the blood incident. The Ft. Jackson blood bank was low, so they called for volunteers. I was happy to step forward. But a funny thing happened: they rejected me!!! Not enough hemoglobin! That means not enough iron! They rejected 11 of the 15 of us! The answer has to be the shit they pass off as "food" around here!

If you flunk Basic, you have to take it over again. I cannot possibly flunk. Either I pass, or I stage a grand rebellion against the entire military establishment. Those are the only two possibilities.

Right now, a tropical thunderstorm is approaching. So, assuming I don't get struck by lightning, and assuming I don't pull guard duty or KP next Sunday, I will write then. 'Bye for now.

Love,
Greg
ALL-AMERICAN FIGHTING (???) MAN

The terms "tear gas," "riot control gas," etc. are misnomers. These products are actually a mist of extremely fine particles suspended in the air after being released from storage under pressure. The particles adhere to clothing and any exposed skin; this gives them the ability to continue to punish the lucky recipient for a period of time after the initial irritating impact on the respiratory tract. Almost certainly it was the classic CS "crowd control" product we were exposed to in the initial chamber.

No one was able to complete the recitation of the personal information required of us in that first chamber. We went as far as we could and had to bolt for the exit door, groping our way with teary eyes. As World War I showed, chlorine gas is a very dangerous material. I rather suspect a little joke was played on us in the second chamber of our gas exercise. Since I noted no effect from being in that atmosphere, I have to believe it was just plain air.

"A cheap room for the night" (wink, wink)

After the first four weeks of learning the joys of soldiering, the big moment arrived: our first full Weekend Pass! Full? Well, first there was morning formation, Police Call, etc. Police Call: you spread out over the company compound and pick up any "unauthorized" object you find that's movable. This could be a bit of trash of any nature, but largely it meant picking up cigarette butts.

It was expected that virtually every guy in a unit would take advantage of this first opportunity to get the hell away from Army green for a few hours. If one stayed behind, one was at risk of being assigned endless petty tasks to pass the time. No, thanks. I'm gettin' on line for my pass! This ensured the businesses in nearby Columbia of thousands of young, short-haired customers every weekend. And you may be sure this constituted a significant chunk of the economy of that town. So it is in all towns adjacent to military facilities.

We lined up alphabetically to sign out and receive our written passes. So I naturally fell into a clump, to await a taxi, consisting of Jacobowski (a.k.a. 'Polak'), Ed Larsen, and 'Fat' Lewis. When we finally got a cab, it was driven by a middle-aged crewcut fellow who was likely retired from the Army himself. Larsen, 'Polak' and I piled into the rear seat, Lewis in front. "Where to, boys?" inquired the driver. Lewis: "We're looking for a cheap room for the night." I did not see the wink Lewis must have given the driver; had I seen it, I still would not have immediately grasped its meaning.

We were delivered to a nondescript hotel on the outskirts of Columbia. The check-in process seemed straightforward. I took a room with Larsen; the others had a separate room. Larsen and I weren't buddies; things were falling into place without conscious design. We sent out for burgers, and we started swilling beer immediately. I didn't start this adventure with the intention of getting flat out plastered, but it was "the thing to do." (What happened to my natural tendency to oppose conformism?) It was only when the women magically appeared in our room that I realized our "cheap room" was in a brothel.

It so happened that 'Polak' and 'Fat' Lewis were married men, as doubtless were many of the other customers that night. But men, above all. Getting laid was priority number one. I had had zero experience with prostitutes—indeed, I was a virgin. This was all foreign to me. I upped my beer consumption. One of the gals climbed onto the bed and got behind me. I asked Larsen to pass the can opener. "My" hooker reached down to fondle my genitals, announcing "Mmm, this one's got a <u>nice</u> can opener!" I distinctly remember her making that cute remark, but thereafter I have a complete memory blackout until I awoke around 4:30 AM to go urinate, my head in a fog. Larsen later claimed that I had squirmed out of my bed and tried to climb into his, saying "I don't believe in this." He said he interpreted this to mean that I was "queer." <u>If</u> I actually said that, I merely meant I didn't believe in patronizing prostitutes. I wished to lose my virginity, sure, but not in a commercial transaction with a total stranger.

By the way, the married guys got "rolled" that night. They weren't roughed up, mind you; that wasn't necessary. While they were in drunken stupors, they were relieved of all their cash. 'Fat' Lewis and 'Polak' were a few years older than I. But maybe I, just 19, wasn't alone in being naive. It was a bedraggled lot that made its way back to base Sunday afternoon. We had four more weeks of fun and games ahead of us. Perhaps we should have simply sought some decent food and to catch up on the sleep the Army loved to deprive us of. But boys will be boys . . . especially if they're married, it seems!

The left-handed rifleman

June 25, 1967

Dear Folks,

We are scheduled to graduate July 14. I don't know if I'll make it, for one reason: my damned right eye. Things weren't bad at the 25 meter target range, but this past week, the targets have been 75, 175 and 300 meters distant. The 175s are hard for me to focus on, and the 300s close to impossible. So, I am going to make a courageous attempt to shoot <u>left-handed</u>! Now, that's pretty incredible when you consider how little I use my left hand for anything. If I fail to shoot up to par Wednesday, I will probably have to stay here until July 28 to re-attempt to qualify. That, of course, would mean cancellation of the leave that I might get (ain't no guarantee). As for the location of my medical school, most guys are sent to Fort Sam Houston, Texas. I've always wanted to see Texas, and though I won't see <u>much</u> of it, it would be a good experience.

Time's really flying. Next week we qualify (shoot for record) with our rifles. The following week, we go out on bivouac for three days and three nights. That means C-rations! *Feh!!* Then, the last week, we goof off and do a little rehearsing for graduation.

My third session of KP ought to be coming up very soon. Fortunately, it's the last. I still haven't gotten into trouble! Other guys, who apparently don't hold any moral and intellectual convictions against the war, are finding it harder to adjust to military life! They're getting into trouble, I'm not!

Our Platoon Sergeant, Sgt. Sampaga, picked me and another college drop-out to be on CQ (Charge of Quarters) with him one night last week. This means that we stay up, on alternate shifts, all night to answer the phones down at Battalion Headquarters, while he (the Sergeant) sleeps. Only in case of an emergency would we awaken him. But the phone didn't ring once all night!

Yesterday, the Sarge continued his hilarious ways by personally giving "baldie" haircuts to those who refused to get them voluntarily. With a sardonic grin from ear to ear, he mowed it down to their scalps. I don't mind having my hair this short, but I'll tell you this: when I get out of the service or jail, whichever is my destiny, it'll be a long time before I get a haircut.

I am enclosing a piece of a 25-meter target to show you the size of the rectangle I was hitting. Since we spent last week doing nothing but shooting, there's not much to tell. So, until next Sunday, your broke (till pay day) son says 'Bye.

Love,
Greg

Through most of elementary school, I'd worn eyeglasses. By the time I got to high school I'd managed to ditch the spectacles. But the Army put an end to that happy-go-lucky spell in my life and put a pair of their nondescript gray frames on my face. But my right eye was still too weak to allow me to zero in on the long-range targets on the rifle range. My concern that I might get left behind for failing to qualify with the M-14 the following week was fully justified. At the five-week point in Basic none of us needed convincing that **any** extra time spent in that environment would be abominable; we felt it in our guts. There was no way out of this situation but to learn quickly how to fire the rifle as a southpaw so I could sight with my left eye. I had been approved to move on to Medical Corpsman training, but I had to get over this hurdle.

Sarge "lets his hair down"

Being on CQ duty was just another rite of passage, like walking guard duty around the PX (Post Exchange, a department store with discount prices, underwritten by the taxpayer). Every night an NCO from the battalion cadre had to take a turn minding the HQ building. He got to select two trainees from his own unit to be "runners." We were mainly there to apply some spit and polish to the offices so the big-wigs would be pleased upon arriving in the morning. But I really was privileged to have been selected by Staff Sgt. Sampaga, for he was about to show me a side of himself that I'm sure very few privates would ever see.

We discussed the war that night at Battalion HQ. I explained my moral stance; he listened patiently, even with a bit of sympathy. He addressed some buxom blonde on the screen of the TV he'd brought to HQ that night, informing her: "I'm going to send Laxer over to fuck you!" Thanks, Sarge, but that's not too realistic at this point. It would have been a major shock had he agreed with me about the situation in Vietnam. This man likely already had 10 or 15 years in the Army, with a plan to spend another 15 or 20 before retiring with a nice pension. So he basically held his tongue on the specific topic of Vietnam. Yet, what Sampaga did next blew my mind.

A Permanent Party emblem designates personnel who are assigned to a given base as their duty assignment, i.e. they're no longer trainees or transients. Sarge's PP emblem was in the form of a decal on his helmet liner. The design of the emblem may have changed over the years, but it always featured some symbol of liberty in US iconography (e.g. the Liberty Bell in Philadelphia) surrounded by the motto "THIS WE'LL DEFEND." Suddenly Sarge held up his helmet liner, pointed to the emblem and declared: "This we'll defend . . . United States **fuck!**"

What was this man, whose job was to make our daily lives miserable while preparing us for combat, trying to tell me? He had dropped his guard, he had lowered the mask he was required to wear, the mask of the fierce, ass-kicking Drill Instructor. Here was a lifer willing to verbally fire a spitball at the organization he was committed to serving for decades. I suspect this gentleman was bitter about his own treatment, as a Filipino, in American society.

We shared a good belly laugh at his remark and that's as far as the incident went. But I would never view him quite the same thereafter. We now shared a kind of secret bond. The plain fact of the matter was that I liked this man. But it would have been against protocol to tell him that. We had been warned by one of our DIs: "Don't tell me you like me, 'cause likin' leads to lovin', and lovin' leads to fuckin', and ain't none of you sorry-asses gonna fuck **me**!!" Fair enough. But beneath the *macho* veneer, most of these fellows were decent human beings. They genuinely wanted us to survive. Any doubts they may have secretly harbored about the wisdom of the war in Southeast Asia they had to keep strictly to themselves. I'm sure some eventually called it quits as the war dragged on endlessly, but at this point the majority were likely contemplating making a career of the military, with a decent pension—meager compared to those that would be drawn by the colonels and the generals, to be sure—after 20 to 30 years.

There was one other unforgettable NCO among our training cadre. Sgt. Larry Goodman was a black guy, still in his early 20s, who stood close to 6-foot-6 and probably weighed 220 pounds, without an ounce of body fat. He gave the impression he could run all day, despite his size, without breaking a sweat. It was a bad day for the fatties at the rear of the formation if Larry was in charge of our running. Goodman had been through the most extreme training available short of being a Green Beret. He was an Airborne Ranger and damned proud of it. This was a guy no one was going to try to pick a fight with. He was still awaiting his first assignment to Vietnam.

One day we were given our M-14s, without ammo, and put through an exercise of learning to advance in a line, "firing" without "killing" one another. Since we didn't even have blanks to fire, I compensated for the silence of our weapons with "Ta-pocketa! Ta-pocketa!"—straight out of James Thurber's story, "The Secret Life of Walter Mitty." Suddenly, looming like a tree, there was Larry Goodman. "Soldier, what the hell are you doin'?" he demanded. "Well, Sergeant, if you can't give us ammo I've got to pretend, don't I?" Fortunately, Sgt. Goodman was in a mellow mood that day.

Sharpshooter in the rain . . . and grease

July 2, 1967

Dear Folks,

Well, this has been an incredible week, in a positive manner and a negative one.

Monday, I became a left-handed rifleman. I hit about 50% of the targets; not a dramatic improvement, but it virtually guaranteed that I would be able to qualify later in the week. My left cheek was not ready for the sudden switch from right-handedness, and is now recovering from a small cut and my left eye is recovering from a slight shiner incurred by the recoil. Tuesday came and off we marched to the rifle range again . . . with a slight difference—RAIN. Hard. All morning long. There are no dry spots on one's fatigues to dry one's hands on. One climbs into one's wet foxhole for the first firing position. The vibrations from the first discharge send all the raindrops on the weapon flying up into one's eye. So one takes his wet hand and tries to dry one's eye; then one blows the water from the sight and continues. The next firing position is the sitting position, between the foxholes. Guess what's between the foxholes? A puddle 5 feet across and, without exaggeration, 2 inches deep. Splash. Down we sit and fire away. I still hit for 50%! We came back later to repeat the whole business, but by this time the rain had soaked into me, and I was shivering so much I hit only about 25%.

Wednesday arrives and it's time to shoot for record; you must knock down 30 of 84 targets to qualify. If you fail, you fire over again, and if you still don't qualify, you start Basic all over again. 30-44 targets makes you a Marksman; 45-59 a Sharpshooter; 60+ is Expert.

It's *expose* time: my company officers reek of corruption! I suspect that they reflect the rest of this man's Army. You see, our Company had been doing poorly in marksmanship in past training cycles. So one of our second lieutenants decided he'd had enough of this. The targets ranged from 50-350 meters. He advised, and practically ordered, that we handle the long targets by aiming well above them when we hear the buzzer which indicates that the targets are about to fall (they are "pop-up" style). With the proper timing, it would appear that we scored a hit, when in reality the targets would have fallen whether we fired or not. We would be given the benefit of the doubt and given credit for a hit, the lieutenant assured us. I managed to pick off 47 targets, so you are now the parents of a left-handed Sharpshooter! The lieutenant's method worked well enough to make our

Company number one! I hope the fink is proud of his bunch of cheaters!! And himself.

Thursday's dawn found me reporting to the Mess Hall for my third, and hopefully, last tour of KP duty. This one defied belief. Guess what job I was given? Yup, for the 3rd straight time, I had the pots and pans all to myself! This time, they (the cooks) did a minimum of yelling about how slow I am. They took action. I had to clean out the two grease traps. These are approx. 2 X 3 feet by 4 1/2 feet deep, and contain all the grease from the previous week! (And, in the Army, that's a lot of grease!) Well now, you can imagine how I looked and smelled after dipping into these things with my bare hands and scooping out the contents, which are very similar in consistency, color and odor, to vomit!! I had to take a 30-minute shower and wash my clothes in a utility sink in the latrine. Fortunately, hot water was available for showers that night (usually it's not available), otherwise I might still smell like a garbage dump. The cook said next time I have KP he'll make me do the same thing again. Well, now, if they follow the regular duty roster, I won't have KP again in Basic, but there are never any guarantees here. The next day, while I was on the chow line, the cook reminded me of his promise to return me to the grease traps. So I told him that next time, before I take a shower, I'll roll around on his bed awhile. That left him dumbfounded!

Friday night came the real fun: the Night Infiltration Course. Enclosed is a postcard showing the exact course our company used. Now, this is supposed to be our "baptism of fire," but it's a farce. The machine guns fire about 4 feet above the ground. By staying low, one can be so safe that there's no nervousness, even though they're live bullets flying around. (Nevertheless, one hears stories about someone panicking and actually standing up to flee!) The explosives, which are detonated inside sandbagged bunkers, are only 4 ounces TNT each; in other words, more noise than anything else. Bullets and TNT? Didn't bother me in the least; this charade did not simulate actual combat conditions.

Next week is bivouac. Thanks to July 4, however, we only sleep out in the woods one night instead of the usual 3. Plus, due to a tight time schedule (the June draft was big and they have to get us out of here) we will be trucked to and from bivouac, about 9 miles, which we normally would march. Lucky break for my blisters. Despite the unusually easy facets of our bivouac, I'm not looking forward to it, for we'll be doing a lot of crawling and it's bound to <u>rain</u>!! The following week, we have final exams, which are no sweat, then we rehearse a bit for graduation, and on Friday, July 14, it's all over!

So, it's been a wild week. On the bright side, I made Sharpshooter on only two days' practice (one of those days in the rain), lefty. On the dark side, I was stuck with KP again. MOM: Do not call LBJ to complain about the way the cooks treat me.

Please stop telling me how proud you are of me, Mom. Reality dictates that I will probably end up in the stockade yet. Uncle Sam is going to want me to be a Combat Medic. This I won't be. So that's how it is. *C'est la vie.* So don't talk like they're gonna make me a general, but don't go to the other extreme and worry. I'll keep you posted on what's happening. Until next Sunday, 'bye.

Love,
Greg
DEFINITELY NOT A COMBAT MEDIC
GREASE TRAP CLEANER
COLLEGE DROP-OUT
PHILOSOPHER
CIVILIAN-AT-HEART

A lowly private would have an awfully bare chest on his Class A ("dress") uniforms if not awarded a medal in BCT, and that's where the rifle range award comes to the rescue. A few guys in my platoon did make the Expert level. Some of them doubtless had been handling rifles since they were knee-high to a Kentucky grasshopper. And for the record: the lieutenant's suggested technique didn't really work for me, so I abandoned it and legitimately earned my Sharpshooter award. As an avowed pacifist upon entering the Army, did I have any qualms about firing weapons? None whatsoever. I knew that no force on Earth could compel me to aim down a rifle barrel at a citizen of Vietnam or anywhere else.

Gray, the cook who assigned me the delicious task of cleaning out the grease traps, was a light-skinned black guy. He was a mere PFC himself, but he relished being in a position of authority over me. No doubt he considered me "ofay" ("Pig Latin" for "foe"). Or maybe he disliked "bigheads." But I was set to graduate July 14 and our paths in life would diverge permanently. Little did I know that a new hurdle (literally!) would soon jeopardize my ability to graduate and kiss Ft. Jackson goodbye.

Last letter from Basic Training

July 9, 1967

Dear Folks,

Well, last week we made Army history. We had what was undoubtedly the easiest bivouac of all time. Monday morning we climb on the trucks and ship out. Monday night we truck back home. Tuesday, the 4th, we have off. Wednesday morning, it's back on the trucks. Wednesday night, we pitch our tents and sleep out (4 hours of sleep). Thursday afternoon, it's all over: onto the trucks and home. Now, bivouac was <u>easy</u> only in relation to how it should be: although we were trucked to the bivouac area, once arrived there, we did a good amount of walking, with full combat gear. Good thing they trucked us; when I get tired from walking, you can imagine how the fat guys must feel.

This week, we have final exams. No sweat! They're geared to an 8th grade education. There's no doubt, now that I've qualified with the rifle, that I will graduate this Friday. By sheer chance I saw TIME on the newsstand—cover story on the Hippies, so don't bother sending it to me, I have it. Due to having bivouac last week, there's not much to tell. So, until I write next, or come home on leave, 'bye.

Love,
Greg

Ah yes, the famous mythical leave at the conclusion of BCT. The promise of the **possibility** of such a leave was probably floated before every guy entering the Army at that time, in an attempt to diminish the AWOL rate. During Basic, the likeliest causes for a guy to just skip out were: 1.) just not being able to cope with the bullshit; 2.) a "domestic issue" at home with the wife or girlfriend—'Jody' at work!; 3.) some other family crisis the trainee did not trust the Red Cross to address promptly. 'Jody' was the dirtbag back home who made a beeline for your gal as soon as he heard you were off in the military. I'd never heard of this 'Jody' prior to entering the Army, but he was everywhere, it seemed. No doubt enlistees in the Marines, Navy and Air Force heard tales of 'Jody' as well. One tireless SOB. Well, I had nothing to worry about. I was "blessed" with no girl back home. But worries about 'Jody' did cause some guys to take off.

Remember the Night Infiltration Course? Though low-crawling 75 meters through loose sand, which quickly got inside one's fatigues, and crawling over logs and under barbed wire fence was not fun, you'll note that I criticized the set-up as being insufficiently scary. This wouldn't be the last time, believe it or not, I'd complain to my parents that I found the Army "not Army enough." Also of note is the fact that the Training Company immediately adjacent to ours made our treatment at the hands of Cadre look like a picnic. Those poor bastards were subjected to extra PT and Drill & Ceremonies, and the icing on the cake: "Chinese Fire Drills"! What is a "Chinese Fire Drill"? A Drill Instructor enters the barracks at an ungodly hour of the morning, blows a whistle and yells "Fire!" And heaven help any "dud" who isn't out on the company street in 30 seconds, **carrying his footlocker!** It seemed like the Army was conducting a sociological experiment to determine which approach produced the most reliable soldiers, the "easy" or the "hard." But I'll never know if my company or the adjacent one housed the guinea pigs.

As the weeks raced by, whenever a weekend pass was available, I took to walking to a nearby motel that was respectably clean, affordable and, of course, air-conditioned. Paying for a room with a color TV was the only way I could be assured of getting to watch what I wanted to, like Track & Field meets. It was "The Summer of Love" for longhaired youth in America.

But my hair was absent, I was a long way from San Francisco, and I had zero experience with illicit drugs. Were those married guys still "chasing tail" on their weekend passes? And if so, were they doing a better job of minding their valuables? I didn't know and I didn't care. I was content in having found a way to escape the base, do some good reading and eat what I wanted.

Close call before moving on

Nearing the end of our eight weeks in Hell, we were likelier to be addressed as "young studs" by Cadre than as "maggots" or "duds." The atmosphere finally lightened. We practiced riot control formations, popularly known as "the National Guard shuffle." Perhaps an army of hippies was assembling in Columbia, preparing to storm the base?

As it turned out, the physical element of final exams was not a pushover for me. I scored <u>zero</u> points on one of the five events! No do-overs, either. This happened in the Run, Dodge and Jump: one snakes his way around and between barriers—hurdles like used in Track & Field, or to steer traffic around a road repair site—jumps a trench maybe four feet wide, executes more barriers, then negotiates the course in reverse direction, racing against a time limit. The problem was that I failed to cross the trench diagonally to dodge around the final barrier. I made my turns very sharp and tight; really, I had never moved so nimbly in my life. I was concentrating so hard on the turns that I didn't watch where I was going closely enough and failed that particular event. I managed to avoid being "recycled" back into BCT by the skin of my teeth, or rather of my feet, enclosed in the combat boots that my unusually narrow feet never did get used to. My time in the final event, the Mile Run, was 6 minutes 31 seconds, and that gained me enough points to just squeak by in overall score.

Graduation Day is a blur in my memory. We all had our orders detailing where we were heading next for Advanced Individual Training. But first we had to hit the Parade Ground. It was a nice, sunny, South Carolina-hot mid-July day. We had to show the reviewing Brass Hats that we knew our Manual of Arms and could pass in review and execute "Eyes . . . right!"

Few relatives of graduates were able to attend. Mostly it was a show to entertain colonels and generals. The base commander and a guest general made standard speeches that went in one ear and out the other. "The great tradition continues . . . "; "Defending peace and democracy around the world . . . "; "Stopping Communist aggression . . . " and blah, blah, blah. Predictable bullshit.

"Dis-**missed!**" Bam, outta there and back to the barracks to grab our already-packed duffel bags and head for buses to the airport. Quick handshake and "Good luck!" with some of the NCOs and fellow graduates. I was off to beautiful Texas for phase two of my Army "career."

CHAPTER III

Weird times in Texas

Fort Sam Houston, Texas
July 15-October 13, 1967

Upon arriving at my new duty station, I was instantly tossed into limbo, a victim of the calendar. It would be three weeks before the next basic Medical Corpsman (MOS 91B-10) course would launch. This left those of us waiting with the decidedly unappealing prospect of being sent on endless Police Calls and other petty time-filling activities around the base. But a way out was soon offered: we could sign up for Truck Driving School.

July 20, 1967

Dear Folks,

When we (15 from Ft. Jackson) arrived here, we were asked if we'd like to be truck drivers. I said I don't drive standards; "That's okay, we'll teach you." So, I signed up. This first week, we do nothing but work: cleaning out warehouses; breaking up lumber; folding blankets. Next week, they ship us to nearby Camp Bullis for a week of practice driving; the third week, we drive, at last.

Tuesday, we were given an eye test which is impossible to fail unless one be totally blind; part of it involved depth-perception—I flunked that part (no wonder I can't catch a pop-fly baseball!) but passed the overall test. The food is much better than in Basic, and, joyously I report that the milk is <u>unlimited</u>! The wildlife is abundant here—a large (Texas-style) hare ran across the runway as we landed in San Antonio; I wasn't on the fort itself more than five minutes before a lizard scampered by; there are birds and insects too numerous to mention; and this morning, one of the guys discovered a very un-Texas-like (closer to Rhode Island-like) frog: exactly 3/8 of an inch long!! He could only hop about 6 inches at a time; how he manages to escape from his enemies, I don't know.

Some of the guys helping us truck drivers fold blankets today are finished with their 10-week course and will graduate tomorrow. They revealed the following good news: those who were drafted are being sent to 'Nam; enlistees are being sent to hospitals in relatively-safe Korea.

The earliest I could possibly come home is mid-October, so keep my LPs dust-free; I'll be home eventually. 'Bye for now.

Love,
Greg
YOUR SON, THE TRUCK DRIVER

Truck driver adventures

August 13, 1967

Dear Folks,

Truck Driving School was unbelievable. Here I was, hardly having driven a stick before, and the first thing they put me into to drive is a monstrous cargo truck (the classic "deuce-and-a-half"—13,000 pounds of steel). Well, before I knew it, I was climbing hills with it. These trucks are fantastic in their mobility and versatility. One reason is what's under the hood: a 478 cubic inch engine! That is larger than most dragster engines!!

My main problem, of course, was shifting. The jeeps were okay, but the big trucks had the gear selector positions so close that I frequently went from 2nd to 5th, thus stalling out. Fifth and Third were that close! The military license I now hold is good till July 28, 1970. Chances are strong, though, that I'll never use it again, having completed my week of driving chores. I've seen a dead armadillo on a roadside; haven't yet seen a live one. Speaking of Nature, it's frightening how acclimatized I've become to this heat. Friday night it went down to 70 degrees and I found myself actually shivering!!! I dread the thought of going North again; if it went down to 60 degrees, I might freeze to death.

Interesting notes: this post is where Conscientious Objectors are given their basic training. In talking to them, I've found that they're nowhere near fanatical as I am: these are the kids whose religions (Seventh Day Adventist, Southern Anabaptist, etc.) require them to be COs. There's really no intellectual foundation at all behind their refusal to bear arms. Some are religious to the point that they say grace for themselves before each meal. SUICIDE: I've heard from other guys about soldiers in their Basic Training companies attempting, and some succeeding, in suicide by jumping in front of trucks. Also of interest, two tornadoes showed up south of here the night it went down to 70 degrees. I've been here a month now, and it's only rained appreciably once.

I'm writing this at the PX, and guys are making all kinds of distracting noises as they drink their beer (yes, the main PX has a "beer garden"), thus ruining my concentration. To complete my comments on suicide, I meant to add that just yesterday, a guy in our company (D-1) took an overdose of sleeping pills. Two guys were walking him around for an hour, at the end of which the ambulance had not yet shown up. GRAFFITI: written on latrine wall at Camp Bullis—"Peace is a never scene," and "San Francisco's where I ought to be, loaded to the gills with LSD." So you see, I'm not alone. There are other would-be hippies here.

Well, this is my last sheet of paper, and it's almost time to shine my boots, shoes and brass. Next week I'll have impressions of this medic course. 'Bye for now.

Love,
Greg
NON-COMBAT MEDIC NOW BEING
TRAINED AS COMBAT MEDIC!

* * *

August 20, 1967

Dear Folks,

Not much to tell this week. Here's what the course has covered thus far: Anatomy and Physiology; taking Temperature, Pulse, Respiration and Blood Pressure; control of Hemorrhage; Making a Hospital Bed, including one with a patient still in it; Positioning the Patient; Observing the Patient; Ward Duties; Equipment Maintenance; Assembling Tents (for field hospital or aid station)—which is fun!; and basic information on how the Army operates in "the field" (COMBAT). You see, I am being trained as a Combat Medic because I enlisted for Medical in general. This, of course, I refuse to be. Thus, I'm a "<u>Non-Combat</u> Medic Now Being Trained as a <u>Combat</u> Medic." But I might have found a way to stay out of 'Nam and Korea.

You can never be certain of anything in the Army, but I've found a pretty sure way out. There is one and only one course of further training that we (enlisted personnel) may apply for <u>before</u> they ship us to a regular Unit ('Nam). Apparently there's a critical shortage of Practical Nurses (MOS 91C20), so a course, 40 weeks long, is available to us volunteers who qualify (draftees cannot take it; those poor slobs are guaranteed to go to combat). I got 59 of a possible 60 points on my first test, so I'm looking good. Upon graduating the 40-week course, I'm required to serve 2 years as a Practical

Nurse, but if it means an Honorable Discharge, rather than the other kind, it will be worth it. NOTE: 91C20s **are** sent to 'Nam, but not in vast droves like Combat Medics. So, once again, I'm gambling. I just might come out a winner, though. There could even be an extra bonus: one of the 8 hospitals teaching the course is in San Francisco!

Please <u>do</u> forward (<u>cheaply</u>) articles on 'Nam, hippies, sports, etc. That is my only request for now, except for this (which is more like a direct order): DON'T get too depressed and DON'T overdo the pill-swallowing. That's all for now.

Love,
Greg

Weirdness breaking out all over

August 26, 1967

Dear Folks,

This won't be long; it's Saturday night and I have KP tomorrow. I've already had it here once, and, miracle of miracles, I did <u>not</u> get on Pots 'n' Pans!! And I was one of the last to arrive at the Mess Hall; it doesn't matter when you arrive, it's purely luck. I hope my luck holds out tomorrow.

As for writing to Congressmen, to vent your frustrations (that's all you'll accomplish; no one can get LBJ to pull out), go right ahead. It's safe. The only way you can get me in trouble is to make a complaint, naming me. (Ex.: Pvt. Laxer is being picked on, abused verbally or physically, etc.)

As for the wildlife around here, in this fantastic state (the sunsets are gorgeous), I have these notes: 1.) today, there were two big, healthy cockroaches crawling around the Mess Hall; and, 2.) Thursday, a louse bit me on the hand!

Ridiculous things have been happening this week (so what else is new?). Thursday night, MPs were all over the place. We soon learned that some fool had taken a handful of tranquilizers, mixed them with something that made him high as a kite, and staggered off into the darkness. Fearing that he might have taken a fatal dose, the company's executive officer had us searching for him from 10 to midnight, assuming he might be unconscious. So, we got to bed at 12:30, and had to get up at the usual time, 5:00, Friday morning. The search, which covered a golf course and a cemetery, was fruitless. Apparently, since no corpses have turned up, he didn't take much stuff after all. He seems to have managed to get off the post and succeed at going AWOL. Now he's really in trouble.

We were supposed to have a parade this morning, so we got all dressed up. We assembled; we prepared to head for the parade grounds. Inexplicably, the parade was then cancelled. Typical Army maneuver.

Well, I have more to say, but lights are about to go out. 'Bye.

Love,
Greg

Get religion or get to work!

The atmosphere at Ft. Sam was looser than the extremely controlled, harassment-around-the- clock scene in Basic Training. Perhaps this explained propensities for self-destructive conduct suddenly surfacing in some of the trainees. Or maybe there was just "something in the air" in Texas. There would be more weirdness to follow. The first couple of weekends saw us pretty well restricted to the company compound. It was made clear to us that if we didn't opt to attend religious services Sunday mornings, some kind of time-filling work assignment would be found to occupy us. My, what a pious fort! So I partnered with a bright guy of Japanese-American descent named Seito, and we went off to explore a bit of religion. Seito was a Protestant of some denomination, but we went to the Catholic chapel that first Sunday. We had at least one Jewish guy in our barracks, and I teamed with him to attend a Jewish service the following Sunday. The Jewish Sabbath starts at sundown on Friday, of course. But the Army outranked

God, so to be a rabbi in the Chaplaincy Corps required flexibility. Suffice it to say, I was not won over to any of the creeds being offered.

Where was God?

The Laxer family was not a churchgoing household. My mother expressed vague Christian feelings on occasion but Dad was another story. Despite his own Lutheran mom—or perhaps as a reaction against her, since she'd insisted he be baptized—George raised himself a hardcore atheist. He considered the contents of the Bible to be sheer poppycock. Among the books I read on his advice were Thomas Paine's The Age Of Reason, and the collection of Mark Twain's satirical pieces on religion posthumously published as Letters From The Earth.

Despite his own attitude, my dad had urged me in childhood to keep an open mind to matters of religion. In fact, he pledged that he would personally chauffeur me to the church or synagogue of my choice if I desired to get a taste of what those institutions had to offer. I never took him up on that offer, for two chief reasons. First, I was already immersed in studying the natural world. I was quite convinced that no supernatural cause is necessary to explain how we *homo sapiens* came into existence. The second reason I could muster no enthusiasm for exploring mainstream religion arose from simple observation: Look at the godawful (pardon the expression) mess the world was in. Every night, through the miracle of television, we could watch the murderous mistreatment of civilians in Vietnam. In the name of democracy. In the name of the people of America. The bombs were actually blessed by US military chaplains. So yes, in the name of God.

The issue was not one of crying out "If you're up there, God, how can you allow this to happen?!" The issue was that policies of great evil were being concocted and carried out by people who claimed to be adherents of the great mainstream religions. And the US war in Southeast Asia was only one component of the inhumanity of Man on display globally. I did not possess the words to describe my revulsion with the state of the world and the Conventional Wisdom that helped keep it mired in these horrors. Bob Dylan had addressed these cosmic questions of morality in his song

"With God on Our Side," severely questioning the Conventional Wisdom that "you never ask questions" about the propriety of what government decrees to be justified. And so, it took the threat of Sunday morning Police Calls to drive me to the chapels on the base. Subsequent weekends became more relaxed and the base atmosphere was actually tolerable enough that I didn't feel a need to take a motel room to escape.

September 3, 1967

Dear Folks,

Well, things are just as crazy around here as ever. Friday morning, I was awakened at 4:15 AM by loud bawling—I mean, this guy was really sobbing his heart out. He was pacing the street, wringing his hands, crying out, "Oh God, please . . . " Well, I considered this a rather serious situation, so I got out of bed and looked out the window. He seemed to be clutching one arm, so I immediately thought of attempted suicide (slashed wrists) or some serious injury. I pulled on my pants and was stepping out the door when he entered another barracks. I assumed he would be safe then, so staggered back to bed (which wasn't too helpful, since everybody had to get up in another 20 minutes anyway).

How's this grab you? I had KP last Sunday; I have it tomorrow, Labor Day! My only opportunity for a day off since July 4, and I have KP. Damn it to hell!!! By the way, I have avoided Pots and Pans so far.

I have been officially tapped for 91C20, the Practical Nurse Course. I have gotten 97 out of 100 questions correct on my tests; if I maintain a 90% average and get the Company Commander's recommendation (which simply entails staying out of trouble, which, miraculously, I have done) I have it all wrapped up. The course starts Nov. 15, at 2 hospitals. One is in the mecca of the hip, San Francisco!! But only California residents can go there. I'll be going to Valley Forge, PA. This is reasonably close to home. In 9 more days I make E-2 automatically. At the end of the 40-week course, I will be E-4. Pretty good deal, huh? As for leave: if I'm to get off for Christmas, I must take a short (4-7 days) leave at end of my present course (Oct. 13).

Then I will serve in the hospital for a few weeks in the role I'm now being trained for, basic Medical Corpsman. I simply must get to bed, so, till next week, 'bye.

Love,
Greg
PERPETUAL KP

P.S.: Please send a book of 5-cent stamps.

"Summer of Love"

Clearly, I was obsessed with getting to San Francisco, but that would take a while. The Beatles had released *Sgt. Pepper's Lonely Hearts Club Band* and on those rare occasions when a radio was nearby, we could hear some of the tunes released as singles. The music of Jefferson Airplane and other Bay Area bands was drawing this New Yorker inexorably toward the West. The Monterey International Pop Festival had taken place in June, while I was still mired in BCT. D.A. Pennebaker was there to document the event. In the meantime, Mr. Pennebaker had just released a movie that caught my attention: *Don't Look Back*, taking us behind the scenes, and on stage, with Bob Dylan during his tour of England in 1965. Quite by accident, I learned that this film was being shown in San Antonio. I used a precious weekend pass for a pilgrimage through dusty backstreets of that city, finally locating the little "art house" cinema where it was being exhibited.

September 16, 1967

Dear Folks,

To answer some of your questions: Of course, I wasn't the only guy stuck with KP on Labor Day, but I was unfortunate enough to be one of the group of 28 out of close to 900 men whose luck ran out. As for the tests, they are ridiculously easy, with the result that many guys get 90s, but thanks to my good memory, I get in the <u>upper</u> 90s. I've taken 3 tests since I last wrote, with these scores: 94, 96 and 100. My overall average: 97.4.

What have I been doing lately, you ask. Well, I've managed to take a rectal temperature without doing too much damage; I've given an injection with a morphine syrette (a syrette is a "baby syringe," with everything pre-measured and sterilized so that it's real easy to give the injection under combat conditions; of course, we only injected glucose and water, not morphine). In the near future, we'll be getting the "good stuff": giving each other enemas (yecch!) and intravenous injections. Yesterday, amazingly, was the <u>first time</u> in my four months in the Army that I was subjected to hardcore propaganda. We were shown two movies, one on Communism in the US, the other on why we're in Vietnam (naturally, they couldn't explain it to <u>my</u> satisfaction). The latter movie featured some of our beloved Lyndon's speeches, and ended with a real cornball, cliche sequence of the Statue of Liberty at night. That wraps it up for now. 'Bye.

Love,
Greg
WORLD'S GREATEST MEDIC

P.S.: I think I heard something about a big Peace demonstration this weekend (SEPT. 16 & 17). So please look through NY Times for Sat., Sun. and Mon., the 16th, 17th and 18th and send any and all articles. Thanx.

It's a sign of the degree to which we were isolated on Army bases that I felt compelled to ask my mother to keep me informed on a major national peace demonstration. We had no daily access to radio or TV newscasts, and we were kept so busy that most of the time I didn't bother buying newspapers (available at the PX or in coin vending machines). Oh, and that business about we trainees having to administer enemas to one another? Fortunately, that never happened!

Breaking out in a cold sweat

I was never particularly squeamish about the sight of blood. In fact, it's accurate to say I was, and am, less squeamish than the average person. But one day we were subjected to a class that nearly put me on the floor.

The class was held under a large tent on a particularly hot, humid Texas day. We were shown a training film that gave a very real-life look at what happens in a field hospital near a combat zone. The footage probably dated back to World War II or Korea. A soldier had suffered a serious wound to the muscles of one of his calves. The field surgeons proceeded to carve away huge chunks of this man's flesh, like the proverbial hot knife moving through butter. The muscle tissue had been deemed beyond salvation.

Before long, as this operation continued to unfold on the screen before us, I broke out in a profuse sweat. It was a very cold sweat! Next time you see a movie or TV show depicting someone experiencing this phenomenon, you have my word that the phenomenon can be all too real. The combination of the stifling atmosphere inside the tent and the images on the screen put me into what is called, in medical terminology, psychogenic shock. By the time this class concluded, I was right on the brink of passing out. Only my pride—the desire to avoid embarrassing myself—kept me conscious until we trainees got outside into fresher air and I was able to recover. I was soaked in this cold sweat; it trickled down my torso under my t-shirt and fatigue shirt, and down my legs inside my fatigue pants. An experience I don't wish to ever go through again.

"At the Zoo"

Guys who surrendered entirely to their hormones started using weekend passes to ride the bus south, patronizing brothels in Mexico. And pretty wild were the tales they brought back from "Boys' Town." The more sedate Private Seito and I settled for an expedition one Saturday to explore downtown San Anton'. Seito was "different"—different by ethnicity, part of a quite small minority of Asian-Americans on the base; different by dint of being very bright and open-minded. He certainly was no lover of the concept of war.

We started, naturally, by going to the Alamo, which is right downtown. The exterior I found not that exciting, and I didn't feel inspired to pay for a tour of the interior. We pushed ahead, along the famous River Walk. I again succumbed to the idea that a soldier on weekend pass should drink. I acquired some brews and, inspired by the Simon & Garfunkel hit single "At the Zoo," we headed for San Antonio's version of such an establishment.

Once I'd gotten beyond being merely tipsy, I decided it was time to find out what all the fuss over marijuana was. I accosted some poor Chicano fellow who was innocently walking by and demanded to know where I could find some. He was taken aback at this interrogation and professed ignorance. Indeed, he might have thought this shorthaired guy getting in his face was a plainclothes cop! I remember with complete clarity my next statement (my speech slurring): "Well, it's a goddamn **Mexican** word, ain't it?!" That did not go over at all well with this gent. Thank goodness Seito was there, and mostly sober, to step between us and beg forgiveness for his drunken companion's rudeness. The aftermath of that binge was predictably unpleasant. It would be the last time I'd get "stinkin' falling-down drunk."

September 24, 1967

Dear Folks,

On Friday, I had my last KP. I'll have Guard Duty 2, possibly 3 more times, but the KP roster is closed. It was my fourth KP here, and, for the fourth time, I escaped Pots and Pans. Hallelujah!

This past week we had all kinds of repulsive movies—tubes being shoved up penises, down throats, noses; emergency surgery where they just slice a guy's belly wide open, without even putting on sterile gloves, etc. We also had a helluva lot of rain, thanks to Hurricane Beulah.

Some guys have already received their orders; they're going to Thailand. The guys being ordered to 'Nam should be getting their orders this week; I should get mine the following week.

As for your questions: 1.) Yes, I get some news on Vietnam, but no details. I simply read the headlines on the front pages each day as I walk past the paper-vending machines at the PX; 2.) Yes, I got the $25.

Well, please keep searching for articles on hippies, 'Nam, etc. Until next week, 'bye.

Love,
Greg

The best time I ever had on KP was on one of these Ft. Sam assignments. There was a sweet, goofy Seventh Day Adventist named John Kiplinger working in the sink area with me. He had one of those big gaps between his front upper teeth. John lived in a different barracks, so I normally had no contact with him. He explained to me the SDA philosophy that made it mandatory to apply for Conscientious Objector status. All the religious COs I encountered during my stay in Texas seemed like really nice kids. John and I discovered, quite by accident, that when enough soapsuds spill over from the sink onto the floor—a floor made from large tiles with a brick-like, but quite smooth, surface—you can go "skating" on them. And that's exactly what we did: skated from end to end of the clean-up area to our hearts' content, laughing our butts off. Versatile footgear, those combat boots.

Evicted from a movie theater

Fort Sam, like any military base of significant size, had its own movie theaters. They showed the major studio releases, not just jingoistic drivel, but with a delay. So it was that the highly-praised 1966 film *A Man For All Seasons*, the story of Sir Thomas More's struggles with King Henry VIII over matters of principle in 16th Century England, came to be exhibited on our dusty Texas home away from home. A fight over matters of principle; yes, I could relate to that.

In Army movie theaters the first order of business, before the running of coming attractions or anything else, was the National Anthem. An image of the flag, waving in a make-believe breeze, would appear on the screen shortly before the music of "The Star-Spangled Banner" would blare from the speakers. Some lifer would yell "ON YOUR FEET!" The entire audience was expected to fly up from their seats in a fraction of a second and stand at rigid attention until the music ended. I had two objections to this practice: 1.) I was tired of being required to snap to attention multiple times in a typical day in the life of a soldier; 2.) I was not fond of what the US flag had come to symbolize in the contemporary world. So I remained seated while everyone else followed standard procedure.

No one immediately surrounding me made a peep about my action, or rather refusal to act. Several minutes passed; the opening titles of the movie had started to roll, the auditorium lights dimmed. Good Lord, was I going to get away with it? No! Someone had reported me to the management after all, and I was duly escorted to the main entrance and sent on my way into the glaring Texas sun. No refund. This was a weekend matinee and I was wearing civvies. No one took down my name to report me to my unit, so this first act of political resistance brought no further consequences.

"My name's 'Bull' Miller and I tip my hat to you!"

My days at Ft. Sam were dwindling rapidly. Due to a time lag before the next round of Clinical Specialist training courses would commence, those of us accepted into that program would actually get to go home for a while. Our First Sergeant for Company D was 'Bull' Miller. This senior NCO was actually very seldom seen around the company compound. Perhaps he spent most days on the golf course. His appearance fit his nickname to a 't': a stout fellow with very muscular forearms and shaved head. My fellow trainees and I, in this particular training company, had scored considerably higher in our exams than the average on the base at the time. As we were in formation and just starting to march off to the graduation ceremony, "Top" (slang for a First Sergeant) suddenly appeared on the side of the street. Lifting his helmet liner from his smooth-as-glass scalp, he bellowed: "My name is 'Bull' Miller and I tip my hat to you!" Despite all the bullshit that being a soldier entails, I don't mind telling you this sudden apparition and his proclamation made us rather proud.

Summer was over, but the war certainly was not. A major peace demonstration was scheduled to be held outside the Pentagon during my leave. Regular Army troops would be deployed in a defensive perimeter around that immense building and that day's events would inspire Norman Mailer to write <u>The Armies of the Night</u>. My next stop would be Valley Forge General Hospital, in Pennsylvania. I had thrown the dice and won a ten-month delay in my inescapable confrontation with the War Machine.

CHAPTER IV
"Happy Valley Days"

Valley Forge General Hospital
October 28, 1967-September 22, 1968

Valley Forge General Hospital was one of eight such institutions the Army maintained in the continental US during the Vietnam Era. These facilities were larger and practiced medicine more comprehensively than standard base hospitals. VFGH, which we of the Student Detachment came to call "Happy Valley," was not located at Valley Forge itself, but just outside the little town of Phoenixville. It was about a 40-minute train ride from downtown Philadelphia.

I had had my first leave after completing the Medical Corpsman course at Fort Sam. My mother, as mothers tend to, thought I looked very impressive in my Class A uniform when I got off the plane at JFK Airport. I, of course, was bursting with impatience to strip those threads off and be a temporary civilian. It was impossible to spend a tranquil time at home in Syosset, due to Mom's deteriorating emotional state. It was a relief to borrow a car and go record shopping, or to hole up in the den to catch up on the luxury of watching TV. In due time I reported for my advanced medical training, having the misfortune to arrive at the start of a weekend. Stuck in limbo yet again!

October 31, 1967

Dear Folks,

This is my first opportunity to write, now that I know my address. I wasn't given a permanent place to live until yesterday (Monday); Saturday & Sunday I had to sleep anywhere I could find a bunk! Where have we (the students) been settled? On a hospital ward, that's where! There are advantages, however. The mattresses are thick, and the head of the bed can be elevated almost to the vertical to convert it into an easy chair. The food is excellent; civilians do all the work. I forgot to mention that the ward we're living on is right next door to one containing real patients..........mental patients!!

The personnel here seem real nice, and so they should be, with the chow and other things so nice around here.

I'll be wearing civvies around here a lot, probably every evening, so the one shirt I brought ain't enough. So, please grab an assortment of my shirts (your choice), put 'em in a box, and mail them to me. And how about throwing my beer mug in the box? Thanx. My address is:

STUDENT DETACHMENT (3416)
VALLEY FORGE GENERAL HOSPITAL
PHOENIXVILLE, PA 19460

There's nothing more to say, at this time, except Happy Birthday to Linda. Until next week, 'bye.

Love,
Greg
MEDICAL CORPSMAN OUT IN "THE STICKS" FOR 42 WEEKS

The former ward housing us students was built of brick, like the rest of the hospital complex. It was one large open bay, with a large latrine at one end. There were a few NCOs enrolled in the course—something of a surprise, lifers who'd decided to change direction in mid-career—who lived in Bachelor NCO housing or off grounds. Staff Sgt. Pell, a very decent fellow, was our "remote" platoon leader; though he didn't live with us, he would inspect our quarters in the morning and relay vital information about schedule changes, special work details, etc. There were even three or four WACs (members of the Women's Army Corps), housed separately of course, enrolled in the program. That took us by surprise, even though nursing in the civilian realm was traditionally a woman's occupation. The world of military medical personnel, in contrast, was very male-dominated. Female military personnel at the time were not put in combat situations.

Reality quickly settled in: no private or semi-private rooms, no TVs. So we were not accorded the privileges of being Permanent Party, but we could leave the base on pass almost daily after classes. Those of us most into music would eventually bring portable record players into our environment, and put up personal wall art. Military discipline did not go out the window, of course: we each still had to maintain a properly organized footlocker, display our highly shined footgear, etc.

My fellow students had come from different training classes at Ft. Sam, so these guys were all strangers to me. Getting acquainted became one of my first tasks. I made no secret whatsoever, from day one, of how I felt about the war in Southeast Asia. This brought no outright hostility, nor did it evoke rousing cheers. There were about 18 of us privates in the converted ward, including a gentleman originally from Ecuador. Lumping in the NCOs and WACs housed elsewhere, we were a class of about 30, and some would start flunking out fairly quickly. Ours was, after all, to be an intense course of study.

November 5, 1967

Dear Folks,

A very hip place, this Philadelphia! Could it be the Quaker influence? The people are friendlier, politer than in New York. Hippies are everywhere.

Friday was frantic! At 2 PM, I chanced upon a newspaper, and discovered that Joan Baez was giving a concert at the U. of Penn. at 8:30. I got off work at 4:00, and what should happen but that I got assigned to an extra work detail until 4:45. But I made it! And I didn't get lost once on the Philadelphia subways! Joanie is fantastic, but got only a lukewarm reception. These U. of Penn. kids are frightfully conservative.

Next Saturday night, I'll be seeing James Brown in person for the second time.

The work I've been doing is mostly janitorial! Since we'll only be working a week before school starts, they (the administration) aren't involving us much in patient care.

Well, until next week, 'bye.

Love,
Greg
US ARMY JANITOR

A most unusual Mormon

Fellow student Richard M. John, who preferred to be called 'Mike-Jack,' was a most interesting character. I had never met a regular Mormon, and here was a member of a sect whose founders had been excommunicated from the mainstream church for heretical views. This sect actually demanded its adherents enlist in the military and volunteer for Vietnam duty! 'Mike-Jack' spoke of encounters with "psilocybin monsters" (from psychedelic mushrooms) and claimed his own counter-chant for marching and running in Basic Training had been: "I want to be an Airborne Medic, I want to go to Vietnam; I want to be an Airborne Medic, I want to **heal** the Viet Cong"!!

This rotund fellow was a little weird, but fun. He was most definitely "different." That made him a kindred soul. He never engaged in serious proselytizing for his sect. He was the only fellow student who accompanied me to Philly to attend anti-war meetings. I know the majority of the others had serious qualms about what the US military was doing to the people of

Vietnam, but they had grown up accepting the philosophy my own father had urged: "Don't make waves."

November 12, 1967

Dear Folks,

Well, Friday was my last day as a Corpsman. Wednesday, school starts, and Monday and Tuesday I suppose will be orientations to the course, textbook issue, etc.

My morale is high, despite the presence of some pathetic cases around here: both legs amputated, many cases of arm amputation, deep bullet wounds, maimed faces, etc. Friday, a new patient was brought in. Apparently, his trachea was no longer usable, so the doctors had taken skin grafts from his stomach and actually constructed an <u>external</u> windpipe—a tube made of his own skin running from his lungs to his mouth <u>outside</u> his body.

Needless to say, I am more anti-war than ever. I am more militant about refusing orders for 'Nam. I have placed over my bed a large (about 42 X 30 inches) poster portrait of Joan Baez. I don't expect this to cause any trouble; wall decorations are allowed, and the only people we were told not to post pictures of are the likes of Mao, Soviet Premier Kosygin, Stalin, Ho, etc.

James Brown was out of sight last night. The reaction of the colored people has to be seen and heard in person to be believed. Unfortunately, the show lasted till 11:30 and there were no more trains out of Philly. The YMCA was full, so it cost me $8.40 for a hotel room.

Love,
Greg
FLOWER POWER KING OF THE ARMY

Soul Brothers and others

The James Brown concert was in an outlying black neighborhood, serviced by an elevated train line. It was a good-sized theater and it was packed. Yours truly was one of only a handful of white people in the crowd, bringing some curious stares. The whole production was brilliant showmanship, and JB must have expended as many calories as a marathon runner in each performance. He really was 'The Hardest Working Man in Show Business.'

We had two black guys living in the barracks. Sam McIntosh was from Texas, and he and his brother had been active in the Civil Rights Movement down there. Once we students learned of the liberal wall art policy in our domicile, Sam hung a poster of Malcolm X. This had to make the administration more uneasy than my own poster of Baez, but it was tolerated. All I knew about Malcolm in late 1967 was that he was considered "a menace to society" and had been assassinated.

Our other resident soul brother was Bill Kaiser. Bill was an old-school Baptist from the Deep South whose playing of gospel records in any spare time available drove me up the wall. My attitude earned me a stern lecture from McIntosh: "Man, don't you understand that, where Bill comes from, Jesus is all there is to cling to for hope?!" Coming from the social environment of my upbringing, no, that hadn't occurred to me. But Sam duly set me straight.

Philadelphia, "City of Brotherly Love." This name doubtless is a vestige of the Quaker influence in Pennsylvania. There was definitely an "alternative scene" there, and hippies all over. When they tried to assert a right, as citizens, to hang out in Rittenhouse Square—a haunt of the very well-heeled—there was quite a row. The first "Progressive Rock" FM radio station I ever heard was based in Philly; some of the on-air staff referred to their little city as "Psychedelphia."

My letters home became less frequent, and shorter, now. Getting from Phoenixville back home for a weekend wasn't all that time consuming when you traveled with Bob Griggs, who applied the nickname 'Clyde' to himself. He was a New Jersey guy and had his own car at the post. He drove at an average speed of 100 m.p.h. on the New Jersey Turnpike. Bob was a good 6-foot-3 and skinny. He definitely did not see eye to eye with me about opposing the war, but he was a decent enough guy to give a wannabe-hippie a lift now and then to the outskirts of NYC, from which I could make my way to Syosset via Long Island Railroad. Failing that, there was always Greyhound. I took advantage of one of these weekend trips home to fetch my portable stereo record player.

Among the other guys who would make it to the end of the course and become friends were Dennis Kirkland, Bob Crossley and John Colson. Dennis was a wiry kid from South Dakota, where anti-war protesters were probably akin to Martians. Crossley was a bright, good-looking, soft-spoken guy from Texas. But he'd made a poor judgment in his youth, he would eventually reveal, leading to a judge giving him the choice of some jail time or military enlistment. Colson, a.k.a. 'Jon-Jon,' was a local Pennsylvania fellow. Essentially good kids, far from "gung-ho" for the war, but not willing to actively oppose it.

And then there was Harry 'FUBAR' (his own choice of nickname) Connell, a Princeton Man. He had red hair and, not surprisingly, a billion freckles. I decided he should be known as 'Harvey,' as in the six-foot-tall red-haired rabbit imagined by Jimmy Stewart's character in the movie of that name. On one of his own weekend jaunts home, 'FUBAR' secured a copy of *Sgt. Pepper's Lonely Hearts Club Band* and brought it back to the barracks. Finally, I got to hear what all the fuss was about. But the impact of this album on my generation wasn't confined to what lay in the grooves of the LP. The album art presented to the world its four most famous living musicians sporting mustaches or beards. I made a vow that on day one of our forthcoming winter holiday break, I would allow my mustache to start growing. Anything to show resistance to the Established Order.

From "Mustache Power" to Carnegie Hall

Army regulations allowed the sporting of a mustache after Basic Training if it appeared on one's Military Photo ID Card. How to arrange this? Upon returning to VFGH in early January 1968, I claimed to have lost my ID

Card. I went to Personnel and a Polaroid photo was taken showing my new upper-lip decoration. The final step was obtaining our First Sergeant's signature on the paperwork for issuance of the new card. When I presented him with the form, 'Top' was so busy with other paperwork he signed my form without even glancing up at me. I won't claim credit for a full-fledged revolution, but my mustache victory did open the door to facial hair for low-ranking EM on our base, and several of my fellow students immediately started to cultivate hairy upper lips.

Meanwhile, I was building a little LP library, to supplement what 'Harvey' provided for our entertainment. I'd discovered, courtesy of the progressive FM station in "Psychedelphia," the existence of the second **Country Joe & The Fish** album. This was *I Feel Like I'm Fixin' to Die*, containing a song highly relevant to everyone in the military at the time, which I made a point of sharing with my fellow students:

> *And it's 1, 2, 3 what're we fightin' for?*
> *Don't ask me I don't give a damn,*
> *Next stop is Vietnam.*
> *And it's 5, 6, 7 open up the Pearly Gates.*
> *Well, there ain't no time to wonder why . . .*
> *Whoopee, we're all gonna die!*

—I Feel Like I'm Fixin' to Die Rag, *by 'Country Joe' & The Fish*

(Copyright Joe McDonald, 1965; renewed 1993, Alkatraz Corner Music; all rights reserved. Used with permission.)

But the big news on the music scene was a concert tribute to Woody Guthrie, who'd died in late 1967, to be held at Carnegie Hall the evening of January 20. Most of the major performers on the Folk scene wanted to be on the bill, but the buzz about the event got louder when it was announced that **Bob Dylan** would be there. Yes, Dylan was scheduled to give his first public performance since having reportedly broken his neck in a motorcycle crash. Tickets had been on sale over two weeks before I even learned of the concert, but I'd been able to secure decent seats for my sister and myself directly from the box office during the visit home for Christmas.

An in-ranks barracks inspection was called on very short notice for the morning of the concert, but failed to derail my pilgrimage to Carnegie Hall. Cisco Houston and Odetta were stand-out performers that evening. Dylan's set was brief, but the crowd was electrified. Accompanying Bob were musicians who would go on to attain legendary status of their own as The Band. Dylan sang "I Ain't Got No Home," "Dear Mrs. Roosevelt," "Grand Coulee Dam" and "This Train is Bound for Glory." I felt very fortunate to have successfully gained entry to this historic gathering.

The war grinds on

At the end of January, the liberation forces mounted an offensive of stunning scope against Saigon's puppet military. This was the Tet offensive, Tet being the Vietnamese celebration of Lunar New Year. American public opinion was starting to turn against the war, as US casualties mounted into the hundreds per week. We citizens were supposed to accept that, because those on the other side were reportedly dying in much greater numbers. The body count game was underway. There were by now hundreds of thousands of US military personnel in Southeast Asia. Dr. Benjamin Spock, the epitome of humaneness, became one of the first public figures to feel the prosecutorial lash of the Establishment's wrath after encouraging draft resistance.

The training we were receiving in 91C School was closer to a college program to become a Registered Nurse than a trade school course to be a Licensed Practical Nurse (LPN). Green Beret medics would be expected to perform actual minor surgery in the field, like removing a burst appendix. We were being trained to perform one notch below that. Sooner than I'd expected, a fresh batch of fellow students would be departing, on academic grounds. We survivors kept on chugging ahead.

Another of our "college boys" was Ron Huska, who actually held a degree in Anthropology from the University of Texas. Like myself, he didn't have to spend much time reviewing to do well on exams. This allowed him to apply his considerable intellect to coming up with nicknames for some of his fellow students. He proclaimed himself to be 'Hot Rod' and our naturalized citizen by way of Ecuador to be Luis 'Go-Go' Zagata. Huska said that under the latter's calm exterior he detected a "party animal."

February 10, 1968

Dear Folks,

The situation in 'Nam gets more ridiculous every day. After the VC penetrated all the way to the embassy in Saigon and raised hell in general, the US claimed a smashing victory in the whole affair! What utter horse shit! Meanwhile, a story leaks out of Washington that nuclear weapons are being considered for use in 'Nam. When the day comes that they are used, that same day I am no longer a member of the Army.

This past week in school we practiced giving injections to one another. I'm pretty good with a needle, in light of the fact that I don't have any great amount of manual dexterity.

I'm swallowing iron pills, hoping I'm not found anemic on Thursday, when I'm supposed to donate blood. That's all till next week.

Love,
Greg
CLEAR-MINDED COLLEGE DROPOUT

* * *

February 18, 1968

Dear Folks,

Well, there's something big happening or going to happen in Korea. You remember my friend the religious fanatic who wanted to go to Vietnam so badly to render medical aid? Well, he put in his request for Vietnam. Request denied. They're sending him to Korea in March. There were about

15 other flunk-outs, basically half our class. Guess where they're being sent? Thirteen to Korea; 2 are staying stateside but are to be attached to Airborne units which are liable to be shipped out to Korea at any time. When a guy volunteers for 'Nam and Uncle Sam won't send him, you better believe there's something big building up in Korea.

See you on the 23rd, but don't ask me when. 'Bye.

Love,
Greg

P.S.: They took my blood, but can only use part of it because I'm allergic to Penicillin. I felt no ill effects from the loss. Naturally, I'm off the iron pills. Next time I go to donate, I'm gonna see if I can pass the hemoglobin test without pills.

'Mike-Jack' subscribed to the L.A. Free Press. One week along came an issue carrying a mail order ad for a short-sleeve sweatshirt bearing a very good likeness of Muhammad Ali. The champ's name appeared above the portrait, and below it was stated simply: "The Greatest." I just had to have one of those and duly launched my order. It arrived in time for me to sport it in Philadelphia when the weather warmed, and it won the admiration of a young black man I encountered downtown. He inquired as to why I chose to wear it. I explained it had as much to do with Ali's refusal to be drafted as with his skills in the ring. "Solid!" exclaimed the young fellow.

'Mike-Jack' and I had started attending weekend meetings of anti-war organizers at the American Friends Service Committee offices in South Philly. This was the social activism arm of the Quakers (formally, The Society of Friends). Initially, this made some attendees nervous. Our short hair gave away the fact that we were on active duty, and it was already known that the US government was infiltrating the anti-war movement at any opportunity. But our sincere interest soon allayed the fears of most of the civilians involved in these meetings.

"Happy Valley" nearly becomes Death Valley

Valley Forge General Hospital was a closed military installation. Relatives of patients recovering from war wounds were allowed to visit, of course, but the general public was not invited to observe the carnage of the Vietnam War. Military Police manned the main gate, armed with standard .45 caliber pistols. Despite the modest "military assets" of our facility (a motor pool!), as spring approached someone up the chain of command decided we needed to conduct a security exercise. A handful of soldiers would play the role of infiltrators of the base and the response time and "counter-terrorist" methods of the base MPs would be evaluated. With the anti-war movement gaining momentum, a base commander couldn't let his guard down when it came to security. What could be more menacing than flower-wielding peaceniks, after all?

One of our own in Student Detachment—Ron, a college-educated guy with curly reddish hair—was appointed to play one of the infiltrators. We all knew in advance of the night-time security exercise, and the exact date it would be held. It doesn't seem likely that the MPs would somehow not have been tipped off in advance. And yet . . . Ron would never return to our barracks after that night. An overzealous MP blew a gaping hole through his abdomen with his .45. Thank goodness, Ron survived his injury and was quietly ushered out of the Army. Very quietly, and doubtless with a generous disability payment for life. I don't think the story of this sad affair ever made it to the outside news media.

April 5-6, 1968: night of gunfire, day of decision

Saturday, April 6 was being targeted for a local anti-war action in Philly by the peace activists who met at the Quaker offices. 'Mike-Jack' and I had been sitting in on these planning sessions, but by April he'd been shipped to Korea. National protests were being planned for later in the month; this would be simply a "sit-down for peace" on a grassy plot of land outside the Philadelphia Navy Yard. I was wrestling with the question of my own participation. If I was arrested, or photographed and recognized later as active-duty military, there would be repercussions. Though the likelihood I'd be ordered to ship out to Vietnam at the end of my training was growing stronger every week, at this time there was still some dumb-luck chance I could serve out my commitment without a direct confrontation with the powers-that-be.

The situation became more complicated when Reverend Martin Luther King, Jr. was cut down by an assassin's bullet in Memphis, Tennessee the afternoon of Thursday, April 4. Word of this event, which was about to shake the United States to its foundation, spread like wildfire as soon as we students finished our final classroom session for the day. We were no less stunned than the population at large. There were people who quietly rejoiced at being rid of "that agitator," but among the young, less than thrilled about being in Army green, we felt a great gap open in the Universe. Sam McIntosh later told me he was incensed that I didn't offer him sympathetic words that day, but I'm not sure what I could have said. I headed the next evening to South Philly to attend the anti-war planning meeting. I even procured a cheap hotel room for the night, in city center. I was determined to attend the protest planned for Saturday, and would decide on the spot whether or not to actively participate.

The atmosphere in the meeting that evening was heavy with grief and somewhat subdued anger over the awful event in Memphis. None of us could know at that moment of the rage that would erupt that very night, and continue for days, in many major urban areas of the USA. The only real issue to be discussed was: do we go through with the action as planned, or postpone it in light of the national tragedy? A consensus quickly developed that the best way to honor the life and spirit of Dr. King would be precisely to carry out this demonstration as planned.

What happened within minutes of this discussion astounded us. Through the door burst an uninvited guest for a chat: none other than Frank Rizzo, Police Commissioner and future "law and order" Mayor of Philadelphia—by which time he'd have earned the sobriquet 'Ratzo Rizzo.' Rizzo had come to argue that the demonstration must not go forward in the current inflamed environment. A wall of resistance met his rant. He gave us his personal assurance that to engage in this protest would lead to our being arrested. Indeed, any public gathering of two or more people would be deemed a riot in the making: martial law, in essence. There was no reason to doubt the sincerity of the Commissioner's promise. But by a large plurality, we voted that the demonstration would go forward.

After the meeting, I went immediately to my hotel room. Sleep was hard to come by. Sporadic bursts of gunfire could be heard through the night, and the sirens of emergency vehicles. Arson was widespread in the downtown areas of many cities, including the nation's capital, for the next several days. Come morning, I went to a nearby coffee shop for a quick bite to eat. There I was accosted by a middle-aged working-class black man who reeked of liquor. Face contorted with grief, he demanded to know: "Why they had to kill that boy?!" Was I authorized to apologize on behalf of "the white race"? All I could sputter was that I, myself, was a follower of Dr. King.

I made for the site of the demonstration, just outside the Navy Yard. Peace activists materialized, as promised. Rizzo's cops were waiting. Protesters formed a large circle, seated on the grass. The atmosphere was very somber. I hovered on the periphery, declining to sit. What should I do? When the police commander announced by bullhorn that the crowd must disperse immediately or be arrested, I opted to avoid confrontation that day. There were 138 women, children and men who chose to not disperse and they were duly loaded into paddy wagons. My day in the City of Brotherly Love was over by noon, and I made my way to the train station for the ride back to Phoenixville.

April 14, 1968

Dear Folks,

The weather is superb. (Usually, almost without exception, it rains on Saturdays in Philly.) The sunshine brought out a lot of strollers. Lots of young black people with natural hair styles and African necklaces. Good to see racial pride, but the fact remains that nothing has changed. Even the death of so great a man as Dr. King cannot sway the course of this nation: America is going to hell. College kids, some of them really good-looking chicks, were out campaigning for Senator McCarthy. Passersby ignored them—they don't care about peace. Nixon will probably win—or maybe Humphrey! Every day brings us closer to disaster. I <u>urge</u> you to write in Dick Gregory and Benjamin Spock—the only other meaningful thing to do in November is to say to hell with voting, nobody on the ballot is worth expending the energy to pull a lever for; and that's dropping out, which is not what the country needs. So vote for Gregory and Spock! (I say this on the assumption that they won't be assassinated in the near future.)

The big thing in the near future should be the Poor Peoples Campaign in Washington. And, of course, watch for articles on protests aimed specifically against the war.

In the hospital, I just finished two weeks on a ward with neurological type patients. There was a lot more work involved than on the first ward. Tomorrow, I start 2 weeks on the Psychiatric wards, which will include assisting the doctors in administering electro-shock therapy. See you soon. 'Bye.

Love,
Greg

The Psychiatric Wards were, indeed, of interest to me. Who was mentally ill for real? Who was just trying to get out of the Army by any means available? Naturally, I had nothing but sympathy for those in both camps. I encountered some guys who seemed genuinely messed up, some of them apparently as a result of consuming copious doses of hallucinogenic drugs. Unsurprisingly, most of the patients were being heavily medicated. Thorazine was the go-to drug for slowing people down, inducing the "Thorazine shuffle." The experience of assisting with electro-shock was disturbing, to say the least. But its use was justified by the professionals on the grounds that it was a means of last resort to shake suicidal thoughts from the severely depressed individual's mind. Unfortunately, it did this by pretty well scrambling the whole mind.

May 12, 1968

Dear Folks,

Well, today I've been in the Army exactly one year. All I can say is: thank goodness the time is going quickly.

As for the fundraising plea from McCarthy, I burned it. A vote for Kennedy is a vote for McCarthy is a vote for Hubert is a vote for Rockefeller is a vote for Nixon is a vote for Reagan is a vote for Lyndon: they're all the establishment and to _hell_ with them. Vote for Gregory and Spock!

I'm following the peace talks closely. I maintain that there will be no peace until the US withdraws. Thanks for the articles, you're doing a good job. See you in a few weeks.

Love,
Greg

Codeine + beer + giant fly = bad night for 'Go-Go'

More than a year had passed since I entered the Army. I was 20 years old and still had never experimented with illicit drugs. This had to change! Purely in the interest of scientific exploration, of course. I enlisted Luis 'Go-Go' Zagata to join me in dabbling in opiates. Opiates and "cool Jazz."

At the time, cough syrup with codeine was sold over the counter, but there was a limit on how many bottles you could purchase in one visit to a given drug store. 'Go-Go' and I borrowed a car one weekday evening and made the rounds of area pharmacies until we'd accumulated what we deemed an adequate supply—two or three bottles for each of us. Since the flavor of this product was famously unappealing ("cherry flavor" indeed!), we decided it would be dandy to chase it down with beer. A six-pack of same was duly purchased.

Back at the barracks, we set up shop on the screened-in porch that used to allow the Psych patients to take some fresh air. I brought out my phonograph and an LP by Miles Davis called _The Cool World_. "The cool world, yeah man! Let's enter that world!" To augment the experience, I had grabbed the "trip glasses" I'd acquired in Philly. These featured translucent, amber-colored lenses in the form of prisms, intended to deliberately distort one's view.

It wasn't easy forcing down all that cough syrup and chaser, but I reminded myself: this is a scientific experiment to study the effects of opiates. And the effects duly exerted themselves. I started the Miles record spinning and donned the "trip glasses." In short order, we valiant volunteers were nodding off.

At some point, 'Go-Go' started from his stupor and, disoriented, looked in my direction. He leapt to his feet, screaming. After struggling with the doorknob, he fled back into the barracks. He later explained that, in the dim light of the porch, the prism eyeglasses made me look like a giant fly!

The profound aftermath of this experiment manifested in the morning: I puked my guts out. Amazingly, my intrepid partner agreed to a repeat of the experiment a few nights later. We were hoping that we could avoid the after-effects. The results were identical. I took this as scientific confirmation that opiates weren't for me. This was one of those adventures I did not write home about.

June 3, 1968

Dear Folks,

Well, there's not much to be said this week. I'll probably come home Friday night, but I'm not sure yet.

In the hospital, I'm working in the Recovery Room, where the patients come right after surgery. The main task is to wake them up. Today, under the influence of sodium pentathol (the famous "truth serum"), one poor kid, all of 18 years old, thought he was back in 'Nam, under fire.

Well, aren't the "peace talks" making marvelous progress? Ha! Ha! What a joke. McCarthy's Oregon primary victory was encouraging. I'm still a Gregory-Spock man, but I prefer Gene to RFK.

The killing of the Saigon big-wigs by an American rocket is quite appropriate. Just another reminder of how f-cked up this war is.

Love,
Greg

Little could I know that the day after I wrote the above, the question of who would represent the "peace candidate" among the Democrats would be decided by an assassin's bullet. Robert Kennedy bled to death on the basement floor of a Los Angeles hotel after celebrating victory in the California Primary. This event shocked me but did not sadden me like the murder of Dr. King. I had doubted RFK's sincerity all along. But it was another momentous event in a year of earth-shaking developments.

On a lighter note, I was in the process of acquiring an authentic Uncle Sam hat in Philadelphia. My big head necessitated a custom order from The Theatrical Hat Company. This set me back the princely sum (for 1968) of twenty dollars. When I finally got the finished product in my possession, I affixed a Resistance button on the front: the *omega*, the last letter in the ancient Greek alphabet, was their adopted symbol. Needless to say, this hat could only be worn on "special occasions," off the military reservation.

July 14, 1968

Dear Folks,

I wonder if they need English-speaking practical nurses in Sweden??? As you know, I've been insistent on staying in this country but things are really going downhill. I read about the Bronx sniper; 4 Philadelphia youths have been killed in gang warfare in the past week.

Meanwhile, the puppets who rule S. Vietnam are predicting that the next VC offensive will be a last-ditch, gasping, dying effort. Well I've heard that line of bullshit before—didn't believe it then and don't now. The US can't win this war, but they'll still be trying come September when I get my orders.

Things are going smoothly on the wards. As a matter of fact, time is flying at a fantastic pace. In just seven weeks, we'll be done on the wards. A week after that, we graduate and go to Fort Dix for 3 days of Vietnam orientation, then 30 days of leave begin.

Well, that's about all for now. See you next weekend. I'll call when I reach Manhattan.

Love,
Greg
FUTURE SWEDISH CITIZEN?

Today's lesson: "The Music of Phil Ochs"

There were no more letters home from VFGH. As we neared completion of our training, it was looking more and more inevitable that my orders would be for Vietnam. I had set this in stone: the only course of action my conscience would permit would be to refuse. There were wrenching arguments with Mom and Dad on my weekend visits. My father still counseled that I not "make waves." Mother was distraught about the potential consequences of a court-martial. It was almost a relief to return to the base on Sunday nights.

Occasionally, a graduate of the Clinical Specialist course would be sent somewhere to be an instructor for other medics. To prepare us for this vague possibility, a couple of days were devoted to having each student do a 20-minute educational presentation to the class, to be graded by the instructors. We could lecture on any topic under the sun. The idea was not to gauge our medical knowledge, but to look for talent as a teacher.

The Philadelphia Folk Festival that year was held at the Academy of Music starting Friday, August 23. I had managed to secure a ticket for one day of the event. Phil Ochs was a featured performer, already a star of anti-war, generally anti-Establishment "protest music." His song "Cops of the World" appeared on the LP *Phil Ochs Live* (1965, Elektra Records), a copy of which was in my possession at the barracks.

And so, I chose "The Music of Phil Ochs" as the topic for my educational presentation. I gave a biographical sketch, with what details I could get my hands on, including Phil's role in the founding of the Youth International Party (YIP), whose members became popularly known as "Yippies." This brought hostile glares from the lifers in the room. Undeterred, I moved on to the best part: I had brought my phonograph to the classroom and proceeded to play "Cops of the World." The song is a hard-hitting *expose* of the gross hypocrisy of the USA, which pretends to encourage democracy in "the underdeveloped world," while conveniently extracting profits from natural resources and human labor. And if resistance is encountered, a local dictator is conveniently found to suppress it. And failing that, "send the Marines."

Did I impress the instructors with my pedagogical skills? Well, they didn't flunk me for this phase of training, but neither did I find myself selected to become an instructor. I had definitely made a statement, and by this time (early September) I was firmly informing my fellow students in the barracks that I would **not** report for duty in Vietnam.

Finally came the day when we headed north to Fort Dix for "Orientation to RVN" ("Republic of Viet Nam"). We went to the rifle range for our first introduction to the M-16 (AR-15) fully automatic rifle, which was finally replacing the M-14s we'd used in Basic Training. Traditionally, medics carried .45 pistols in combat. But anyone assigned to duty in Vietnam was required to qualify on the M-16. We were allowed to fire ever so brief a burst with the weapon set on full automatic, just to get a sense of the kickback. The rest of the "information" disseminated during our stay at Dix I tuned out as best I could. No need for it, thank you.

In the third week of September 1968, we survivors of the intense course were graduated and promoted—I was now a Specialist 4th Class ("speck four"). And I was in possession of multiple copies of orders to report to Oakland Overseas Replacement Station for shipment to RVN on October 22. We newly minted advanced medics said our good-byes all around and began our 30-day leaves. For me, this was the start of a countdown to becoming a fugitive from "justice." Farewell, "Happy Valley." Hello, life of an AWOL.

CHAPTER V
An AWOL at large

New York and Boston
October 22-November 22, 1968

Mission one, day one of my post-school leave was to start growing a full beard. All the better to disguise my status as an active-duty GI when my reporting date for overseas shipment came and went. I would be going underground in 30 days, a new experience. The offices of the War Resisters League (WRL) were on a high floor of 15 Beekman Place in lower Manhattan, at one time the tallest building in the city. I went there seeking advice on battling the military from within. The WRL brought to my attention the existence of the American Servicemen's Union (ASU), headquartered in a low-rent office building at 156 Fifth Avenue.

The ASU was still a young organization, having been founded specifically to try to throw a monkey wrench into the cogs of the War Machine. Its Chairman, Andy Stapp, had taken on the Military Establishment at Fort Sill, Oklahoma in a battle over whether GIs have constitutional rights like freedom of speech, assembly, and seeking redress of grievances. Andy had been booted from the Army because the military's answer on those issues was essentially a loud and clear **"No!"** Stapp would tell the story of the founding of the ASU in Up Against the Brass, published by Simon and Schuster in 1970.

ASU was unique among anti-war organizations precisely because it was recruiting active-duty personnel to its ranks, and because it modeled itself after a labor union. The handful of office staff were almost all veterans of recent vintage. I immediately felt comfortable dealing with these people:

mutual understanding, sympathy and solidarity were palpable right from the start. Veterans know in their guts the bullshit that soldiers are subjected to in a way civilians, no matter how deep their sympathy for the cause, can't quite grasp. Mr. Stapp was, himself, a brilliant fellow. He could slip into a casual conversation a relevant observation on the life, exploits or tactical military errors of some Roman emperor, knowledge he had gleaned from Edward Gibbon's classic The History of the Decline and Fall of the Roman Empire, unabridged version.

The American Servicemen's Union was not just opposed to the Vietnam War. It also agitated against racism and exploitation in general. Just to take one example: The US Navy had a tradition of using Filipino enlisted men, wearing white gloves, to serve meals to the officers on its ships. The wall of separation enforced between the officer caste and the enlisted people in the military was seen as analogous to civilian life's division between bosses and workers. The fact that these low-paid workers had come from a nation conquered by the US military at the turn of the century was yet another wrinkle. This is the kind of analysis I would now start learning. It was socialist, it was radical, it was "far left"—it was new to me, and this way of looking at the world made sense to me. [See **APPENDIX 6** for more discussion of the "caste" system in the US Military.]

The ASU had an eight-point (later expanded to ten, and ultimately twelve) platform of demands around which to agitate and organize. It was understood that for the US military to grant even one of the more radical demands would be suicidal for their oppressive system. That's why the list was simply a tool, a starting point for discussion, and it touched on matters of class exploitation as well as of war and peace. As of September 1968, the demands read as follows:

UNION DEMANDS

1. *An end to saluting and sir-ing of officers—let's get off our knees;*
2. *Election of officers by vote of the men;*
3. *Racial equality;*
4. *Rank-and-filers' control of court-martial boards;*

5. *Federal minimum wages;*
6. *The right of free political association;*
7. *The right of collective bargaining;*
8. *The right to disobey illegal orders—like orders to go and fight in an illegal war in Vietnam.*

Obviously, that final plank in the platform especially didn't sit well with the Pentagon. Week after week, month after month, the dead kept piling up in Vietnam. Mostly, of course, they were Vietnamese, but the toll of Americans was also on the rise. Politicians spewed hot air and made empty promises. Senator Eugene McCarthy had actually done quite well at the Democratic National Convention in late August, yet Vice President Hubert Horatio Humphrey was that party's nominee. He made no noises which could give hope to those of us craving peace. Repression was escalating, exemplified by Mayor Daley's cops rampaging through the streets of Chicago while Humphrey was crowned, lobbing tear gas and indiscriminately smashing heads with their batons. Because of this atmosphere, I decided to buy a football helmet to wear to any demonstrations I might attend in the waning weeks of the presidential campaign of 1968. On the bright yellow helmet I painted, in red, the word "Oink!" on the front and back. This was a swipe at the police, who were now known as "pigs" among anti-Establishment youth.

"Oh my God [shudder], a Yippie!"

Not long after I attended an anti-Humphrey rally at the Waldorf Astoria Hotel, early in October—Hubert made his fundraising speech and then ducked out the "back door" to avoid us—the Republicans came to town for a fresh infusion of cash from their well-heeled supporters. Nixon's running mate, Maryland Governor Spiro 'Ted' Agnew, was to address a weekday rally in the Financial District in lower Manhattan. I decided this would be a splendid opportunity to put my Uncle Sam hat to use. I festooned it with an official 'Yippie!' button and headed into town.

By the time I reached the site of the rally, the street and sidewalks were packed. It would have been hopeless to try to work my way through the crowd to get near the speaker's podium, so I merely lingered on the periphery, taking the scene in. I had never attended an open-air rally related to a presidential race. For that matter, I was too young to have voted. Much as I loathed the conduct of the war by the Democrats, I knew in my gut that Nixon-Agnew would be bad news for the country. But all I could do was present a frowning countenance and a silent button on front of my hat. Had I shouted in opposition to the war, I would have quickly been drowned out, if not physically assaulted, by the partisan crowd. From my vantage point, no signs of protest were visible.

I did accomplish one thing, though. I gave a fright to some matronly, fur-wearing Republican stalwart. She was apparently departing early to try to beat the crush of bodies and nearly walked right into me. Seeing the button on my hat, she recoiled in horror, muttering "Oh my God, a 'Yippie'!!" It's a good thing for her she didn't faint, because I was not prepared to catch her.

Still officially on leave, I was at liberty to trek into Manhattan several times more to discuss strategy with my new friends at the ASU office. They were keeping tabs on acts of GI resistance and chronicling them in The Bond. Every month, thousands of copies of this modest (usually 8 pages) publication were mailed to subscribing troops around the world at no charge. Handwritten home addresses of ASU staff were used as return addresses, to try to disguise the nature of the envelopes' contents. As The Bond proclaimed on the front of every issue, GIs had a legal right to receive, read and retain literature of their choosing. That was the theory, at least.

Deserter or merely AWOL?

Per the Uniform Code of Military Justice (UCMJ)—so called because it applies to personnel of all branches of the Armed Forces—if you are not at your assigned work station during your scheduled duty hours, then you are Absent Without Official Leave (AWOL). If you remain in this status in excess of 30 consecutive days, then technically you are a deserter. On day

31, you are Dropped From the [personnel] Rolls (DFR'd) at your assigned base and become a fugitive, ultimately destined to face legal proceedings. So the surest way to avoid being shipped to an assignment in a war you object to, is to keep your body absent long enough to be DFR'd.

There was also the question of intent. If you got arrested in a barroom brawl after exceeding 30 days of absence, with your Military ID Card in your wallet, and were turned over to Armed Services Police, odds are you would only be prosecuted for AWOL. If, on the other hand, you had tried to destroy all evidence you were on active duty, and had an airplane ticket for a flight to Canada, England or Sweden in your pocket, it could be argued that you intended to never return to the military. You could then be charged with desertion. Though I was growing a beard, and had every intention to be away longer than a month, I made a point of always keeping my Military ID on my person.

Precisely because the military was having a mammoth problem with people going AWOL during the Vietnam War, the services could not possibly prosecute as a deserter every GI who was gone more than 30 days. Their judicial system would have bogged down; Navy brigs and Army stockades would have burst at the seams. Indeed, many were filled to overcapacity as matters then stood in 1968. It was in the military's own interest to apply minimal disciplinary measures, and move the personnel in question back into their assignments as quickly as possible.

October 22 rolled around soon enough, the day I was supposed to arrive in Oakland for processing and shipment overseas. Instead, I borrowed my mom's car and hit the road to visit my friends at Syracuse University. I assigned myself the codename 'The Shadow' for checking in by phone with the ASU office. Assuming their phones were tapped was simply common sense, not an exhibition of paranoia.

Dick Nixon, up to his tricks in Syracuse

Booth Memorial Hall, 4th Floor. Back to the site of my very brief college "career." Most of the guys I'd met as a freshman, when they comprehended my status, were afraid to give me temporary sleeping space. But Alan

Sanderson, from Maryland, was totally cool about putting me up for the night. Next day, I tracked down Dan Weber in his off-campus apartment. I would bed down on his floor for the next 10 days or so, before shifting my location. While Dan was at classes, I busied myself reading Ernesto 'Che' Guevara's recently-published diaries of the guerrilla campaign in Bolivia, or hung out at bookstores. A college campus is a great place to hang out if you don't have the irritating obligation to actually attend classes. And, of course, I blended right in with the student body with my scruffy appearance.

Election Day was right around the corner. Flyers were going around campus advertising a Nixon appearance in downtown Syracuse on October 29, just one week prior to Election Day. There were also leaflets circulating, issued by the local chapter of SDS (Students for a Democratic Society), that called upon opponents of the war to infiltrate the crowd, as the event was stated to be an open one, not a by-invitation-only GOP rally. By this time, John Carlos and Tommie Smith had riveted the world's attention with their protest against racism at the 200 Meters Sprint Medals Ceremony at the Olympics in Mexico City, arriving shoeless and each raising a clenched fist, inside a black glove, overhead. In emulation of that act of defiance, protesters were urged to wear a black glove on one hand, or at least place a black sock over one hand to simulate a glove. The Olympics had been held later than usual in '68, and I'd had the privilege of watching most of the TV coverage, including that protest, and American Bob Beamon's phenomenal smashing of the World Long Jump Record.

It was an easy decision that I should participate in this protest. As soon as I arrived at the arena, I encountered strange goings-on. There were no Secret Service Agents apparent, but the head of Syracuse Police Department's "Intelligence Unit" (popularly known to leftists as "the Red Squad" in numerous cities) was positioned right at the entrance. (I learned his identity from one of the student leaders.) The bigshot was directing his cops to grab every member of the local SDS he recognized, and put them aside in a makeshift holding pen. So this was an event "open to the public"? The quarantined protesters started chanting "This is America! This is America!" Since I was a perfect stranger to the gentleman in charge, and had my black sock concealed in a pocket, I entered the venue unmolested.

As I was working my way toward still-available seats, there were young people in the aisles distributing mimeographed copies of the lyrics to "Sound of Silence," the song that had been a huge hit for Simon & Garfunkel a couple years earlier. These leaflets were signed by "The Nixon Reception Committee."

As soon as candidate Nixon appeared at the podium, most of the younger people in the crowd started to sing, as the leaflet requested. Older, die-hard Republicans immediately started to boo loudly, trying to drown us out. But Nixon raised an arm and stilled the partisans, saying "Wait, let's hear what these young people have to say!" There was something most peculiar here. We had been duped by ol' 'Tricky Dick'—this was no protest at all, but part of the show! The leaflets had been distributed by the Nixon organization itself. For now the speaker seized the opportunity to put forth the fiction that he had a plan to end the war in Southeast Asia, that he was now breaking the "silence" he'd been accused of maintaining on this issue. In their coverage of this rally, the mainstream media did not catch on to the fact that the "protest" in the form of singing "Sound of Silence" was a staged, pro-Nixon stunt.

Some local anti-war activists who had managed to slip past the watch-dogs at the entrance jumped to their feet, raised their black-gloved (or black-socked) fists overhead, and started to chant "End the war now! End the war now!" This was the cue for the rest of us so inclined to do likewise, and get ready to walk out of the arena in disgust. As soon as I joined the protest, Nixon partisans in rows behind me started shouting for me to "Shut up and sit down!" Among them I recognized none other than my conservative freshman roommate from my sole semester in 1966. "Yep, that figures!" I said to myself. He gave no indication of recognizing me, and that was fine. The protesters proceeded to exit without further incident. The captive SDSers were released when the rally was finished. For me, this was an eye-opening lesson in how casually the "right to freedom of speech and assembly" can be tossed aside.

Meandering toward my fate

I was ready to hit the road again the day before Election Day. Dan Weber and I had a philosophical discussion of methods of civil disobedience. He didn't like the idea of my suffering imprisonment for my opposition to the war. Since I was determined to not flee abroad, I considered it absolutely inevitable that such was my coming fate. He urged me to not give up on the notion of seeking Conscientious Objector status, and I promised to look into it when I was back in the tender hands of the Army. As I was walking to the car, Dan leaned out his apartment window and implored me one last time to not go to jail. What could I do but shrug my shoulders?

I drove south from the campus and put up for the night in a motel somewhere in upstate New York. As history records, the next day Richard Milhous Nixon was elected to the presidency and somehow the world went on. Lyndon Johnson was now, in a sense, a doubly broken politician. First, he had declined to seek another term, in the face of military setbacks on the battlefield and growing opposition to the war all around the planet. Second, his VP had been defeated by a man offering a "secret plan" to end that war. But LBJ was still Commander-in-Chief, and I would soon have a message to send him.

Having been informed on the telephone by my mother that no police officials, military or civilian, were snooping around on the homefront, I returned to Syosset. I didn't want to spend money on motel bills and outside meals needlessly. But when 'The Shadow' checked in with the ASU, he learned something interesting was happening on the Upper West Side of Manhattan.

Sanctuary on an urban campus

Bill Brakefield, a young soldier who said he'd enlisted in the Army in hopes of acquiring skills useful later in life, had become disillusioned with military ways and gone AWOL. He was opposing the war in a very public way. Some students associated with SDS, along with some radicals from the surrounding community calling themselves the City College Commune, were sheltering Bill in the Grand Ballroom of the Finley Student Union on the City College of New York (CCNY) campus. This was about a mile north of prestigious Columbia University, where protest activities by students were becoming more common. The CCNY action was deemed a "mobile sanctuary," with Bill and others addressing rallies at various locations around the campus, but bedding down for the night in the Grand Ballroom. A core of supporters always surrounded Brakefield to try to fend off—non-violently, at the young soldier's insistence—any attempt to arrest him. Traditionally, it is a church which grants sanctuary to a fugitive from social injustice. And that activity had already been put into practice in various cities and towns in opposition to the Vietnam War. But this was something new, this "secular sanctuary." I felt a need to get involved.

The sanctuary had been initiated in the wake of a protest against the presence on campus of recruiters representing Dow Chemical Company. This corporation was the proud (or at least, profitable) manufacturer of much of the napalm being used to scorch living beings, and the very earth itself, in Southeast Asia. As if that wasn't reprehensible enough, they also made the Agent Orange herbicide that had been in use since the early '60s to destroy food crops and natural forested areas. That protest was on Halloween; I arrived at the campus around November 6 to lend my moral support. There had already been an attempt by Federal law enforcement to arrest Bill, which his supporters had successfully thwarted with the technique of surrounding him tightly and linking arms. Bill Brakefield was totally committed to waging peace instead of war, and he positively radiated honesty, integrity and sincerity. I bonded with him instantly and shared with him the secret of my own AWOL status. Since I was still weeks shy of hitting the 30-day mark, I could not make my status known to the news media. I was just another bearded face in the crowd of supporters. Two or three other guys also identified themselves to Bill as being underground AWOLs at the time.

In the evenings, there were cultural presentations by people from outside the campus confines. One night, I found myself sitting no more than twelve feet from Allen Ginsberg, who likewise was seated on the hard floor, playing a harmonium and chanting/singing. I hadn't explored Allen's works at that point in my life, and knew nothing about Hindu or Buddhist chants—whatever it was he was doing—but I knew this was a special occasion. Another very memorable event was a performance by the Bread & Puppet Theatre. This troupe performed little morality plays—political parables—using larger-than-human-size "puppets" and a few percussion instruments. They usually did this at open-air demonstrations. Their performance in the closed space of the ballroom, in an already charged atmosphere, doubled the impact of their message.

I slept in the ballroom, with the other supporters, that first night. I didn't have a sleeping bag, so had to scrape together what somewhat-soft articles I could to put between the hardwood floor and myself. Late the following night, a rumor rippled through the building that several truckloads of Tactical Police (a sanitized name for the Riot Squad) had mobilized at the 24th Precinct Station, some 35 blocks south of campus. A reporter present on the scene actually telephoned that facility, and the story was denied by the police. The rumor was deemed a false alarm, one of many that had circulated during the sanctuary action.

Around 1 AM, reality fully asserted itself as 150 Tactical cops flooded into the ballroom. The college administration had decided this disruptive activity, which partially involved people from off campus, had gone on long enough. Supporters instantly crowded tightly around Brakefield. Bill addressed them, making sure the cops heard as well, insisting that no resistance, other than purely passive, be offered. The commander in charge announced one last opportunity for people to vacate the premises and avoid arrest. But that was a flat-out lie, for the police had already hermetically sealed the room by then, blocking every exit. So we were all destined for a ride way downtown. Some personal belongings I'd brought along, including my Syosset High School Class ring, were lost to me forever. My being arrested—one of more than 160, including 135 students—was definitely not part of my plan. My Military ID Card was still in my wallet.

An overnight at "The Tombs"

"The Tombs" is the popular designation for the complex of jail cells in Manhattan's main Judicial Building, way downtown at 100 Centre Street. On the long ride, we sang and chanted to keep our morale elevated. Upon arrival, we were placed in the largest holding cells available, segregated by sex, to await formal booking on Criminal Trespass charges. Our holding pens were in a different part of the massive building than the regular cells in which prisoners convicted of serious offenses awaited shipment to prisons upstate, like Attica. So we were spared the sights and sounds of the "real" Tombs, with its reputation for routine brutality by guards. This was one of the largest mass arrests of anti-war protesters in the city up to that point, and the processing of paperwork quickly bogged down. We radical troublemakers would each have to appear before a judge for a formal, if only three-minute, arraignment. Regulations required our jailers to feed us at some point. This consisted of a baloney sandwich and a cup of coffee. All the coffee was prepared the same: "light and sweet." Since there was no source of drinking water and the hours were dragging on, I drank my very first cup of coffee. I'd never been tempted to try this beverage at home, probably because I associated it with my parents' habit of smoking at a meal's conclusion. Thus, I have the NYC court system to thank for putting me on the path of caffeine consumption.

Because this had been a mass arrest, the cops did not take time to meticulously search us. I had to show my driver's license as proof of identity, but my Army ID Card remained safely tucked away. By early afternoon, I was back on the street, "Released on My Own Recognizance." The same thing happened to the other "secret" AWOLs. But Bill Brakefield, having been a very public AWOL, was turned over to military custody to face prosecution. The American Servicemen's Union would help defend him. As for myself, it was time to think about how I could return to military custody in a timely manner, to get my punishment over with, while contributing to the movement against the war.

Continuing education

More trips into Manhattan were made to discuss my options with activists. Armed with recommendations from Andy Stapp and others at the ASU, I started to build a personal library of literature on the current war, and to read about past wars that now seemed less than just.

The first book I acquired was Vietnam! Vietnam!, by British-American journalist Felix Greene. Published in 1966, this book featured many photographs, including the aftermath of atrocities committed against the civilian population by US troops, or soldiers of the ARVN under their direction. Among the images seared into my brain permanently are the body of a suspected "VC" being pulled by a rope behind an armored personnel carrier, and one of a woman fleeing an attack on her village. She is chest-deep in a river, trying to cross to safety on the other side, looking back toward the camera in dismay. I quickly came to believe that the women of Vietnam were the most beautiful on Earth. Though I'd never yet met any Vietnamese, I was forming an emotional bond with them.

Green Beret Master Sergeant Donald Duncan had made a big impression on the public while I was still in high school. For his service in Vietnam, the Army had offered a battlefield promotion to rank of Captain, a quite rare event in modern times. Duncan's response was to very publicly quit the military. His article about the war—"It Was All A Lie!"—was the cover story in a new magazine called Ramparts. I had read that article prior to my enlistment, and now I acquired his book-length indictment of the war, I Quit! "Yes," I thought to myself, "that's what I need to do!"

No more ammo for my moral opposition to this war was required; that had been firm since my high school days. It was historical facts I was now absorbing. I intended to argue, in my coming inevitable showdown with the Army, that this war was a criminal enterprise routinely violating the "laws of war," escalated on false pretenses, and unconstitutional because, as with Korea, Congress had never formally declared war. Around this time, I also discovered the works of Wilfred Burchett, an Australian journalist who, like Felix Greene, had been granted access to the northern part of Vietnam to observe the activities of the liberation forces and how the civilians dealt with US bombing raids. Burchett's writings on what the US military did to the people of Korea in that earlier war were a revelation: execution of civilians, use of napalm and a bombing campaign so intense that, by the 1953 ceasefire, only a handful of buildings still stood above ground north of the Demilitarized Zone. The more I studied the aspects of US history I **wasn't** taught in school, the queasier I felt about being a US citizen at all.

Message to LBJ

In the Boston area, there was a local chapter of an anti-war group calling itself simply The Resistance. One of the volunteers in their office was a disillusioned former Army Captain who'd been in "Military Intelligence," no less. There are many colleges in the Boston area, which proved ripe for recruitment of activists. I had never really spent any time in "Beantown," so when I learned that an anti-war teach-in was scheduled for Boston University on November 22, I seized the opportunity to see the sights up there and make my public stand. The timing would be perfect to take me right to Day 31 of my period of AWOL, and get Dropped From the Rolls out in Oakland. At that point, technically a "deserter," I could surrender myself to the military in any geographic location with the same results: prosecution at the new location.

To make my position crystal clear to the very highest authorities, I decided to send a little message directly to the Commander-in-Chief. This was entirely on my own initiative. The depth of my revulsion at what "my" government was doing in Southeast Asia demanded my protest be loud. I took one of the numerous copies I'd received of my Vietnam orders and penned my message over that with red magic marker. Unfortunately, I did not make a photocopy of the finished product, but it read pretty much like this:

TO: President Lyndon Johnson, The White House, Washington DC
FROM: Spec. 4 Gregory Laxer, US Army
DATE: November 18, 1968
SUBJECT: My resignation

I hereby accuse you of waging an illegal war against the people of Vietnam and of committing crimes against humanity. I am returning my orders for Vietnam duty to you and hereby inform you that I quit the US Army effective immediately.

[signature]

Of course, I was well aware that a regular enlisted person has no legal right to simply quit the military. As a highly decorated veteran of the war, Donald Duncan had been in a unique situation when he made his protest. And I certainly had no expectation that President Johnson would ever personally see this document; his secretaries and aides would intercept any such "rude" message. But I did, indeed, duly post it to 1600 Pennsylvania Avenue in the nation's capital. I would later have confirmation that, yes, it reached its destination.

I find I have company in Boston

When I arrived in Boston, it was love at first sight. The Public Gardens and adjacent Common, the lovely female college students strolling everywhere, Harvard Square in neighboring Cambridge, ample record stores, book shops, movie houses—what was not to like? It was clearly, to me, "a happening place."

Checking in at the offices of The Resistance, I set about engineering a role in the teach-in, and a means for publicly surrendering myself to military control (i.e. custody). I was informed that another AWOL soldier, Martin Gross, would also be participating, and I welcomed that news. Martin, who preferred to be called 'Mate,' and I put our heads together to plan strategy. He had friends in town putting him up; I was given living accommodations, for a couple of nights, by members of The Resistance.

Though I by no means had all my Army-issue clothing in my possession, I had made a point to bring a set of fatigues—well-starched, mind you, in keeping with Army protocol—right down to combat boots and fatigue (baseball style) cap. 'Mate' would appear at the teach-in in civvies and make a public statement of his own refusal of orders. I felt it was important to present the actual appearance of an active-duty soldier. I shaved all my facial hair, except my mustache, the day of the event, which was scheduled for the evening of Friday, November 22.

I had typed my speech at the offices of The Resistance, to make copies available to whatever media might attend the teach-in. 'Mate' and I sat in the audience while a panel discussion of GI resistance was held. Andy Stapp himself, Chairman of ASU, had come up to Boston for this event. Then it was the turn of the active-duty resisters. There was no way of knowing if Federal or other officials were present, waiting to arrest us AWOLs. I prefaced reading my official statement by declaring: "I'm no hero. If you were sitting upfront here you'd see how my hands are shaking" (as I held a microphone and the written speech). For ease of reading, I have re-typed the text of the front-page article in the December 16, 1968 issue of The Bond detailing the Boston event. [See **APPENDIX 3** for a summary of the FBI's report on the teach-in.]

* * *

Soldier-Unionist Defies War Machine Orders to Vietnam

Calls on GIs to "Liberate America"

By Sp. 5 Bob Lemay (ret.)

"There is no one in a better position to stop the slaughter than the GI himself. The Pentagon is scared to death of the power we could wield if we organized against the racist, imperialist system which sends us out to kill and to be killed. We must seize this power, now.

"I ask you, my comrades-in-arms, to join me. Liberate your minds, then your bodies, and let us liberate America before it is too late."

--Sp. 4 Greg Laxer, speaking to a Boston University audience as he refused duty and defied orders to Vietnam.

* * *

An ASU member publicly stated his refusal to go to Vietnam at a Boston University rally on November 22. Another active duty ASU member, a sailor, spoke in support of the Union, and two ASU organizers from New York described the progress of the American Servicemen's Union.

The meeting was sponsored by the New England Resistance, a student group which is active in resisting the war.

Sp. 4 Gregory Laxer said he would not go to Vietnam though under orders to do so. He had been scheduled to report to Oakland on October 22 to be sent to Nam.

"Today," he told the audience of 300 students, "I end eighteen months of complicity with the War Machine. I hereby declare myself liberated from the United States Army. My flesh and blood are no longer government property; my mind, I am happy to say, never was and never will be."

Greg said that he had hoped to be able to serve in the Army without being ordered to Vietnam so he could leave the Army with an honorable discharge but, he said, "I knew that I would go to jail before I would prostitute myself by participating in the war in Vietnam in any manner whatever. Then, in August, along came Chicago, proving that the government of the people, by the people, and for the people has vanished from the face of this nation. It was then that my conscience would not permit me to serve anywhere in the world while wearing the uniform of the United States Army."

Mentioning the use of troops to suppress the rights of Americans and the use of napalm against the people of Vietnam and elsewhere, Greg said: "I can no longer give sanction to these actions by my silence. I know from personal experience that many other GIs feel the same way. The time to speak out, brothers, is NOW."

Union brother Greg Laxer ended by saying: "There is no one in a better position to stop the slaughter than the GI himself . . . I ask you, my comrades-in-arms, to join me."

Andy Stapp, Chairman of the ASU, who had been invited to speak, described the program of the ASU and the problems and progress of the growing union. He told the students of the conditions that GIs face in the military chain gang.

On open mic for GIs, Norm Gelnaw, a Union sailor on the USS Randolph, drew great applause and stated: **"The American Servicemen's Union is where it's at."**

Also on open mic, Bob Lemay, a Vietnam veteran recently out of the Army at Fort Sill, Okla., related some of his experiences in Vietnam and urged civilian support for the GIs' Union.

GREG LAXER WAS TAKEN INTO CUSTODY THE FOLLOWING DAY [emphases in original].

* * *

The intent of my statement was plain: to exhibit maximum defiance on the personal level, while acknowledging I was part of a larger movement, and to encourage acts of resistance by others. Challenging an institution as immense as the US military is a little intimidating, and I was groping my way. A soldier going AWOL may be likened to a worker going on strike, denying the bosses his or her body on the production floor. I was acting individually, but as part of a larger movement. The immediate task was to face whatever my punishment would be, while getting in some good licks at the Establishment.

After the teach-in, Martin Gross and I left the campus, unmolested by law enforcement personnel, to get what sleep we could that last night of freedom. A bus had been rented to carry us and civilian supporters to the gates of Fort Devens—in the town of Ayer, some distance west of Boston—the next day, where we would turn ourselves over to the tender mercy of the Army.

CHAPTER VI

The first court-martial

Fort Devens, Massachusetts and Syosset
November 23, 1968-June 30, 1969

Having surrendered ourselves to "military control" at the main gate of Ft. Devens, Martin Gross and I were now in the custody of the Provost Marshal. And there we would stay for the next 48 hours. Having been seduced by the timing of the Boston University teach-in, vis-a-vis my crossing the 30-day mark for absence, I'd forgotten the curse of the weekend: there would be no one around to process us into the Post Stockade until Monday! We were confined in individual holding cells (cages would be the better word) with literally just a wooden bench upon which to sleep—no mattress, no sheets, no pillow. The clothes I had on, which were my Army fatigues, provided the only cushion between me and the hard bench. Radio traffic between the PM Office and MPs on patrol did not aid us in our quest for sleep. At least we were more coherent conversationalists for our guards than would be the typical occupant of those cells—someone who'd had several drinks too many and gotten into a brawl.

It's also indubitable that the case of a drunk and disorderly GI would not generate FBI documents, with copies going to the Secret Service. Apparently, anyone publicly expressing disagreement with the policies of the Federal Government was automatically deemed a potential threat to the President. Strange times were upon us. [See **APPENDIX 3** for FBI summary of the teach-in.]

November 28, 1968

Dear Folks,

Well, it took a while to write, but here I am. I surrendered Saturday here at Ft. Devens and am now in the stockade waiting for the Army to make its move.

I won't know for a while just what they plan on charging me with, but I believe they're required to court-martial me within 90 days. I can't make any genuinely accurate guesses at what my sentence will be. I shall file for Conscientious Objector status as soon as possible, but slim are my chances of receiving it and getting out under honorable conditions. My lawyer (arranged by The Resistance), in case he hasn't been in touch with you, is Edward Rudnitsky; I don't know, to be honest, how much he'll cost. In reserve, should I need him, I have Mike Kennedy of the Emergency Civil Liberties Committee in New York.

Now dig this news: I'm allowed to have books up here, so for starts, how about sending 3 paperbacks up here? In the upper right drawer of my desk is a list of at least 200 books I should read, so pick out any 3 that you find to be available in paperback. And you can add to the list an expensive paperback ($3.95) called <u>Ten Blocks from the White House</u>, about the D.C. riots last April [**in wake of Dr. King's assassination**]. This is a great opportunity to catch up on reading.

Well, that about wraps it up. I'm writing to my lawyer next; he'll be coming out here to see me whenever something develops. I'm doing fine, there's nothing to worry about so cool it. 'Bye for now.

Love,
Greg

Ft. Devens Stockade: something less than 5-Star accommodations

The Devens Stockade was modest in capacity and, like all such facilities, wasn't purpose-built as a prison. One lived in barracks, the same venerable "temporary structures" one knew from Basic Training, guarded by tall razor wire fences and MPs. But this particular barracks, at this particular moment, had a problem. Someone had clogged the toilets, flooding the latrine. We had to wade through a feces-wafting pond to reach the shower stalls; the showers lacked hot water. My life as a prisoner was off to a dandy start. Fortunately, the plumbing crisis was resolved fairly quickly.

Applying for Conscientious Objector status after one is already in the military is a complex process. Those who will sit in judgment of one's sincerity wear the uniform of the war-makers, and harbor an inherent bias against the applicant: the military needs bodies and is not wont to turn them loose casually; they were losing enough personnel via drug use and mental instability. Now, add the wrinkle of someone who is openly defiant of their whole regime and the applicant's chances of success slip farther. But even in a seemingly hopeless case there's a saving grace: once you file the application you go into administrative limbo and cannot be shipped elsewhere while the decision is pending. This is the straw I was grasping at as I awaited the Army's decision on how harshly to prosecute me.

Mechanics of the military "justice" system

There are three levels of courts-martial: A General Court-Martial deals with the most serious offenses, e.g. murder, mutiny, desertion in face of the enemy, etc. It can carry the death sentence. A Special Court-Martial is employed for mid-level offenses. The judicial remedy for the most minor offenses is the Summary Court-Martial.

The military also provided for punishment of really minor offenses without resorting to trial. This was the proceeding known as an Article 15 ("Article" numbers refer to the Uniform Code of Military Justice). This is like a plea bargain in civilian life. The procedure is not designed to allow the accused to genuinely offer a defense. Punishment—a fine and/or tempo-rary loss of some privileges, extra duties, etc.—is decided on the spot. This expedites returning a soldier to regular duties.

Because I had made my opposition to the war politically pointed and very public, speaking out while in full uniform, I anticipated a Special Court-Martial, at the least. It was unlikely my personal message mailed to President Johnson would be a factor in my prosecution. News of that almost surely had not trickled down to Ft. Devens.

I initiated the paperwork for the CO application while still held in the Stockade. I found I needed letters from people testifying that they believed my opposition to war was sincere, not an act launched the day I got my orders to 'Nam. I wrote home in early December, urging my mom to expedite getting me current addresses of my classmates from Valley Forge General Hospital.

By the second weekend of my confinement in the Devens Stockade, I received a very pleasant surprise. A guard came to fetch me and announced "You have visitors." "I have visitors?" I responded in puzzlement. "Yeah, your girlfriend and your cousin Dave." Now here was a mystery. It turned out that the good folks at The Resistance in Boston had sent two young people to check on my welfare. Sally Bachman, a beautiful young Boston area college student, greeted me with a surprise kiss on the lips. "Cousin Dave" proved to be Dave Reichert, who was a junior at Syosset High School when I was in my senior year there. I'd had no way of knowing he had become an anti-war activist while attending Massachusetts Institute of Technology in Cambridge. I assured my visitors I was doing fine. I wasn't kept in the stockade long enough to merit another visit, but I would stay in touch with Dave for a while upon my release. Sally vanished from my life as mysteriously as she had entered it.

"The Perfect Soldier"

Around the time of my confinement at Devens, my mother received a note from 'Hot Rod' Huska, writing from his duty station in Germany. Ron perhaps had won assignment as an instructor for other medics, or by sheer dumb luck had not been sent to Vietnam.

Dear Mrs. Laxer,

Thank you for helping me write to Greg. I enclose this letter to him. If you would like to read it, please do. No one will ever praise Greg for what he has done, Mrs. Laxer, but in my book he has done a noble thing, which although I could never do I agree with in principle. When I went to college I majored in anthropology and spent a great deal of time studying civilization and man's slow climb upward. There are many fools in the United States who believe that we are fighting for humanity, civilization and noble goals; your son is much too intelligent to fall for that. If mankind is ever able to defeat war and work for himself rather than against himself, then it will be because somewhere there was a beginning, because somewhere sometime we quit listening to the shibboleths of patriotism and those who would endlessly lead us down the path of man's inhumanity to man.

Ronald Huska

I include this note not to blow my own horn, but to show that by casting its net of conscription far and wide, the military had reeled in soldiers unwilling to embrace the spirit of "Kill! Kill! Kill!" Another Texan, Robert Minor, had drawn a cartoon during World War I, published in a socialist newspaper of the time, The Masses. This cartoon would circulate again in the Vietnam Era. A massive, muscular male body stands in front of an Army Medical Examiner. But this mighty specimen is minus a head! The doctor exclaims: "At last, the Perfect Soldier!" The cartoonist had been jailed thereafter, and there he stayed until the war ended. Freedom of speech in America? So much for theory. In practice, the "need" to go to war trumps the US Constitution.

"Special Troops" are we . . .

After just under three weeks of incarceration in the stockade, I was released to the Special Processing Detachment. Our housing there was standard barracks, but no surrounding wire or guards. The occupants of SPD were, like myself, men in limbo. We were awaiting trial for non-violent offenses; we were waiting for orders to be cut assigning us to another geographical area; we were awaiting a determination of our "fitness" to continue in uniform; we were waiting for rulings on applications for discharge; we were finishing up a sentence on minor charges, getting ready to return to regular duties. We were waiting, waiting, waiting. Have I mentioned we did a lot of waiting in the Army? What privileges we might have, such as permission to leave the base on days off, were decided on an individual basis. Did the Military Establishment look down on us as riffraff, troublemakers, losers and ne'er-do-wells? Absolutely! Did that bother us one damned bit? Hell, no!

Interesting characters presented themselves immediately. I met Ray Kroll, who had been an AWOL in sanctuary at Boston University prior to my arrival in town for the November teach-in. And there was 'Sully,' a kid with local roots who was unmistakably a "head." When it came to use of consciousness-altering substances in the military, there was division between "juicers" (drinkers) and "heads" (users of marijuana, psychedelic drugs, etc.). Lifers tended to be juicers, while younger troops, especially draftees, leaned toward softer drugs. One day 'Sully' returned to SPD from a record-shopping trip with the first Led Zeppelin LP under his arm. He announced enthusiastically: "It's **mental**, man! Heavier than Hendrix!" Well, that's a matter of opinion, but it typified how 'Sully' spoke. I am sure that once he hit the street again he grew his hair down to his waist. Another kid who just wanted to be left alone, to live and let live, but the government had had other plans for him. Multiply 'Sully' by tens of thousands and you can see why the military's heavy reliance on conscription assembled an uneasy, and significantly unwilling, pool of manpower. It was said: "We are the unwilling, led by the incompetent to do the unnecessary."

My 21st birthday was approaching and I still had never smoked "weed" (marijuana), or "dropped acid" (taken LSD). But my new-found acquaintances in SPD had cures for such deficiencies. What else would you expect from a bunch of ne'er-do-wells? And special treats for "stoned" ears were magically appearing from out of the ether: Jimi Hendrix's *Electric Ladyland* and The Beatles' so-called *White Album*, both 2-LP sets. There was something in the air. I wrote to my mom requesting at least one of those for Christmas that year.

December 11, 1968

Dear Folks,

I completed my CO application and turned it in. Attorney Ed is supposed to come see me tomorrow to discuss strategy. I shall demand a court-martial and try to convince the Army that it's not worth the energy or money to try to send me to 'Nam. Until my CO application is approved or rejected they can't put me on an Asian-bound plane. If they really wanted to send me quickly, the application could be rejected in as short a time as one week. Just because I'm out of the stockade doesn't mean I'm safe.

Over here in SPD they put me to work; in the stockade I laid around and read. Already I regret leaving the stockade. I don't need any more books now. But for heaven's sake, send me news of what the peace movement's up to. The last time I read the NY Times was Nov. 22! Forward anything The Resistance might've sent. There's no political censorship here.

Don't worry about me. I do not regret my actions. I've got to write to billions of people, so I close for now. Perhaps I'll see you around Xmastime. 'Bye.

Love,
Greg

"Just an Article 15?! No deal!"

December 16, 1968

Dear Folks,

Today I was offered punishment under Article 15; I refused it, which will result in a Special Court-Martial. Since I refused the Art. 15, I might be sent back to the stockade (which wouldn't bother me in the least—there I goofed off, here I've had KP every other day!).

The major who offered the Art. 15 thinks like a typical career officer (e.g. he thinks SDS is run by Commies), but as an individual is a real nice guy. He's the officer to whom my CO application was submitted, and he appears to be sympathetic! This could mean a lot in my favor, but let's not get up false hopes.

Ed came out Friday and found out first-hand how stubborn I can be. He thought accepting the Art. 15 wouldn't be a bad idea, but I said it would equal abject surrender. I convinced him that he couldn't dissuade me from making a stand at a trial.

The major is trying to arrange for me to work at the hospital while the disposition of my CO application is pending.

Despite all the KP, I'm ready for 2 or 3 more paperbacks. Incidentally, you can scratch off the list: The Algiers Motel Incident, The Autobiography of Malcolm X, and Men and Apes. Please add these, both by Frantz Fanon: The Wretched of the Earth and Black Skins, White Masks.

That's about it. Will let you know when I get more info on my court-martial. Thanks.

Love,
Greg

Frankly, I was amazed to be offered a paltry Article 15 for my 31 days of politicized AWOL. I had been preparing myself, and my civilian attorney, to take on the Military Establishment in a frontal assault on the very underpinnings of the war. Something told me there was more than met the eye going on here, more than merely the Army's desire to move quickly through the backlog of cases. I had to conclude that the War Machine was real anxious to hand me a fresh set of orders to go to Vietnam, given the declared critical need for my MOS over there. I had thwarted them, temporarily at least, by submitting my CO application. I now exercised my legal right to refuse to settle for Article 15 and force the Army to bring me to trial. Normally, a serviceperson would be grateful to get off with such light punishment, but I was not a normal soldier.

Taking advantage of the relative idleness forced on me by being in legal limbo, I was devouring all the books of interest I could get my hands on. The Autobiography of Malcolm X had a great impact on me. Here was a man who knew he was marked for death—he felt himself shadowed by government agents, even while he made *hajj* (pilgrimage) to Mecca—but doggedly continued to fight for the principles he upheld as morally right. Someone in ASU circles had brought to my attention the writings of Frantz Fanon (1925-1961). Born on the Caribbean island of Martinique, ruled by France at the time, Fanon earned the positions of physician and psychiatrist. He made a specialty of examining the psycho-social impact of colonial rule, the effects of being deemed inferior by a self-appointed "master race." This yielded the book Black Skins, White Masks. Equally well known was The Wretched of the Earth, which asserted the right—nay, the duty— of oppressed peoples to struggle to attain independence. Fanon, himself, participated in these struggles in France's northern Africa colonies in the years following World War II.

The Summary Court-Martial

My trial was convened on January 8, 1969. It was a Summary CM, not the Special CM I'd initially anticipated to result from my public opposition to the war. Representing me were Ed, my civilian attorney, and Lt. Gurian of JAG (Judge Advocate General Corps), my assigned Army defense attorney. The only other person present in the hearing room was the Court, in the form of one Captain Mencl. Prosecutor, judge, jury, all in one. The marvelous efficiency of military "justice"! The Court had in front of it the only evidence that mattered to it, a pair of Morning Reports. These are documents that account for the presence or absence of all personnel assigned to a given unit on a daily basis, like an Attendance sheet in school. The report from Oakland of October 23, 1968 indicated I had failed to report the previous day, as ordered. My next letter home recounts the full story.

January 12, 1969

Dear Folks,

Here, basically, is what happened at my trial:

1.) The Court (Capt. Mencl) read my charges (AWOL from 22 Oct.-23 Nov.). I examined the Charge Sheet and found no errors; 2.) Ed moved that the case be dismissed on these grounds: a.) that I'm a CO; b.) that my enlistment was coerced; and c.) that the war is illegal; 3.) The Court rejected a.) and c.) but agreed to hear an argument on the coerced enlistment; 4.) I was sworn in; 5.) I explained about the threatened (or at least hinted-at) suicide of my mother had I been incarcerated in a civilian prison for refusing the draft; 6.) The Court agreed to listen to my ideas on being a CO and on the illegality of the war, although he had already ruled the arguments out. The Court was skeptical about why I waited so long to apply for CO status. About the war, I explained that in my oath of enlistment I swore to uphold and defend the Constitution, and that this is what I'm doing by refusing to participate in a war undeclared by Congress; 7.) My plea was entered as Not Guilty; 8.) I was permitted a final statement. I merely said that there are higher laws than the Uniform Code of Military Justice, and that I'll continue to obey the higher laws regardless of the outcome of the trial; 9.) The Court recessed himself for 10 minutes to deliberate; 10.) The Court said he had taken into consideration my clean past record and the fact that I'd already served 18 days in the Stockade and that I'm working in the hospital (thus hinting or implying that he was going to be lenient) and then proceeded to hit me with a heavy sentence: reduction to rank E-1 and forfeiture of pay for a couple months. End of trial.

There's not much more to say except that it's a hell of a drag cooperating while awaiting the decision on my CO status. I wish they'd hurry up and tell me "No!" so I can sock it to 'em with both barrels. 'Bye for now.

Love,
Greg

That I would be found guilty was the most foregone of conclusions. Perhaps Capt. Mencl enjoyed a cigarette or a cup of coffee during that ten-minute recess. I characterized the sentence as "heavy" because I would have to start working my way back up to my former rank from "Buck Private" (E-1, lowest rank in any branch of the military). This would take some time. The official Summary of the trial recorded not a word of my legal or moral arguments against the war, but just the hard fact of the length of my absence.

Meanwhile, I had shared a few times in the communal activity of smoking weed with some of my SPD cohorts. According to popular belief, the first time you indulge in marijuana you don't feel any significant effect; that comes with your subsequent intake. But I seemed to have a problem: it was as if my consciousness was armor-plated, very hard to penetrate. After several tries—and believe me, I was inhaling deeply (to my throat's chagrin) and holding the smoke in my lungs as long as possible—I still was not getting high! The cure for that proved to be using LSD. After my first "trip," the barrier around my brain came crashing down like the walls of Jericho. But, of course, these adventures went in the folder marked "Not to be divulged to Mom and Dad."

February 2, 1969

Dear Folks,

They're starting to work me in the base hospital on evenings, weekends, etc., whenever they feel they need me most. It could easily be another 3 months before a decision comes from Washington re: CO application. All I can do is wait and be as filthily, viciously subversive as possible in the interim.

The ward is a Medical ward, you might call it the Miscellaneous Ward: there are cardiac patients, ulcer & diabetic patients, plus a few paranoid schizophrenic patients! There's really not much work to be done, but there are good people to rap with (talk to), so boredom doesn't become too big a problem.

Please scratch <u>Black Skin, White Masks</u> off the list, in case you haven't yet done so. Also, <u>The Armies of the Night</u> by Norman Mailer, which I picked up in Boston last weekend. You don't seem to have understood, by the way, that that trip to Boston was illegal, but I (like everybody else) got away with it. That's all till next weekend.

Love,
Greg

Flying high in Harvard Square

We "Special Troops" were not being monitored all that closely. One weekend, several of us who were restricted to base decided we'd had enough of that bullshit and took off for Boston/Cambridge. I partnered with Ray Kroll, who knew the area better than I, and just happened to have some good LSD to share. It was a cold weekend in what was an exceptional winter in the area. We headed straight to Harvard Square, the very heart of Cambridge with its restaurants, pubs, music clubs and numerous shops. There was snow and slush on the ground and a chilly wind was blowing; the sun had already gone down. We each swallowed our tablet without hesitation. It takes about twenty minutes for one's digestive juices to break down the material and get the psychoactive element to the brain. Once LSD kicks in, there's no escaping its effect until the drug is excreted by natural means. This usually makes for an eight-to-ten-hour trip.

Were we crazy to even contemplate consuming "street drugs" of who knows what quality, what real ingredients? Well, in our defense I'll just say: we were young. I knew I was tripping for real when a city bus approached an intersection in slow motion, then stretched itself to twice its length, the central part becoming some fantastic liquid "slinky toy," the rear end finally catching up to the front on the other side of the intersection. Wow, man! This is crazy! Color, light, sound, texture, flavor . . . all the things we perceive by our senses were intensified. The very act of walking on the sidewalk was a new experience. This was called "body tripping"; a larger dose, as I'd later learn, could take one way beyond these effects.

Ray had a friend known as 'Walrus' who lived in the area. He stepped into a phone booth to call his pal and get permission for us to go hang out at his apartment. We needed to get out of the wicked cold. My altered sense of hearing perceived Ray's end of the conversation like it was taking place in an echo chamber. 'Walrus' said we could come over in about a half-hour. To pass the time sheltered from the cold, we went into a Brigham's Ice Cream Parlor. I ordered a hot cocoa and it was an ordeal to consume it: where did the rim of the mug end and my lips begin? Was the liquid too hot? Was I burning my tongue? It was hard to say, so I proceeded with caution.

When we arrived *chez* 'Walrus,' we were eager to listen to music on his stereo. This is one of the great joys of acid, but things can get a little weird: you haven't lived until you've heard Bobbie Gentry sing "Ode to Billy Joe" sounding like a 45 RPM record played at 33 1/3! Our host provided various taste treats to titillate our senses. We all stayed up until our trips had pretty well run their courses, then caught some token sleep. I won't even try to describe the sensation of urinating while under the influence of acid; let's just say it's a tad peculiar.

A wall locker is no place to stash a "nickel bag"

One day, entirely unexpectedly, I was approached on the company compound by a black woman sergeant whom I'd only seen occasionally; I think she was Company Clerk. She asked me if I could get her a "nickel bag," that is, five dollars' worth of loose marijuana to be rolled into joints, sealed in a neat little plastic bag. Not wishing to look like a "square ofay doofus," I cheerily declared "Sure! No problem!"

Not only was I absolutely not a drug dealer, I never even mastered the art of rolling joints. I was all thumbs when it came to such feats of manual dexterity. I was always dependent on the kindness of strangers when it came to illicit drugs: I smoked or ingested what was being passed around, never seeking to keep my own stash. Nevertheless, I now needed to procure a supply in order to keep my word to a virtual stranger. This proved to be not difficult at all in the US Army of 1969, especially among the riffraff of SPD. I planned to sell the bag to the sergeant for exactly what I'd paid. I placed the bag of illicit material on the little shelf in my wall locker, secreted behind other items toward the rear.

Since my release from the stockade, I had wasted no time resuming the role of agitator against the Establishment. Having already gone AWOL and been court-martialed for it, I could be more openly defiant. I was not going to emerge from my active-duty stint with a clean record. In no time, I was distributing anti-war literature in SPD, and also at the Medical Company barracks. That's how it came to pass that, among the items on that shelf in my wall locker was a stack of anti-war newspapers I had received via The Resistance.

Apparently, someone had observed my activities and squealed, for on February 6 there appeared in my barracks a second lieutenant MP from Provost Marshal's Office, demanding that I open my wall locker for his inspection! "Oh, you mean **this** wall locker, with the nickel bag in it?" I said internally. The wisdom of cooperating in this particular situation pressed itself upon me. Instead of putting up a fight over freedom of speech, as I normally would, I sheepishly surrendered 27 copies of a publication designated "Vietnam GI" on the Military Police Receipt for Property,

Department of the Army Form 19-31 (Revised 1 JUN 55) I was given, and closed the locker before prying eyes could peer deeper. Talk about a close call!

I completed the transaction with the woman sergeant as quickly as possible. In the coming days I would ponder this affair, and try to make sense of it. I have to admit: that sale was one of the most colossally stupid things I ever did in my life. Without a doubt, I was being set up for further prosecution. Yet, the seizure of the literature could only have been a coincidence, in this sense: that lieutenant was not looking for drugs in my locker. Some time after I had passed that bag of marijuana to the sergeant, Lt. Gurian said to me: "What the hell are you doing?! Don't you know you're being *watched*?" For a while after that, I did steer clear of the drug scene. But the allure of drug use, as a badge of rebellion, tugged strongly at me and my colleagues. I made a point of never having drugs on my person longer than it took to consume them, or mixed in with my personal belongings. As fate would have it, no one up the chain of command opted to come after me on drug charges. Neither did the Army attempt to prosecute me for distributing anti-war literature on base. Mysterious, indeed, are the ways of the military.

A winter to remember

By the time I was taken off restricted-to-base status, the winter of 1968/69 was proving to be a humdinger. Eventually, the snowdrifts between some barracks at Ft. Devens reached the second-floor windows! Concurrently, an icy blast of repression bore down on some young soldiers imprisoned in California. The results became a major story in the anti-war movement. The Presidio of San Francisco was a modest Army facility inside city limits. At the base stockade, a mentally confused young soldier confined for a non-violent offense, Richard Bunch, had been blown away by a shotgun-wielding guard October 11, 1968. Authorities claimed he was attempting to escape. Monday morning, October 14, in protest of Bunch's murder and overcrowded living conditions, 27 young inmates sat down in the yard of the facility, demanding redress of their grievances. The powers that be decided that examples needed to be made of these young men: they would be prosecuted for **mutiny**. They were convicted, of course. In February 1969, the first few defendants received sentences of 14-16 years at hard labor. Ironically, three of the four accused ringleaders had escaped the stockade, taking refuge in Canada, before they could be tried. Ultimately, under review, the charges and sentences would be reduced. The sordid history of this affair would be recounted in The Unlawful Concert, by Fred Gardner, which I read as soon as it came out in paperback.

A college chum with some very interesting information

Charly Coleman, my anti-Establishment buddy (and drinking mate) at Syracuse University, had also dropped out of college and he'd landed in the Navy. He'd been sent to some facility in the Boston area for an advanced course in electronic communications. He'd written to my home address to alert me, and my mother had passed word to me. A very disgruntled sailor, he was on the brink of flunking out of the class he'd been involuntarily enrolled in.

I had set up a rendezvous with Coleman at the Devens PX. (Anyone on active duty in any service branch could shop at a PX or BX, the Navy's equivalent, by showing his or her Military ID.) Charly sported a full, though trimmed fairly short, beard; the Navy allowed leeway in such matters. We went and sat in the snack bar section, to shoot the breeze and compare notes on our respective military experiences. Coleman revealed that he'd been a crew member of the USS Banner, practically an identical twin of the Pueblo. The latter had been seized by "north" Korean patrol boats in 1968, having violated Korean sovereign waters. Following standard practice, the US Government had vehemently denied it had been conducting electronic espionage from that location. The Banner was designated AGER-1: "Auxiliary Geographical Environmental Research Ship #1." I started scribbling notes furiously as Charly confirmed that the mission of both vessels was, most definitely, electronic espionage. What Coleman revealed would be published in interview form in The Bond, Vol. 3, No. 3, March 17, 1969. Of course, we withheld the identity of our source. These are excerpts from the interview:

Q.: What were you told your mission was?

A.: To conduct oceanographic and electromagnetic research.

Q.: What percentage of the crew knew the real mission?

A.: 100%.

Q.: To your knowledge, was it at all possible for the Pueblo to be scuttled?
[The command staff had been severely criticized back home for allowing the vessel to fall into "enemy" possession.]

A.: No, it was impossible. It would take more time than was available.

Q.: Did the men have confidence in outside help in case of attack?

A.: As to the use of our support, it once took between one and two hours for a helicopter to find the ship in order to remove two sick men because it was such an infinitesimal dot.

* * *

I had gotten a resupply of anti-war literature quickly, in the wake of the seizure from my wall locker early in the month. I was showing Coleman a copy of the issue of The Bond with the front-page article on my November public act of resistance. A uniformed MP appeared from out of nowhere and grabbed the newspaper. What the hell?! Were MPs now routinely spying on customers of PX snack bars, with orders to ferret out subversive activities? Or had I been tailed from my barracks to the PX? I certainly wasn't conscious of having been followed. It was enough to make a fellow just a tad paranoid. Fortunately, no repercussions descended on Charly in the wake of this event, though we were evicted from the PX for that day.

Upon automatic review of the findings of my court-martial, some lieutenant colonel decided to reinstate the one-time $64 fine—above and beyond the pay I lost by being busted to lowest rank—that had initially been voided in an earlier review. In revenge, I vowed to cancel the US Savings Bonds purchase agreement so many of us had been coerced into. But the news wasn't unrelievedly glum.

March 2, 1969

Dear Folks,

Major Crimmins is granting me a pass starting late Saturday, March 8. This permits me to go see Country Joe & The Fish legally (in Boston). There's no time, of course, to make it home that weekend. [Technically, I wasn't supposed to be eligible for a pass until March 10.] Ed wants me to get together with him for a general discussion of things; perhaps that can be arranged for Sunday, March 9.

I received two envelopes of clippings last week. Thanks. On the book scene: Miami and the Siege of Chicago by Norman Mailer; Dick Gregory wrote a book, The Shadow That Scares Me, that's probably only available in hard cover. You might try ordering it at the bookstore; I don't know the publisher. The Naked Ape should be out in paperback soon.

Have you seen any mention of Spiro Agnew lately? He seems to have vanished; or does 'Tricky Dick' keep him out of sight?

That's all for now, see you in less than 2 weeks.

Love,
Greg

Working on Hospital Ward 34 introduced me to ambulatory patients John Roget and Bob Frieden. Roget was only about 5-foot-6, slight of build. He had fine blond hair, a wispy blond mustache, very fine facial features. Women must have found him irresistible. Hell, I'm hopelessly heterosexual, and I found him adorable! He was a Massachusetts native, and had a girlfriend in a suburb of Boston. We bonded immediately, based on shared love of "progressive Rock." Frieden was also a local. He walked with a cane, being in the advanced stage of recovery from a leg injury in Vietnam. He was at Devens awaiting further evaluation of suitability to be returned to regular duty. The three of us understood the Army very well, and we were all against it. This newfound friendship came with a really big bonus: John had wheels right there on the base. This would soon empower the three of us to experience some phenomenal live music events, enhanced by the charms of LSD.

John Roget, himself a medic, was in the hospital to undergo a whole battery of tests to try to determine the underlying cause of his occasional *petit-mal* seizures. I soon learned the actual cause: John had a sensitivity to Darvon, the painkiller often abused for kicks (though I'm sure it produced what I would have found a not particularly pleasant "high"). Since I had access to the locked meds cabinet in the ward's Nurse's Station, I made sure Roget had a supply of Darvon—which he hid under his mattress—whenever he wanted to exhibit his peculiar affliction. GI solidarity!

'Country Joe' & The Fish, live! ... ever so briefly

March 10, 1969

Dear Folks,

Well, Saturday was really disastrous. Country Joe was saved as the last act; he started playing at 3:25 and at 3:45 he had to stop because the joint had to be prepared for two goddamned hockey games that evening. The other acts weren't bad, but still, it boiled down to paying $5 for 20 minutes of Country Joe!

Yesterday (Sunday) I got together with Ed in Cambridge. He's going to write to the Commanding General and inquire as to the whereabouts of my CO application; it's my understanding that the paperwork has not yet, after all this time, departed for Washington. I told him that my thinking right now is that upon rejection of my application, rather than go AWOL again and shoot for a BCD (Bad Conduct Discharge) I will cease to cooperate and have Ed file suit in Federal Court to force the Army to discharge me honorably as a CO.

I'll be bringing home a mess of records bought at PX prices. Just finished Revolution for the Hell of It by Abbie Hoffman. If things work out like I want them to, I'll start my leave about 5:30 PM Thursday and have to return by 5:30 PM Sunday. See y'all soon.

Love,

Greg

P.S.: Recently released figures show that a soldier, sailor, marine or airman goes AWOL *every three minutes!* I'm proud to be part of that statistic.

The concert, the only occasion for me to ever be inside the old Boston Garden, with its famous parquet floor—the site of so many legendary duels between the Celtics and the '76ers, Bill Russell at war with Wilt Chamberlain—was a crushing disappointment. We booed when CJ & The Fish were ordered off the stage after only 20 minutes, to no avail. Commerce is commerce, and the arena was to host a collegiate, followed by a Bruins, hockey match that evening. But at least I got to see the famed soul duo of Sam & Dave, as one of the warm-up acts.

As part of the application process for Conscientious Objector status, I'd been sent to be interviewed by a Theology professor at a seminary on the outskirts of Boston. I stuck to my guns (pardon the expression) and clung to my internal logic of advocating strict pacifism. Essentially, all my arguments against war were based on human-derived morality and ethics. I saw no need for belief in supernatural beings to grasp how wrong my country was in its actions in Southeast Asia. [See **APPENDIX 4** for text of my statement.] The waiting game with Army bureaucrats would go on for some time more. And speaking of bureaucrats, it was around this time that a polite letter from a lieutenant colonel at the Pentagon finally caught up with me. It had been forwarded several times until the Army finally figured out where I was currently stationed. The gentleman patiently explained that there was no legal mechanism by which I could simply "quit" the Army. Naturally, I'd been fully aware of that reality when I undertook my protest. Now I knew my personal message to LBJ had, in fact, at least been noted in the corridors of power. Was I, as a result, under closer surveillance at Ft. Devens than I could have imagined?

March 24, 1969

Dear Folks,

I spent the weekend in Boston so am now writing on Monday evening, which means the letter will reach you late in the week.

The most notable thing to happen was the scene on the ward today. A 21-year-old guy was admitted deep in a coma; the docs thought it was a diabetic coma, or possibly the result of ingestion of something like ethyl alcohol. He seemed to be improving when suddenly his heart decided to stop beating! Something you don't expect a 21-year-old's heart to do! Soon the room was a sea of white-coated doctors; external massage did the trick (one doctor was all set to cut his chest open!) and got the ticker going. It was a frantic Monday all right; I ended up working 40 minutes overtime. When I left, we had a machine doing the kid's breathing for him. I wouldn't want to lay odds on walking onto the ward tomorrow and seeing that kid alive.

Well, I have to go do subversive things and then get some sleep. Kind of a short letter, but *c'est la vie.* 'Bye.

Love,
Greg

And indeed, I soon discovered that that young man departed this life by the next morning, the cause of his cardiac arrest still undetermined. Death has a way of arriving on stealthy feet, and it wasn't necessary to be in combat to exit life prematurely.

A church in which I could worship

Before I started hanging out with John Roget, I was unaware of the existence of a concert venue called The Boston Tea Party, on Berkeley Street. The building had been a Unitarian Meeting House, built largely of stone. You'd think such construction would make it too "bright" (reflecting a lot of sound waves off the interior walls) for loud Rock music, but you'd be wrong. I have been in New York's great concert halls, but music never sounded better to me than at The Tea Party. Doubtless, illicit chemical substances coursing through my blood vessels played a major role in that perception. The stage had been the church's altar, and across the back wall the exhortation, PRAISE THEE THE LORD, was still emblazoned in large letters. The first show we caught there, last weekend of March, featured The Ainsley Dunbar Retaliation and Rhinoceros.

Later that spring, we were blessed to see the Jeff Beck Group, with The Nice as opening act. I had the weekend off, and John was allowed to sign himself out of hospital on a pass. We were lucky enough to secure some very good acid, and we were deliciously high by the time we arrived for the show.

The centerpiece of The Nice was the multiple-keyboards work of one Keith Emerson. One of Keith's tricks was to cause massive distortion in the output of his Hammond organ. This was accomplished by rocking it back and forth, even lifting one end and dropping the whole thing to the stage! A Hammond organ weighs plenty—this guy was a madman! Jeff Beck was simply Jeff Beck, that is to say one of **the** great electric guitarists, schooled like so many Brits in the Blues, and even Jazz, roots music of the USA.

March 31, 1969

Dear Folks,

Things are really getting "Mickey-Mouse" here in SPD. The cadre is now "playing Army"—in other words, they're running the place as if it were basic training; they've instituted the very policies and attitudes that cause so many guys to go AWOL in the first place. Fortunately, I really haven't all that much longer to put up with it. I should hear the results of my discharge attempt within a month and a half.

I still have plenty of books, so don't worry about that matter. My money is holding out okay—I can even afford more records; now if only I can find time to listen to 'em!! That's all for now.

Love,
Greg

From this point, I no longer had a need to write letters home from Fort Devens. I made the trek home to Syosset several times, on days off. Attorney Ed kept my parents updated on my legal status, and I could access a pay phone to call home if something critical developed.

Such a matter was my learning, in April, that new orders to ship me to Vietnam were being issued. I was told I must fill out an insurance form, to designate a beneficiary, in the event of my death overseas. I had declined to do this after completing my training at Valley Forge General Hospital. Now, I would have a little fun with the Army.

I produced what must be a rather unique document during the Vietnam War, perhaps for any war. On my Servicemen's Group Life Insurance Election, VA FORM 29-8286 (NOV 1965), I designated as my beneficiary "The National Liberation Front of South Vietnam." I signed the document on April 16, 1969, duly witnessed by the Personnel Officer. No questions asked. File it away! This clerk was a civilian employee of the Federal Government, and I reckon he just didn't get the joke. Had I written "The Viet Cong," instead of the formal name of the liberation forces, I imagine someone would have noticed.

Lessons in LSD and music appreciation

One weekday, when my varied schedule at the hospital had me off duty, I went to hang out at Dave Reichert's MIT dorm room while he was in classes. A few months had passed since he'd visited me while I was in the Devens Stockade. I found my way to his dormitory on the campus without too much difficulty. A tablet of LSD accompanied me on this visit. Swallowing it, I was again at the mercy of whatever the street chemists had concocted.

On one of the walls hung a large poster of Frank Zappa & The Mothers of Invention. Zappa was a brilliant social satirist, highly-skilled composer, and guitarist. His band embraced the term "freaks" used to describe hippies and other perceived social malcontents. These guys deliberately cultivated a crazy, unkempt appearance. Long, long hair and wild configurations of beards and mustaches adorned them. By their very appearance, they were confronting Mr. and Mrs. Straight-Laced America: "Freaks? We'll show you freaks!" Zappa composed many songs of social commentary. "Hungry Freaks, Daddy," from the 1966 album *Freak Out!*, is but one outstanding example.

When Frank and his bandmates came to life, conversing among themselves "in" that wall poster, I knew I had taken a bigger hit of LSD than I preferred! I had finally crossed the line into a true "head trip." That is to say, I was flat out hallucinating. I sat—absolutely immobilized, staring at, and listening to, this scene—for a full two hours, unable to look away. (I always checked my watch frequently while tripping, curious as to how time seemed to be flowing while I was under the influence.) The antics of Frank and the Mothers were not frightening. I can't recall a single thing that was said in their two-hour discussion among themselves. But ultimately I **was** frightened by the fact that I had lost control of my own mind; technically, I was quite <u>insane</u>, albeit temporarily. Had a fire erupted in the dormitory, would I have just sat there, paralyzed, enjoying the beauty of the flames as they closed in on me? The effects of the drug lessened in intensity after those initial couple of hours, and I became capable of operating Dave's record player, making choices for my sensory input. The LPs available included the first 'Country Joe' & The Fish album, *Electric Music for the Body and Mind*. Good choice, Dave!

In 1969, recordings of the British trio called The Cream, or simply Cream, had achieved great prominence here in the US, though they had already ceased performing together. Listening to their extended versions of Blues-oriented material under the influence of LSD, I discovered how to fully appreciate music. I could focus on what Jack Bruce was playing on his bass guitar, and how he was interacting with Clapton's guitar, and Ginger Baker's drums, without losing track of the overall sound and progression of the piece. Likewise, I could zoom in on what Eric and Ginger were doing individually, simultaneously appreciating how they contributed to the bigger picture. Once my brain was thus rewired, I retained this new skill of deep, analytical listening even when I wasn't stoned. Graffiti of the times: "LSD: Better Living Through Chemistry." Amen!

John Wayne meets LSD!

I had gone to see *The Green Berets*, produced by and starring John Wayne, during my period of AWOL. I'd wanted to determine for myself just how ludicrous was this piece of pro-Vietnam War propaganda. I was not disappointed, let's say. When I learned the movie was playing at a theater right on Ft. Devens, I rounded up a small gang of fellow n'er-do-wells from SPD and we went together to see it strictly as a goof. I dropped acid myself, and the other "Special Troops" took care of their own heads as they saw fit. This was my first trip to an Army movie theater since the eviction incident at Fort Sam Houston. When the National Anthem was played prior to the start of the movie, rather than remaining seated this time I raised a clenched fist overhead, another homage to the actions of Tommie Smith and John Carlos at the previous year's Olympic Games. I cheered when the "Viet Cong" attacked, and booed Wayne's appearances on screen. I can't say that LSD actually made suffering through the execrable film enjoyable, but it made for a "different" movie-going experience for sure.

When everyone exited the theater afterward, we SPDers walked back down the long hill toward our barracks in the chill air. I kept glancing behind me, and it felt like a mob was following me, personally—with what intent? Had some lifer types observed my conduct and decided to pounce on me in retribution? It was commonly known in those times that the amateur chemists who made acid for street sale "cut" it, or diluted it, with speed. That was said to be the basis for the paranoid feelings so often experienced when high on these substances. At any rate, the troops at my rear gradually peeled off to head to their own destinations and I got "home" unmolested. A military facility is not the most conducive environment for pleasant highs under any circumstances, but this night's trip was especially weird. And a lousy rightwing movie is still a lousy rightwing movie.

Phil Ochs, up close and almost personal

At some point in April, an anti-war demonstration was held in Boston, culminating on the famous Common, where a sound system had been set up for speeches and live entertainment. Phil Ochs performed his best-known songs protesting the Vietnam War. There was still a chill in the air, after the unusually cold and snowy winter, and Phil was wearing a quite weathered brown leather bomber jacket.

After the formal ceremonies of a typical demonstration had concluded, I lingered a while on the Common. My time in the Boston area was running out and I wished to savor the sights and sounds. Strolling around, I found I was moving closer and closer to the gazebo under which the speakers and musicians had been gathered. In no time, I was able to walk up right behind Mr. Ochs and eavesdrop on his conversation with others. His back was to me, and I could have reached out and tapped him on the shoulder, but didn't want to startle him. The organizers of the rally had obviously not made adequate security provisions—a rightwing thug could have easily assaulted this bard of the left! Had I waited patiently for Phil to conclude his conversation, I could have related to him the tale of how he became the subject of a lecture in an Army medical training program the year before. But alas, I was too shy, and the opportunity slipped away.

CO application rejected; next stop Federal Court

As anticipated, the Army rejected my application for discharge as a Conscientious Objector in April. Despite my unwavering adherence to a philosophy of total nonviolence, in the spirit of Martin Luther King, Jr. and Gandhi—which was, truthfully, my firm belief system at the time—the "expert witness" who had interviewed me at the seminary had issued the opinion that I was a "selective objector" to the war raging in Southeast Asia. The Army seized on that one opinion and wielded the rubber stamp that said "DENIED." The war being waged against the peoples of Indochina was the only war I was being ordered to participate in and, yes, I objected to it with every fiber of my being. But the military always acts in its own interests, and the Army needed senior medics very badly.

To the Army, the matter was closed. They proceeded to cut my second set of orders to report to Oakland US Army Overseas Replacement Station on May 12, second anniversary of my enlistment. I had repeatedly stated, in public and at my Summary Court-Martial, that I wasn't going to go. I was fully prepared to again wield a GI's ultimate weapon: denial to the military of the use of my body in its war effort. But there was one more delaying tactic to employ, though attorney Ed, my parents and myself knew full well how heavily the odds were stacked against me: we filed suit in Federal Court in Boston, suing General Cushman, Ft. Devens Commanding Officer, and the Department of the Army itself. The basis of the suit was that the Army had cavalierly dismissed my CO claims because my beliefs weren't part of an established religious denomination.

There were precedents for such lawsuits and it wasn't difficult, in Boston, to find a Federal Judge willing to at least hear the case. An actual ruling in my favor was a truly long shot. Our lawsuit was filed April 25 but, amazingly, the Army dragged its heels in responding. On May 9, with my reporting date imminent, an injunction was issued forbidding the Army from reassigning me from Ft. Devens until a ruling was issued. It felt good to have a civilian telling the Army what it could or couldn't do . . . temporarily, at least. To my pleasant surprise, I was told in late April that I could go home, on unpaid leave, until the judicial matter was settled. So it was farewell to John Roget and our live music excursions. John was about to be returned to regular duty, anyway. Though the doctors never solved the mystery of his ailment, they'd decided he was healthy enough to be discharged from hospital.

Back home in Syosset, in legal limbo, opportunities for enjoying live music were coming fast and furious. I learned that The Who would be performing their "rock opera," "Tommy," live at Fillmore East in May. When you think about the Fillmores, East and West, normally offering three bands in a single show for a few bucks' admission, you know that was

The Golden Age. But for this tour, The Who were the whole, multi-hour show. The energy level was incredible. I have no doubt The Who were at the peak of their powers that year, and I was privileged to be a witness. I seized the chance in June to catch the following triple bill: Jesse Colin Young & The Youngbloods opening; Chicago Transit Authority; Frank Zappa & The Mothers of Invention. Better to see Zappa in the flesh than as part of an insane hallucination. In a concentrated span of time, I also was present, at the Fillmore, for the New York debut of Alvin Lee & Ten Years After, as an opening act for Joe Cocker. Woodstock loomed over the horizon, and some of these groups would soon be documented in legendary performances.

I also seized the opportunity to see and, above all, listen to, legendary performances from The (first and only) Monterey International Pop Music Festival that took place in June 1967. The documentary film of that event, made by D.A. Pennebaker, was playing continuously at the Kips Bay Theater in Manhattan. This was a moviehouse that would run a "cult" film as long as an audience for it kept showing up. Stoned or otherwise, enough customers were showing up to see *Monterey Pop* that I attended the screenings twice, each time sitting through the movie two or three times consecutively. LSD powered me through these marathon sessions. Acid was easy enough to score among acquaintances I had made in "the community of AWOLs" loose on the streets of New York City.

The Federal Court issues its ruling

The court in Boston issued its decision on my suit against the Army June 19, 1969. The case pivoted on how my application for CO status had been handled or mishandled, i.e. administrative procedures. My application had been denied in Washington, D.C. with the finding that my "objection to service is not based upon sincere religious beliefs and training." This could have been appealed to a higher Federal Court, because the regulations governing Conscientious Objector status allow for a belief system "equivalent" to traditional religious tenets. I never saw the inside of the courtroom myself. I was home when arguments were made in the judge's chamber.

My attorney was opposed not by Army lawyers, but a US Attorney and an Assistant US Attorney.

The judge ruled that, yes, my objection was specifically against the Vietnam situation and he had no choice but to rule in favor of the Army.

The court ruling was issued on a Thursday. Suddenly, the stateside Army was working on Saturday! Quite a contrast with no one having been available, back in November, to process me into the stockade on a weekend. Thus it came to be that on June 21, Special Order Number 147 was drawn up and mailed to me at home, instructing me to report to Oakland on July 1, for shipment to Vietnam. Amidst all the standard military lingo was inserted this thoughtful reminder, all upper-case letters: "FAILURE TO RPT [report] TO THE APPROPRIATE PLACE AT THE PRESCRIBED TIME MAY RESULT IN PUNISHMENT UNDER THE UNIFORM CODE OF MILITARY JUSTICE." **"May"** result in punishment? Did that mean they might pin a medal on me instead? There was also some Special Distribution mandated for these orders: five copies to Fort Meade in Maryland (East Coast HQ for "Military Intelligence"), plus five copies to the Office of Personnel Operations in D.C.

July 1 was very fast approaching. There were more anguished scenes at home, my mother fretting over the potential consequences of my continuing resistance. My parents understood what this second set of orders for Vietnam meant: I would have to go AWOL a second time. I consulted some more with my friends at the ASU. They could provide lodging in the big city for me the first few days, just in case MPs or Federal agents came knocking on the Laxers' door out in Syosset.

A couple of days before my reporting date there came a phone call from a Lieutenant Colonel Kelly, at Ft. Devens. Would I like him to make special arrangements for transportation to Westover Air Force Base, in western Massachusetts, so I could hop a military flight to Oakland, avoiding the hassle of commercial airlines? Kelly seemed sincerely concerned for me. Therefore it was with respectful politeness that I firmly declined his offer.

CHAPTER VII

AWOL again, going through changes

New York, Hawaii, California
July 1-September 18, 1969

Don't scab for the bosses,
Don't listen to their lies;
Us poor folks haven't got a chance
Unless we organize.
Which side are you on,
Which side are you on?

—Which Side Are You On, *by Florence Reece*

(Copyright ownership information not obtainable;
Fair Use Doctrine asserted.)

Came the first of July and I was a long way from Oakland. To be specific, I was riding the subway in New York City, en route to the American Servicemen's Union office. There I knew I would be welcomed with open arms, in solidarity with my act of defiance. Since the Army had thoughtfully provided me an excuse for self-reflection upon the start of the second half of the year, by ordering me a second time to report for duty in Vietnam, I decided to invest this date with a special significance. From this day forth, I declared, I am no longer a pacifist. I am a **revolutionary**. A Communist revolutionary. I'd come to understand that I had *no right* to advise the people of a nation under attack by a brutal invading military—that of my own country—that they should lay down their arms.

It is gross hypocrisy to put an equal sign between the warring parties in such a situation. One side was a brutal aggressor, the other simply striving to defend itself.

My views had been evolving in this direction for some time. The writings of Frantz Fanon and Malcolm X argued forcefully for the right of colonized peoples to take their liberty and independence by any means necessary. In the real world, that almost always meant by force of arms. Mao Tse-Tung had declared that "Political power comes from the barrel of a gun." His reward for this truth-telling was to be vilified as a "violence-monger"—by the representatives of **the** most violent nations on Earth! Anti-colonial struggles for independence had erupted in Africa in the wake of India's achievement of independence from Britain (1947), and the Chinese (1949) and Cuban (1959) revolutions. Having been booted from Indochina, France had lost control of its north African colonies just as the US was inserting its first troops ("advisers") into Vietnam.

Let us be blunt: the American Servicemen's Union was founded and administered by revolutionary Communists. The ASU was set up and supported by Workers World Party (WWP), a "hardline" Marxist-Leninist organization. I make no stunning revelation here; this was well known on the American left and certainly to the FBI. That agency had a surprisingly objective summary of WWP's history in its files, as I would learn in later years when I got to view my own dossier at that agency.

So here I was, a mild-mannered kid from the suburbs, raised to believe the Soviet Union wanted to "bury" us, surrounded by Communists. [The proper translation of Premier Khrushchev's statement was that his nation would "surpass" us in economic and technical endeavors, but this was deliberately mistranslated in the US media. This came to light only after the collapse of the USSR.] And these people were keenly intelligent, often with great sense of humor, and devoted to a cause that seemingly, if it could be realized, would put an end to war by putting an end to exploitation of man by man. The United States was and is the great bastion of capitalism, and one only had to watch the evening TV news to see to what atrocious lengths it would go to preserve its spheres of exploitation in the world. I needed no further persuasion. The System itself was the master teacher of this lesson. Or, as Christ was said to have remarked: "Let he who has eyes to see, see."

I penned the following free-form poem in celebration of my July 1 self-declared metamorphosis:

THOUGHTS OF AN AWOL G.I.

earth shakes, universe smiles at
vibrations of fast-fading empire gasping.
Black babies of malnutrition dying
pig politicians for law 'n' order crying;
government run on paranoid energy, Thought Police
want to know: are you now or have you ever been a commie?
general seeking another star spawns
    on a blood-nourished hill
the future liberators of amerika.
fascism? "it can't happen here" say
white super-liberals as they tap Black saints' phones.
tortured visions of future fester in my head
rockefeller's army marching on peru;
harlem streets enflamed by sheets of napalm
stockade is ugly—sweden like a siren beckons
but i cannot desert my brothers
we must struggle on.
for the proof is in the Viet Cong pudding:
The People shall surely triumph!

[With so much time having passed, it seems advisable to explain the line starting with "white super-liberals . . . " In the wake of Robert Kennedy's death the previous year, it had become public knowledge that, while Attorney General of the United States, he had approved the wiretapping of Dr. Martin Luther King, Jr.'s telephone conversations. This was part of J. Edgar Hoover's obsessive drive to try to prove King a "Communist" and thereby discredit him.]

Acquiring the Forbidden Knowledge

For whence come wars, and fightings, and factions?
whence but from the body and the lusts of the body?
For wars are occasioned by the love of money . . .

—Socrates, from "Phaedo" in "The Dialogues of Plato"

I had started to acquire **the Forbidden Knowledge**. I believed I had received a very good general education growing up in Syosset; indeed, its public schools system was admired by other districts. But there were aspects of how society really worked that had been quite left out of the curriculum. We were decidedly **not** taught that the state is fundamentally a body of armed men defending the privileges of a tiny minority, the Ruling Class. Most of the members of this self-selecting elite come from already exceedingly wealthy family dynasties and, with extremely rare exceptions, never put themselves at bodily risk in the wars they instigate. The world is divided into exploiters and exploited, the latter being the vast majority of people, the former a small minority. Indeed, those who really run the show, who decide on matters of war and peace and thus death or life for millions, are a <u>tiny</u> minority. Not only are these precepts not taught in the United States, one might say a major aim of the "educational" system is to debunk these ideas. As I delved into the classic works of Karl Marx, Friedrich Engels and V.I. Lenin—"the ABCs of Marxist thought"—their way of viewing the world made great sense to me.

Having rejected the conventional wisdom of seeking a college degree for the sake of higher personal income, I had cast my lot with the working class. Was this some dishonor? My parents were of the working class, though they didn't give the class nature of society any thought. For that's how they'd been programmed by society. Who but Socialists even speak of such matters? By good fortune, I had been raised in a household where the racism prevalent in the society at large was not embraced and not inculcated in me. I was thus blessed with not having to overcome fear of "the other." Though I'd been raised in a virtually lily-white social environment, I now supported the Black Panther Party. The Panthers' official Program proclaimed that black people had no business engaging in warfare against other peoples of color halfway around the world while they were being denied basic human rights at home. There was nothing to say to that but "Right on, brother!" [See the **ESSAY** later in this book for an expanded discussion of class society.]

The Case of the Fort Dix 38

On June 5, 1969 an uprising had occurred in the overcrowded barracks of the Post Stockade at Fort Dix, New Jersey, an installation used primarily for Basic Training. Reportedly, around 800 prisoners were crammed into a facility designed for 250, resulting in hours-long waits to get into the Mess Hall and long stints in pre-trial status. A large sign over the main gate to the Stockade bore the slogan OBEDIENCE TO THE LAW IS FREEDOM. When a photo of this sign was circulated by Liberation News Service (LNS)—founded 1967 as an alternative to the mainstream media and deploying its own reporters and photographers—in April 1969, it was widely remarked that the slogan was uncomfortably reminiscent of that over the main gate to the Nazi extermination camp Auschwitz: ARBEIT MACHT FREI ("Work Makes You Free"). I believe the sign at Fort Dix disappeared fairly soon after this public exposure.

The most common offense causing confinement there? Being AWOL, of course. In the incident in question, interior infrastructure was smashed up and fires broke out. At the time, I'd been awaiting the verdict of the Federal Court in Boston and hadn't heard of this unrest via the mainstream media. The ASU staff had filled me in during one of my visits while afloat in that legal limbo.

Had this riot erupted spontaneously because of abusive conditions in the facility, or was it a planned, conspiratorial event? Either way, the Army was looking to mete out punishment. If it could prove the latter theory, the sentences would clearly be much harsher. Thirty-eight individuals were initially charged with participating in a riot, damaging government property, and arson. Six men were singled out initially as "ringleaders," including Terry Klug, Bill Brakefield, Jeff Russell and Tom Catlow. Those four, all affiliated with the ASU, ultimately became the focus of the prosecution's wrath. If convicted of all charges, these guys faced the prospect of 40 or more years in prison.

Brakefield was still in that stockade after being tried for AWOL in the wake of his sanctuary at City College of NY the previous November; he had nearly served out his sentence. I had no doubt that a violent uprising, even if only property was damaged, was not Bill's style. He was the only defendant I'd met at this point. Terry Klug, I was told by Andy Stapp, was a committed revolutionary who'd been designated a deserter and had done anti-war organizing in several European nations via a group called RITA (Resisters Inside the Army). He'd been absent from his assigned "Military Intelligence" unit (!) for about 18 months, then decided it was time to come home and "face the music." Terry had flown to New York City, held a press conference arranged by ASU, and been taken into custody in January 1969. He would be charged with actual desertion, though he had <u>voluntarily</u> returned himself to "military control." Klug was given a three-year sentence on this charge prior to the events of June 5. Russell and Catlow had become involved with the Union only after arrival in the stockade.

On at least two occasions in July I joined the delegation of attorneys and paralegals, plus Chairman Stapp, which would meet with the defendants at Ft. Dix to discuss defense strategy. My presence wasn't even challenged by the MPs; had it been, I would have been passed off as a paralegal assistant. Stapp was there to coordinate the overall defense effort, and I was there to express my personal solidarity. It rather tickled me that, AWOL at the time myself, I could visit with these prisoners unchallenged.

Janis Joplin belts 'em out, and "Whitey's on the Moon"

I was very fortunate to be at liberty (unofficially, of course) in the summer of '69. On July 19 I saw Janis Joplin perform in concert at the world-famous Tennis Stadium at Forest Hills, in Queens. Joplin had left Big Brother & The Holding Company by this time and called her crew The Kozmic Blues Band. Janis put every fiber of her being into her performances. She made remarks from the stage that night about the Apollo 11 mission, which was in lunar orbit, approaching its time to touch down. The very next night I was privileged to watch one of the greatest events in human history unfold in real time, from the comfort of the family living room. I slept at home most nights by this time, there being no sign of law enforcement at the Laxers' door. Neil Armstrong stepped off the ladder onto the lunar crust, and for that one brief moment it almost seemed like humanity was united as one, watching this spectacle unfold in somewhat bleary TV images. But when we awoke the next day, wars were still raging and poverty had not been alleviated. As a person with a very keen interest in all aspects of Science, I couldn't help but feel inspired and thrilled. But I was increasingly bothered by the hypocrisy of the leaders of the nation that mounted this mission. Nixon, in fact, had used the occasion of the lunar success to speak of bringing "peace" to Planet Earth. I was strongly compelled to sympathize with the narrator of "Whitey on the Moon," written and recorded by Gil Scott-Heron, when it appeared the following year (on the album *Small Talk at 125th and Lenox*). He recounts the misery of life in the ghetto, while the mainstream populace—blissfully unaware and largely uncaring—celebrates American astronauts landing on the moon.

August 2, 1969: Waving the flag, but whose flag?

Beyond the first of August I would exceed 30 days of AWOL and again be Dropped From the Rolls out in Oakland. I lacked a firm plan for a date and method to again surrender myself to the Army, to get my punishment over with. Once again, an event was planned for a propitious date: the ASU, in collaboration with SDS, Black Panther Party and other militant groups, called for a street demonstration Saturday, August 2, in front of Pennsylvania Station, above which the new Madison Square Garden had recently been constructed. The theme of this demo was "Free the Ft. Dix 38 and All Political Prisoners."

Clearly, I had to participate, and on my own initiative again decided to participate dressed in full Army uniform. It being hot weather, I donned the appropriate Class 'A' uniform: khakis, nicely pressed, dress shoes and garrison cap (the soft, envelope-shaped headgear, as distinguished from the "saucer cap" with its hard visor). And, of course, an ASU button adorned my khaki shirt. Andy Stapp and other ASU staffers were present. In the sea of banners and placards, as was often the case at militant protests, there were some "Viet Cong" flags: yellow star on a background divided horizontally into fields of red and pale blue. Quite spontaneously, I asked to borrow one of these. Climbing atop a low stone wall abutting a pedestrian plaza, I held aloft the flag of "the enemy." The crowd chanted: "Ho, Ho, Ho Chi Minh! Vietnam is gonna win!" Having concluded that justice was on the side of the people of Vietnam, I was calling for victory for the liberation forces. Did this mean I was cheering the deaths of American military personnel? Not at all. My position was quite simple: they should never have been sent to Indochina in the first place; the US should declare a ceasefire and withdraw its forces as quickly as possible; the Vietnamese people must determine their own destiny.

My flag-waving of the "wrong" variety drew the attention of the crew covering the demo for CBS-TV's flagship NYC station. I was taken aside to a quiet location and interviewed on camera by Dave Marash, a reporter for that station before he became a fixture on "60 Minutes." When asked why I was demonstrating, I stated (this is verbatim): "I support the National Liberation Front of South Vietnam in its struggle against US imperialism." When asked what I expected would become of me after this, I said I would face the consequences: prosecution and imprisonment.

Shortly after I returned to the demo from the interview, Andy Stapp and I noticed at least two uniformed members of the Armed Services Police on the periphery of the crowd, starting to work their way toward us. An instant decision was required: did I really want to end my period of AWOL here and now? If it *had* to end that day, that was okay. But no, it wasn't my keen desire. I made a dash for the Seventh Avenue entrance to Penn Station and descended the long stairway. Removing my ASU button, I ducked into the first vacant telephone booth I came to and yanked off my cap. I turned my face away from the folding door's large window panes and pretended to be speaking on the phone. My peripheral vision caught sight of the ASP guys bustling right past me. I was saved by the simple fact that, at any given time in those war years, there were scores of uniformed military personnel passing through this huge facility.

August 2, 1969: The pinnacle of my public opposition to the war. Outside Pennsylvania Station, with the newly constructed Madison Square Garden above it, I held aloft a "Viet Cong" flag. I was never directly prosecuted for this or other public demonstrations while in full Army uniform.

(Photo credit: Staff photographer/Liberation News Service, published in LNS issue of August 7, 1969.)

Here I am with Andy Stapp, founder of the American Servicemen's Union, during a quiet moment in the demonstration to "Free the Ft. Dix 38 and All Political Prisoners," August 2, 1969.
(Photo credit: Unidentified friend of the ASU; from author's private archive.)

Liberation News Service covered this demonstration in its print issue of August 7, 1969. They ran a photo of me displaying the flag, but made a major error in the photo caption and the text of their brief article. The latter reported: "One GI appeared at the demonstration briefly and held up the flag of the National Liberation Front of South Vietnam; he was later arrested by Military Police in the subway and charged with violation of codes which prohibit soldiers from demonstrating in uniform." In fact, I escaped quite unscathed, though it was a close call. The ASU would later receive a letter from a US Coast Guard officer who said he'd witnessed my actions that day and had intended to <u>personally</u> arrest me, to prevent my getting into deeper trouble. My vanishing act must have sorely disappointed this self-appointed guardian of my best interests.

I spent that evening at the apartment of Andy Stapp and Deirdre Griswold, who would soon give birth to their daughter, Kitty. We confirmed that the local CBS-TV station did broadcast a brief segment on the demonstration, including my interview. If the Army wished to throw the book at me over my actions and words of August 2, all they would need do is subpoena the videotape of that interview. I later learned that this bit of publicity finally brought FBI agents knocking on doors in Syosset. After ascertaining I was not to be found at my parents' home, these snoops inquired of some neighbors as to my character and activities. I learned they got an earful from the son of one of our immediate neighbors, who'd only been in grade school while I was in high school. Seems he'd invited them to "Go to hell!" I stayed with ASU comrades in the city for a few days after that, then returned unmolested to our family domicile.

Soon the epochal event known as Woodstock would transpire. I was "at liberty" to attend, but wasn't adventurous enough to head off with no lodging available. When I learned of the torrential rain that struck Max Yasgur's upstate farm during the festival, I felt vindicated in having stayed away. But that sentiment faded with time. Yes, for the record, I do regret having missed that event.

GI sanctuary in Hawaii

Unbeknownst to me in New York, something significant had pretty well spontaneously gotten underway in early August in faraway Hawaii. Two churches in Honolulu had offered their premises as sanctuary for military personnel who had come to oppose the war. Hawaii was full of GIs, of all service branches, many transiting to or from the war zone. Suddenly, the number of servicemen seeking shelter from the storm of military madness grew to the point of attracting the attention of the mainstream media. Just the kind of publicity to make the generals and admirals at the Pentagon want to hide under their desks. Obviously, I was all for it! Furthermore, I was available to become a participant. John Catalinotto, a non-veteran adviser to ASU on behalf of Workers World Party, had been sent to the island early on to lay support for the brewing rebellion. [John Catalinotto quotes from the early draft of this memoir, and recounts his own involvement in this sanctuary, in <u>Turn the Guns Around—Mutinies, Soldier Revolts and Revolutions</u>, World View Forum; New York, 2017.]

I had a meeting with Sam Marcy, Chairperson of WWP, to discuss what the ASU could contribute to such a movement. We concluded that an effort should be made to raise the political consciousness of the sanctuary participants, and their civilian support network, about the true nature of the war and the military system.

The cost of flying from the East Coast to the Hawaiian Islands obviously would not be cheap. What to do? Having received my fair share of Army orders in my time, 50 copies at a pop—whoever supplied paper to the military had one sweet deal—I had concluded that producing phony orders for travel should not be a challenge. All I needed was a good old manual typewriter, for that's what Army clerks normally had on their desks. Following the format of my own orders to report for duty in Vietnam, I simply drew up a set of fictitious orders assigning me to report to a base in Hawaii on such and such a date. Run off a few photocopies, put on my Class 'A' uniform (khakis again), go to the airport and hand my orders to a ticket agent and, *voila!* I used my real name and Service Number because I would have to show my Military ID Card. I would fly to this assignment, on behalf of the GI resistance movement, on Uncle Sam's dime. The commercial airlines processed millions of these bits of paper over the course of the war and sent them on to the Pentagon for reimbursement. With that volume of paper, my little trick was pretty well guaranteed anonymity.

Flew all the way to Hawaii and all I saw was this church!

My first time actually setting foot on California soil was to change planes at San Francisco en route to Honolulu. With the final leg underway, I changed out of my khakis and donned civvies. The plane set down in paradise and I was off, by taxicab, to The Church of the Crossroads. This was the church then housing the majority of the AWOLs. I had been given the name of Susan Steinman to seek once I got there; she was affiliated with WWP and its youth group, Youth Against War & Fascism (YAWF). My arrival in sanctuary was made public and some reporters hastily assembled. I openly announced to the press corps that I had come to raise the level of political consciousness on the scene! Oops. I got chided for this excess honesty later on. [See **APPENDIX 3** for FBI memo reporting my arrival at the Sanctuary.]

Susan proved to be quite lovely, deeply tanned, with long, dark brown hair. She was just 19 at the time, attending University of Hawaii. Her politics were intense. Susan gave me a guided tour of the grounds and her own political assessment of the people with whom I'd be interacting. The Church of the Crossroads—military personnel who were opposing the war publicly for the first time, by taking sanctuary there, were indeed placing themselves at a crossroads in their young lives—covered a decent chunk of real estate. There were administrative buildings in addition to the church proper, a long breezeway between structures, and a large expanse of lawn. Though not designed to house people around the clock, it provided enough physical space that folks could spread themselves out at night and sleep with some degree of privacy. When I arrived on August 21, the sanctuary was in its third week.

The population of servicemen fluctuated during my stay. Some grew bored and wandered off-grounds in a careless manner and were snatched by MPs; we knew the church was under constant surveillance. For example, The New York Times reported on August 22 that the very day I had arrived at the church, MPs had arrested a sanctuary participant who had left church grounds. I will obscure that individual's identity in what follows. Here is the brief article as it appeared in the Times:

[Headline:] **Marine Seized, but Soldier Enters Hawaii Sanctuary**
Special to The New York Times

HONOLULU, Aug. 21—An AWOL marine who tried to join his visiting parents for dinner at a Waikiki hotel lost his sanctuary at the Church of the Crossroads last night.

But the number of servicemen taking refuge at the church remained at 22 after a young soldier from Syosset, L.I. arrived here from the mainland to seek sanctuary.

The marine, PFC _____ _____ of the Bronx, was arrested by Hawaiian armed services policemen outside the Outrigger Hotel and turned over to the marine authorities.

Taking his place at the Church of the Crossroads was PVT Gregory Laxer, 21, of Syosset, who had been ordered to report to Oakland, Calif., by July 1 for assignment to Vietnam. His former base was Fort Devens, Mass.

Occasionally a new guy would show up to join us, having heard of the protest in the media or by word of mouth. There were about 20 of us at any time at this facility, plus a few others at the second church (Unitarian), making this altogether the largest GI sanctuary in US history. That is why the ASU felt we had to have a presence there. It was local activists of SDS and The Resistance who had proposed the use of the churches. Unlike mainstream Christian denominations, these churches had boards of directors and memberships who believed that faith without deeds was inadequate. They couldn't remain on the sidelines while the nation was being torn by crucial social issues. Church members and other civilian sympathizers saw to it that no one went hungry.

Preaching to the choir

The tactic of political sanctuary has an inherent practical drawback: once you take refuge, you have essentially imprisoned yourself. So, how to pass the time? All we could do was talk among ourselves, talk to the civilians about the experience of being in the military, and talk to representatives of the news media from time to time. Most of the participants in this sanctuary were not very politically aware; they had simply had enough of military bullshit and felt in their guts how wrong this war was. Navy Seaman Oscar Kelly, a light-skinned African-American, could testify personally to racist indignities suffered in the fleets. But most of the guys were white, and not so attuned to such matters. We politicos sought to emphasize the importance of this protest not being the end-all, but that we should continue to work against the war, and the greater Military Machine, at our next duty stations. We all knew we would be back in the military's grasp eventually.

So the days started to blur one into another. Fortunately, there were stimulating interruptions from time to time. John Lewis, a fellow AWOL soldier working with the ASU, arrived a few days after I. He was from coal country in Kentucky, and had steeped himself in the history of militant labor unionism. Indeed, he bore the same name as a famous radical mining union leader. And there was a film crew from the British Broadcasting Corporation shooting a documentary on the sanctuary. I was "elected," as an articulate spokesperson for GI resisters, to be interviewed. I spoke for 20 minutes or more and answered all questions very candidly.

Additional "entertainment" was provided by uninvited visitors. "Young Americans for Freedom" was a rightwing youth group sponsored by the Republican Party, active on college campuses. One day, a member of YAF came to the church to try to instigate trouble. Before he could get far into his speech in favor of the Vietnam War, we challenged him as to why he wasn't backing up his pro-military fervor by donning a uniform himself. "Oh, I'm 4-F. Bad back, you see" was the reply. This was all too typical. Those who made the loudest pro-war noises were often those most shielded from any risk of having to participate themselves. An equally unwelcome visitor was a Major Geary, an Army Chaplain who dropped in one day, in uniform, to try to open our eyes to the holy necessity of combatting Communism. He apparently thought we would cut him slack because he happened to be a black man. In show business parlance, let's just say this preacher's act "bombed." [See **APPENDIX 3** for additional reference to this Chaplain.]

As the ennui grew among those self-imprisoned at the church, drugs were being used more and more to try to offset the boredom. So the most political of us huddled and talked over our options. We concurred that the sanctuary had lost its forward momentum and was stagnating. The grounds were under constant surveillance by MPs, making it intimidating for new servicepersons to join us. We made an expensive phone call to our advisers in New York and it was agreed we should pull out and try to engage in more effective struggle elsewhere. It would be too risky for me to fly out of Hawaii using the counterfeit military orders trick again, so WWP had to wire us the funds for airfare.

The great escape—a comedy of military errors

In the wee hours of Sunday, August 31, five AWOLs and some civilian supporters were to depart The Church of the Crossroads. Susan and I made our way briskly to a Volkswagen 'Beetle' to be driven by a young supporter who knew the area very well. I immediately hunkered down on the floor in the back. We took off and a government car immediately came in pursuit. The personnel in the pursuit car, presumably Army CID (Criminal Investigations Division) agents, decidedly did <u>not</u> know the local streets. The young man driving our getaway car didn't even have to drive at a reckless speed; he shook off our pursuers simply by making a lot of turns onto side streets. We may rest assured that no one in that pursuit car received a promotion as a result of his actions that particular day. We arrived at the airport unscathed. The others did not fare so well: one car was intercepted, its occupants, including John Lewis, seized; the third car was in jeopardy of capture and fled back to the church.

Susan and I had to wait until dawn for a flight to San Francisco. It was a nervous two or three hours. My face had appeared in newspapers the day of my arrival. It should not have required the IQ of an Einstein for Military Intelligence to watch the airport and spot any fleeing sanctuary partici-pants. This was why we were fond of saying "'Military Intelligence' is an oxymoron!" So off we flew to The City by the Bay. Farewell to the paradise I never really had a chance to see, other than gazing out airplane windows.

Susan and I would spend the next few days in the apartment of noted civil liberties attorney Mike Kennedy. Mike was going away to work on an urgent case. Sue and I camped on the floor, cushioned by a sleeping bag. There I made my first fumbling efforts at lovemaking. My lack of experience surely was obvious. Susan was very understanding.

Susan was familiar with the Bay Area and showed me around. We paid a visit to the humble apartment of a certain Mr. Nguyen, a middle-aged gentleman with ties to the liberation forces in Vietnam. Nguyen prepared us a traditional meal, after which he assiduously swept up any crumbs from the kitchen floor—a custom he'd brought with him from his homeland. I was then presented with a silvery ring, unadorned but for the engraved inscription "2000." This ring was said to have been crafted from a piece of the two-thousandth US aircraft shot down over Vietnam in the current war. Such rings were given as symbols of solidarity to foreign supporters of the liberation movement. I would wear this ring for perhaps 15 months before the cumulative effect of thousands of handwashings—mandatory for a conscientious medic—caused it to break into several pieces and slip down the drain of an Army barracks sink.

Homeward-bound is stockade-bound

During my stay in the Bay Area I concocted a plan to surrender to the Army right at the entrance to the Oakland Army base from which I was AWOL, to make a very public statement of opposition to the war. But cooler heads in New York prevailed. They reminded me of the risk of being forcibly shipped out directly from that facility. So back east I would go, and we would work on strategy from there. An occasion would surely arise to permit me to be taken back into military custody in another public show of militant resistance. I returned to home base, cleverly disguised as a civilian, after the brief stay in San Francisco. Susan, meanwhile, returned to the University of Hawaii.

The ASU would soon learn that back in Honolulu, the number of AWOL servicemen in sanctuary had dwindled to a dozen. Perhaps 30 men in all (the figures are in some dispute) had participated for some period of time. In the early morning of September 12, MPs raided the two churches, kicking doors open, and arrested the remaining GIs present. FBI documents I later obtained showed that the military had been discussing with the local civilian prosecutors using a "health and safety inspection" of the church grounds as an excuse for breaking up the sanctuary. But that was deemed a process that could take three weeks, because of bureaucratic procedures. The Brass had tired of the publicity and weren't willing to wait indefinitely for entropy to terminate the protest. The FBI generated a report on the conclusion of what had been an historic, if ultimately somewhat disappointing, event. [See **APPENDIX 3**.]

I split my time between Syosset and staying with comrades in the New York City. In fairly short order, President Nixon provided me an opportunity to prepare for the inescapable process of facing my punishment. It was announced that Nixon would be addressing the United Nations General Assembly on September 18. WWP, in the guise of YAWF (Youth Against War & Fascism) and ASU, called for an anti-war protest outside the US Mission to the UN on East 45th Street in Manhattan. Militant elements of the anti-war movement felt that, as long as the criminal war was being waged, no major US government official should be allowed to visit the city without being confronted.

Before the date of this demo rolled around, I wrote a letter of solidarity to the people of "north" Vietnam, who were being bombed daily by B-52s, and included with it one of the many copies the Army had thoughtfully provided of my most recent set of orders for duty over there. I also enclosed an article about Ho Chi Minh, trying to explain to US soldiers what the Vietnamese were fighting for, that I'd submitted for publication in an upcoming issue of The Bond. Correspondence to and from Hanoi could be routed via peace groups in Japan. It would take several months for a two-way exchange of correspondence to be completed this way.

I reported for demo duty dressed in my Army Green Class 'A' uniform, reflecting the change of season. No parade permit had been obtained for this action, which had been called on short notice. An Associated Press photo of the scene that appeared in some newspapers shows me at the rear of the knot of demonstrators, helping to stretch a long banner across the street. The NY Daily News covered the incident under the headline **"Nab 11 Anti-Nixon Pickets."** Opening paragraph: "Eleven antiwar demonstrators, including a 21-year-old soldier in uniform, were arrested yesterday after they attempted to picket in front of the U.S. Mission to the UN, at 45th Street and UN Plaza, in protest against President Nixon's appearance before the General Assembly." I am identified by name and home address later in the brief article. I only learned by later viewing copies of my FBI files that the Bureau had obtained four items, photos plus articles, from The Daily News, including photos that weren't published. As New York's blatantly rightwing daily paper back then, the News was extra cozy with Hoover's operation.

I was one of the eleven demonstrators grabbed off the street. Though I was resigned to being busted that day, I defiantly told the cop clutching me: "You can't arrest me, I'm military!" His immediate reply was "Oh yes I can!" My arresting officer, Patrolman Goff, turned out to be a decent fellow. He said he was in the Army Reserve himself and sympathized with soldiers who'd had enough of this insane war. We arrestees were taken to the nearest Precinct House for booking. I was called out of the holding pen and escorted to the Desk Sergeant. "What's going on?" I inquired. "Just look up at the Sergeant" someone instructed. As I did so, flashbulbs went off. Though I had never heard the expression "perp walk," that's what I'd just been put through, doubtless as a favor to The Daily News. A little later, Patrolman Goff made a point of bringing me this news: "The boys at Military Intelligence were creaming their jeans when they found out you're in custody." Well, it was nice to know I'd made somebody happy!

In fairly short order, I was separated from the civilian prisoners, handcuffed, and transported by van to Brooklyn Navy Yard. That facility had seen major reductions in utilization by the 1960s; the brig there was certainly wanting for customers. I was given a private cell for the night on an upper level; I don't recall any other prisoners being on that floor. At some point in the evening, a voice bellowed "Where's Laxer?!?" "Up here!" I shouted, having no clue who was seeking me. A fat little Chief Petty Officer appeared, puffing from having to climb the stairs. He came to my cell and shouted at me: "You don't demonstrate in your uniform!!" My response was "You do if you have a political point to make!" That was the full extent of our dialogue. The CPO waddled back downstairs and I was in splendid isolation for the rest of the night.

I had been AWOL for 79 days this time. If I was not to be sentenced to either a Dishonorable or Bad Conduct Discharge, my days AWOL would be added to my days in pre- and post-trial detention. This was called "Bad Time," and I would have to live an additional day in olive drab servitude to offset each and every day in the "Bad" category. Surely the Army wouldn't want to keep me around after my most recent activities. In the morning, I was back in handcuffs for the long ride to Ft. Dix, New Jersey. I didn't know when I would see Susan again, next attend a Rock concert, get stoned, or simply indulge in the luxury of walking down a sidewalk in the World. But what weight did any of those concerns carry while human beings, on both sides of the war, were still being killed and maimed? I had made a conscious choice to be a Soldier for Peace. Now I would face the consequences. Again.

CHAPTER VIII

In the bowels of the beast

Fort Dix Stockade, New Jersey
September 19, 1969-January 27, 1970

. . . You've got a slot to fill
And fill that slot you will.
You'll learn to love it or we'll break you.
What will it take to whip you into line?
A broken heart? A broken head?
It can be arranged,
It can be arranged.
Don't worry, Mister Blue,
We'll take good care of you.
Just think of it as sense and not surrender.
But never think again
That you can think again
Or you'll get something you'll remember.
What will it take to whip you into line?
A broken heart? A broken head?
It can be arranged,
It can be arranged.

—Mr. Blue, *by Tom Paxton*

By the time I entered Fort Dix Stockade, the authorities had reduced the population there as much as possible in the wake of the June uprising. To be sure, the joint was crowded, but it didn't feel suffocating to me. Getting into the Mess Hall was no longer a half-day affair. The "cellblocks" were simply more of those two-story World War II barracks I'd been housed in from day one in uniform, separated one from the other by razor wire fencing to prevent inmate mingling. The exception to this was the "Segregation," i.e. solitary confinement, unit. That was a pair of long, low buildings containing individual cells, fenced off from the general population. The accused ringleaders of the uprising were among those held there. We inmates wore regular fatigue uniforms, but with white rectangular patches on the left shoulder; only that white patch made us stand out from ordinary troops. That and the absence of any insignia of rank.

Having declared myself a hard-core militant, I initially made myself the living embodiment of the demands of the ASU. During the intake process upon arrival, I refused to salute or address as "Sir" a gentleman of captain's rank. Referring to the configuration of the silver insignia of that rank, I declared: "Railroad tracks on one's shoulders do not a Captain make."

September 23, 1969

Dear Folks,

Greetings from lovely Ft. Dix Stockade! I hope you didn't have any great difficulty in finding out what happened to me Thursday, but I didn't even get around to asking someone to call you, because the bust came with lightning speed. The charges were "Disorderly Conduct" and "Resisting Arrest." Ha! Ha! The judge dismissed the charges readily in order to expedite my return to the military. I spent the night in the brig at Brooklyn Navy Yard and was brought out here Friday; had no writing material until today.

Once I got out here, I wasted no time in endearing myself to the Brass. I refused to salute an officer or call him "sir," so am now charged with, in addition to AWOL, "disrespect to an officer." Sounds good for a 6-month sentence to me.

I'm beginning to coordinate my defense now, and estimate that I'll be tried in about two months. Andy or Bob Lemay (ASU Executive Director) can tell you who my lawyer will be, but under no circumstances do I want you contacting him; he's an extremely busy man.

You won't be allowed to send newspaper clippings, so I would appreciate it if you would mention in your letters the important events; just a few details would suffice. I have sufficient underwear and the like; my only problem, really, is blisters from playing basketball.

Please don't be bugging the Union with phone calls; when there's news, you'll hear it from me. There really ain't much more to say, so till next week, *au revoir.*

Love,
Greg

As Ft. Dix Stockade "serviced" the Greater New York City area, it contained a greater racial/ethnic diversity than what I'd encountered at Fort Devens in Massachusetts. I welcomed this diversity, though at times the feeling wasn't reciprocal. Within my first few days inside the razor wire I received word that "Military Intelligence" wished to "debrief" (interrogate) me, and would I be so kind as to report to Administration? I told the messenger I had nothing to say to MI and heard no more of the matter. But someone among my peers decided I must be an undercover agent. End result: a big blob of shaving cream deposited on my bed. Now I was "the other"—my new acquaintances already sensed I was "different." But I was committed to standing in solidarity with the wretched of the Earth, whether they liked it or not!

I had brought along an old bible my family had had at home, as I knew this was the one item of literature that would not be prohibited inside. This ensured I had at least some reading matter. But mostly, at the outset, I passed the time comparing Army experiences with the guys and playing basketball when recreation was allowed, and the weather permitted. Playing in combat boots, especially after not playing for a long time, was a guaranteed road to blisters. That really was my chief complaint of the moment, hard though my Mom found that to believe. She assumed I was being mistreated and concealing that from her. Worse still, she expressed a desire to come and visit me.

Main Gate of Post Stockade, Fort Dix, NJ in spring 1969. Public exposure actually embarrassed the Army sufficiently that the offending sign was gone by the time I entered this portal in September of that year.
(Photo credit: David Fenton/Liberation News Service, April 1969.)

The four primary defendants held responsible for the June 5, 1969 rebellion in Fort Dix Stockade. Left to right: Bill Brakefield, Jeff Russell, Terry Klug, Tom Catlow.
(Photo credit: Photographer unknown; published in Liberation News Service, summer 1969.)

A little *too* militant, perhaps?

Why was my mother bugging me now about visiting me at Ft. Dix Stockade? Doubtless this was because of the place's reputation as a hellhole. She wanted to see what she could of conditions there and complain to the authorities. But of course, from the Visiting Area, she would have seen very little. But the main reason for my desire that she **not** visit was my knowing how the affair would unfold: Mom would collapse in hysterics, clinging to me and creating a major scene. It would embarrass me tremendously and certainly **not** improve my mother's mental/emotional state. Indeed, if the guards decided I was a "mama's boy" they might be encouraged to rough me up. Most of the guards did not have a sadistic streak, though. They had simply been assigned to this facility by luck of the draw. They were ordinary guys who wanted to get through their own tours of duty with minimal hassle and get the hell out.

Some of my ensuing letters home could be interpreted as conveying a degree of harshness toward my mother. I was trying to give her firm guidance as to what she could do to actually assist me in my circumstances. She was becoming a real emotional wreck and I was trying to divert her into activities like scanning news stories on GI resistance, the anti-war movement as a whole, and the course of the war itself. My depth of militancy was no act, but it made my mother fear for the worst outcome in my confrontation with the Military Machine. I *was*, perhaps, "laying it on a little too thick."

In early October, I was presented with the official charge against me, which was solely that I'd been AWOL from date X to date Y. Interestingly, the prosecuting authority at Dix apparently had no information on my having surrendered myself at Fort Devens and been tried and punished there. They were charging me with being continuously absent since October 22, 1968! Such breathtaking competence! Meanwhile, the threatened "disrespect to an officer" charge had evaporated. I do not have a martyr complex, but I confess I was again puzzled by the Army's apparent willingness to be "lenient." Had not the "Military Intelligence" boys been "creaming their jeans" with delight over my having been apprehended?

Introduction to Seg

I'd been advised by Terry Klug, during my visits as a "paralegal" earlier in the year, that the riot defendants requested the right to attend Catholic Mass on Sundays. Other than going on Sick Call or attending a court session, this was about their only opportunity to get out of their Seg cells, stretch their legs, and have some contact with the general population. Even in the chapel they were kept separated from the rest of us by the guards, but at least I could express solidarity with the guys as they passed by, entering and exiting. And so it was that I became a regular attendee at Mass on Sundays my first few weeks in "the pound" (as in dog pound), as the inmates lovingly referred to this facility.

October 15, 1969

Dear Folks,

You'll never guess where I am. I'm in Seg, which is short for Segregation, which is tantamount to solitary.

Before you start writing to Dick Nixon or take any foolish action, allow me to assure you that I'm getting more food here than I was in the regular cellblocks. Physically and mentally I am in excellent condition. My major gripe is simply the illegality of being given corporal punishment without due process of law. But, of course, due process of law is something the military is not at all concerned with. I was put here Sunday afternoon by order of a mere first lieutenant, whose arrogance manifests itself as an inability to tolerate those who won't lick his boots—for my "crime," you see, was to refuse to call him "sir." Somehow, he figures that this will earn him my respect; I guess he thinks basically like Tricky Dick—illogically. So much for Seg—don't worry; I don't.

I've only got about 880 pages to go in the Bible. Some progress, huh? I might have a surprise for you soon concerning my court-martial. That's about all there is to say now, so as the Amazing Mets roll on to victory, I sign off....

Love,
Greg

First Lieutenant Roark was a real piece of work. He may not have been a lifer himself but, while he wore the green, he apparently lived and breathed only to show enlisted men his imagined superiority, especially "maggots" who had bucked the system sufficiently to land on "his" compound. A lieutenant conducting himself in that manner in Vietnam would have been a ripe target for a fragmentation grenade. Major Casey was the Commander of the stockade; Roark was Duty Officer on most day shifts. While we only saw the former on special occasions, Roark was in our faces regularly, accompanied by his ass-kissing buddy, Spec. 5 Jewell. He was no gem!

In all my days in the Army, I never saw a closer relationship between a Commissioned Officer and a low-ranking NCO. It was like these guys were joined at the hip. Their joint reign over daily life in the facility made Ft. Dix Stockade something of a blend of plot lines that could have been collaboratively devised by Franz Kafka and Joseph Heller.

This first trip to solitary was Administrative Seg, somewhat akin to being put under psychiatric observation. We were housed in one of the single-level units; the adjoining unit was for Disciplinary Seg, where naughty boys were sent for actual punishment. Each cell had three solid walls, with the front being classic jailhouse bars. Built into the bars was a rectangular opening through which the food tray was passed. Dimensions were about seven feet wide by nine feet deep, thin mattress on a low shelf across rear wall, individual commode and small sink for washing hands. I would sooner have spent my whole stockade stay in such a cell than address a jerk like Roark as "Sir."

October 23, 1969

Dear Folks,

I was released from Seg on Saturday morning; partially because I didn't give the guards any trouble, and partially because they needed the cell for others. For the entire 6 days, I received regular food; no problems. Of course, I still don't call officers "sir."

I've seen Bob Lemay and Maryann W. [**functioning as a paralegal on ASU's behalf**] frequently lately, at pre-trial hearings for the last of the guys involved in the June "disturbance." Their material keeps me reasonably up to date on news relevant to the Movement.

I feel that you would end up regretting a trip down here. You can do without the emotional strain of having to leave after an hour and driving back home again. It (a visit) can bring me no material gain, and could be spiritually depressing for both of us. It's about time you get used to not seeing me for long stretches, anyway.

Last time I mentioned a possible surprise concerning my court-martial. Forget it. Originally, the government had my AWOL dates wrong; had they gone through with the proceedings as such, I would have been acquitted on a technicality. But they have corrected their data, and thus I will be convicted and given the max: either 6 months at Ft. Riley, Kansas, or 6 months confinement here, or a year at Leavenworth with a BCD (not to mention an extra month, most likely, for "contempt of court"). It would be very impractical for you to try to attend; Bob can tell you the run-around technique the Army sometimes employs. Also, the proceedings and my strategy might well confuse and upset you.

You should have been contacted by now by my attorney, Dan Pochoda, concerning the opinion of Judge Julian in Boston. He's been in touch with Ed [**my attorney in Boston**] already. Dan wants to make an issue of the CO angle; it's not going to do us any good, but he wants all the ammo he can latch onto. He's been quite busy lately, so please don't bug him.

The Bond is a bit late this month, but should include a piece I wrote on Ho Chi Minh. That's all till next week.

Love,
Greg

P.S.: I saw the LIFE article on Camp Pendleton Brig. Good old Marine Corps pulls through again, eh what?

Going to Ft. Riley would mean being deemed "rehabilitatable." On that base, in the wilds of Kansas, stood CTF, the Correctional Training Facility. There, one had two options: go along with the program and be returned to regular duty; or, intentionally present oneself as a hopeless screw-up. A few guys could succeed in making themselves so obnoxious to the Army that they would be put back on the street, but I was not that good an actor.

LIFE Magazine had again made waves with an expose of guard brutality at the brig at Camp Pendleton, California. I guess there's a certain internal logic in the Marine Corps' treatment of its prisoners. They felt compelled to maintain their reputation as the toughest branch of service. In the Nixon

White House, no doubt, they were howling like banshees about "the liberal bias of the news media." I prefer to call it shining a little light in the darker corners of the US military.

October 30, 1969

Dear Folks,

My Special Court-Martial is scheduled for Nov. 6, next Thursday. There's no guarantee that it will materialize that day, however. My lawyer might not be available then, or the government's "efficiency" might pull through. I would say, though, that it's safe to notify the Union of the date; they might already know about it. They probably get this information before I do.

I'm reasonably up to date on the news, including the object lesson in "American democracy" going on in Chicago. With every such occurrence as the shackling of Bobby Seale [**tried for allegedly fomenting riots in the streets of Chicago during 1968 Democratic National Convention**], the system demonstrates plainly that it can't be reformed; it must be destroyed.

Every year when Christmas approaches, the powers that be try to clear as many guys out of here as possible. I think it safe to say that no matter how much time I'm sentenced to, I'll be serving it elsewhere. Ft. Riley remains likeliest destination.

I'm almost halfway through the Bible now; sure is slow reading. Well, ain't much more to be said. Until next week....

Love,
Greg

Stockade life and times

In the barracks-cellblock to which I was first assigned I made the acquaintance of Kenny Simon, a young black guy from Harlem. We quickly discovered a natural compatibility—we could crack one another up with ad-libbed jokes all day long. As it had been in my Basic Training unit, whatever racial animosity may have been harbored among the men was kept mostly suppressed. There was one clique of African-Americans, however, who intentionally segregated themselves, claiming the top floor of a barracks for themselves exclusively. I thought this "Black Nationalism" unfortunate, as it hindered overall GI solidarity within the facility. But there was nothing to be done to alter the situation. I had to respect their choice, while letting it be known that I was a conscious anti-racist myself.

Every time I got some word from the Army about my trial, I could count on soon receiving contradictory news. The only constant was the certainty I would be convicted of having been AWOL. My mother had suggested that I plead for mercy from the court on the basis that she was an emotional, suicidal wreck. This undeniably was true, but I knew such a line of argument would get me nowhere. I was determined to present a purely political defense. My mother felt that my letters conveyed nothing but bitterness. For me, opposing this War Machine I'd been sucked into had become a life's mission. Was I a changed person as a result of my Army experience? Absolutely. Had I remained a civilian, I would still have opposed the war wholeheartedly, but would not have had my eyes opened so widely to the inner workings of American society. My attempts at levity in my letters to my mom, "ordering" her to not worry about me, didn't succeed. I may as well have commanded the sun to stand still in the sky, like Joshua at Jericho.

November 6, 1969

Dear Folks,

Well, as much as I would like to get it over with, we have had my court-martial continued for another week. So now the date will be Thursday, Nov. 13. Dan is digging up interesting evidence on how it was decided at Devens that I'd be ordered to Vietnam again. This evidence will not get me off lightly, but will be useful as grounds for future appeals; there can be no doubt that next Thursday I will be convicted and sentenced to close to six months.

I caught a little bit of Nixon's speech Monday night; didn't hear anything new—same old lies, basically. I understand Bobby Seale was sentenced to 4 years in Chicago yesterday; please confirm this for me and find out exactly what charge he was convicted of. It also came to my attention that one of the pollsters claims that 77% of the American people approve of Dick's approach to the war and only **6%** disapprove. If I were convinced of that, I would be on the next plane, boat or even piece of driftwood, leaving the country. Surely the people aren't that gullible! Good grief!

Well, there ain't much more to be said; I suppose you'll know from Dan or ASU about the continuation before this letter reaches you. I'll write again next week. Until then,

Love,
Greg

To try to bolster the notion that those who marched in the streets to oppose the war were a "tiny, noisy minority," the Nixon administration hatched the notion of "the Silent Majority." "They support me, but they don't boast of it publicly" was essentially Nixon's argument. Unfortunately, it is true that the majority always tend to believe that a war is just and necessary, until the evidence to the contrary becomes overwhelming. Having come to office boasting "a plan to end the war," Nixon had to make speeches offering something that appeared new, like the "Vietnamization" policy. As if the ARVN could really carry the battle to defeat the liberation forces without ongoing massive US operations!

Trial by a jury of decidedly not my peers

November 14, 1969

Dear Folks,

Well, yesterday I once again had the opportunity to observe "democracy in action." Despite a freakish turn of events, the result, as predicted, was the maximum sentence: 6 months and forfeiture of 2/3 pay. This almost undoubtedly means I will be shipped to Ft. Riley, Kansas, possibly within 2 weeks. From there I will attempt to win a discharge by demonstrating that I cannot be "rehabilitated."

I've expected the max, of course, all along. The freakish thing was that the prosecutor, who I am informed also is against the war, ended his case by practically pleading that I be given a light sentence! The court-martial board (jury of 7 men) then chose to ignore the prosecution and impose the max. I never even made a political attack against the board or the method of trial itself—I was terribly polite. Afterwards, of course, I regretted not having told them what I think of them. One of the judge's rulings so blatantly ignored the facts before him that we are appealing. Of course, by the time an appeal can reach a federal court, I'll undoubtedly have served the 6 months. But if we can set a precedent for others, I'll be very happy indeed.

That's about all for now. I will keep you informed of my disposition concerning shipment to Ft. Riley.

Love,
Greg

Excerpts from the official record of my court-martial are reproduced as **APPENDIX 5**. The reader has likely never seen an actual transcript of such a proceeding, and will come to understand why the Uniform Code of Military Justice could well have been penned by Franz Kafka.

Trial began on November 6, 1969 with a hearing on various motions. I was represented by my civilian counsel, Dan Pochoda, and First Lieutenant Ted Volckhausen. Ted was sympathetic to opposition to the war and had also helped defend those accused in the June stockade uprising. Defense presented a motion seeking trial by a jury to include enlisted personnel; motion granted. The jury (the "Members of the Court" in Army parlance) originally proposed by the prosecution consisted of a lieutenant colonel, three captains, two first lieutenants and a second lieutenant. The Defense argued that the proposed roster of all Commissioned Officers could hardly be deemed a jury of peers for a "Buck Private." Captain Weiner, the Military Judge, ordered a one-week continuance so both sides could prepare briefs on this issue.

Trial resumed on November 13 with the court offering a jury with a maximum of three enlisted members, and having specified that they be of rank E-6 or above. Nothing but lifers, in other words. Defense stated these could hardly be considered the accused's peers and moved to have the court dissolved and reconstituted in a manner to protect defendant's Constitutional rights; motion denied. Doubtless military judges are heard muttering "Motion denied" in their sleep! The trial proceeded. I entered a plea of Not Guilty

The Prosecution presented its case. This consisted of two Morning Reports, which indicated the (corrected) dates of my unauthorized absence from duty. Just as in my Summary Court-Martial at Ft. Devens, the Prosecution argued this was *prima facie* proof of my guilt.

More technical points of law were argued. "Motion denied" came the robotic response. Now I took the stand myself to recount the story of how I came to enlist "voluntarily," and the basis of my objection to the War in Vietnam. I stated plainly that I objected to the war on moral and political grounds and would never report for duty in Vietnam. The jury was sent off to deliberate. After maybe twenty minutes, the jury reappeared. The guilty verdict was promptly announced, with a sentence of six months at hard labor and fine of $75 a month for that period. Having been reduced to E-1 (lowest military paygrade) in the first court-martial, my salary stood at only $123 a month. And so it was that "The People of the United States"—for that is in whose name I was prosecuted—achieved their glorious legal triumph over the evildoer, Private Laxer.

Why did the Army not press the much more severe charges against me I'd virtually dared them to, via my public acts of dissent? I have to assume it was an economic decision on their part: they had invested about $10,000 (in 1968 dollars) in my advanced medical training. Additionally, they were fighting legal challenges on many fronts at the time. A show trial would have brought more civil liberties lawyers flocking, and drawn more media attention to the absurdities of "military justice."

Rampant misinformation

On November 18, I wrote home explaining I'd been moved to Cell Block #60, from which sentenced prisoners destined for "rehabilitation" departed for Ft. Riley. I said departure could come as soon as the following week. Again, I'd been misinformed. Delays kept piling up. A class action lawsuit against the Army was said to be underway, concerning the general conditions in Ft. Dix Stockade and specific maltreatment of some individual anti-war GIs. As a possible witness in such a case, I'd been told my own attorneys had requested a delay in my being sent to another facility. But when I wrote home on November 21, I was under the impression I'd be on my way to Riley within a few days. I also stated that I'd rethought my strategy and planned to "go along with the program" at the Correctional Training Facility. That should have seen me released from there in early February.

Attorney Pochoda, working with sympathetic JAG defense attorneys, was pursuing further evidence that decisions on how severely I should be prosecuted were being made in Washington, D.C. This represented improper influence exerted on the local command structure where I was imprisoned and prosecuted. Even though I was prosecuted solely for the simple offense of AWOL, it appeared someone in the nation's capital had sat up and taken notice of my very public dissent. Yet they declined to throw the book at me. It felt increasingly like I was now stationed in "The Twilight Zone."

Evidence had surfaced that the treatment of the accused ringleaders of the June uprising was also being managed by authorities higher than those at Ft. Dix. Our attorneys sought dismissal of all charges based on, essentially, tampering with our cases from outside the proper Chain of Command. But the Federal Courts declined to interfere in the Pentagon's machinations. There were some individual victories, however. A handful of prosecution witnesses suddenly lost their confidence about who did what during the stockade uprising. Terry Klug and Bill Brakefield would eventually be released early from the United States Disciplinary Barracks at Ft. Leavenworth, having served time for the "desertion" and AWOL charges only.

CTF at Ft. Riley was the only prison facility in the Army that dangled this promise before its inmates: complete the program and we will station you as close as we can to the geographical location of your choice. But could the Army be trusted to keep its word? I would have to go on waiting to find out. Thanksgiving was imminent. Would I still be at Ft. Dix for Christmas?

"Rabbit food," and the heinous offense that "earned" it

One day I was on an outdoor work detail, dragging the dusty Yard with a rake. The Yard was a central quadrangle inside the stockade, 99% bare dirt. The crew I was on was ordered to fall in to formation to return to barracks. Bringing up the rear, I started to practice the "stockade shuffle." This was a stylized, exaggerated gait borrowed from black and Latino guys, an exhibition of swaggering attitude, swinging one's arms in a rhythm decidedly not military-approved. I just felt like being a goofball, manifesting the absurdity of the circumstances we were all in. Good old Spec. 5 Jewell took offense at this and ordered me to the office. There I referred to his insignia of rank as "a goonie bird with an umbrella over it." This phrase was not of my own invention, but something I'd heard around the barracks. The goonie bird was the American eagle depicted on the insignia of rank for a Specialist—the eagle alone for Spec. 4 (formerly rank of corporal), the umbrella the single curved stripe above the eagle for Spec. 5 (equivalent to sergeant). This so upset poor, sensitive Jewell that he ran to fetch his buddy, Lt. Roark. Before I could say "Bullshit!" I was bound for Disciplinary Seg.

A special treat awaited those accorded this privilege: "Rabbit food" morning, noon and night. Breakfast consisted of a couple of dry pancakes (that is, no butter or syrup) and perhaps some toast, equally unadorned. Lunch? I don't even recall the details, but it may have been simply a smaller version of supper. The latter was a heaping serving of shredded lettuce (thus the rabbit reference), with no dressing, and mashed potatoes and/or some bread, also bereft of gravy or butter. Only water was served to accompany these meals. The classic "bread and water" punishment diet, with slight variation.

December 1, 1969

Dear Folks,

Guess what? I have been in Seg since Tuesday, Nov. 25. The reason is too absurd to try to explain; suffice it to say that the same Lieutenant who put me here the first time did it again. Perhaps he doesn't like me?? Ha ha. Dan left it to me to inform you of the situation, but based on the belief that I'd be going to Riley tomorrow, I felt it unnecessary. Well, the situation has altered.

It is normal for one's second trip to Seg to result in incarceration for 14 days on "rabbit food." Apparently, I've got 8 more days to go before I go to Riley or anywhere else. For details of just what "rabbit food" consists of, you can contact the Union. Needless to say, I don't enjoy this scene too much. In the meantime, I will make a very tentative guess that I'll be going to Riley on Dec. 9.

Received the books Saturday night. Will let you know when I need more. To answer questions: 1.) There ain't no such thing as a written guarantee for stateside duty; 2.) My weight is still 175-180; 3.) Yes, our blankets are sufficient.

I will now proceed to write to Dan and ask him to apply pressure on the pigs to allow me to serve out what they sentenced me to (i.e. to go to Riley). Once again, I say don't worry about me. I'm a lot stronger than the pigs. You can reply to this letter with confidence that it will reach me before I go anywhere. Till next time,

Love,
Greg

The accused riot ringleaders were still being housed in DS, ostensibly to prevent them fomenting any more trouble. We communicated verbally on occasion but could only actually see one another on occasions like Sunday Mass. I was not in a cell adjacent to any of those guys. Klug managed to slip me a copy of illicit reading matter, another book by Frantz Fanon, <u>A Dying Colonialism</u>. I slipped it under my mattress whenever I heard guards approaching, grabbing my bible instead. There was no general shakedown of cells during my stay, so I got away with this.

One of the guys in DS at the time was named Alan Furman. I only got a glimpse of him once, but mostly I knew him by sounds. His background was sketchy to me, but Furman proved to be a man who had taken resistance to the military to the max. Total non-cooperation wasn't enough for him. He preferred to tear apart the fixtures in his cell with his bare hands. Alan wasn't a big guy, but he was compactly muscled. His strength mostly, no doubt, came from his will to resist. He laid waste (no pun intended) to the commode in his cell, breaking it to pieces with bare hands, while I was on this tour in Seg. Guards scrambled to his cell and we could hear them beat him into temporary submission. The rest of us yelled our solidarity: "Leave him alone, you fucking pigs!!" I doubt that Furman's behavior was an act, but if so, it was brilliantly convincing. I knew I was incapable of such actions as a means to exit the Army early.

By the end of my eleventh day on "rabbit food," my bowel movements had literally turned green. Damn, the Army should have featured me on its recruiting posters as "*The Ultimate Soldier: He Even* **Shits** *Green!*" But alas, that institution was insufficiently imaginative.

December 5, 1969

Dear Folks,

I was released from Seg tonight, and thought I wouldn't waste time letting you know. Got your letter dated Dec. 3 this afternoon and will address myself to it shortly.

This is the Riley situation: I am not listed to go Dec. 9. That shipment may be the last till after the holidays. It seems that a hold was put on me for possible use in Terry's trial, which may be what's keeping me at Dix; this despite my request not to be held so I could get Riley over with. Unfortunately, civil liberties lawyers are not always as efficient as they are erudite, so the hold was never canceled. It's looking like I'll be here for Christmas, so you might as well continue corresponding as if I'd never been scheduled for Riley.

As for my "character" and "changes" you imagine: I am very glad to have been politically educated at the government's expense; I have not become a hate-monger—I have merely identified the enemy.

I could have a dictionary if I really wanted it, but don't need it all that frequently. Thanks for the bread—think of the records and books I can buy (yuk! yuk!).

Yes, I had my Bible. It's the only reading matter you're supposed to have till after 5 PM. I've read about 750 out of 1050 pages. It would be helpful to have some bread for Riley (if I ever get there)—they have a PX there that prisoners are allowed to use. Well, that wraps it up for now. Write soon.

Love,
Greg

The visit that never happened

December 12, 1969

Dear Folks,

I have not seen Dan in some time and have not the faintest idea as to the progress (or retrogress) of my appeal. All I know is that I ain't going to Riley this year. On Tuesday they moved me to the Riley shipment barracks and the next day scratched me from this last shipment of '69. Reason: unknown. Frankly, I'm glad of it; I'm back in the sentenced prisoners cell block and find that it's the best block I've been in. Terry's in here now, too. He still has to go to Leavenworth to serve some time on his desertion rap. The next Riley shipment is Jan. 6, 1970. Will I be on it? You tell me! Perhaps the Brass have decided it's not worth their while to send me out there. One thing's for sure—I <u>will</u> be here at Xmas time.

Be advised, before you come down here, of the procedure involved. There are two one-hour visiting periods each Sunday, 1-2 PM and 2:30-3:30 PM. You are permitted only one of these periods. The stockade advises that you arrive here <u>2 hours</u> early to avoid identity mix-ups (although I doubt that you'll have trouble proving that you're my mother). You will find yourself standing on line out in the cold, waiting to get in. You may even feel after a while like you've been drafted. If you feel it's really necessary to speak to me personally, you might as well come down on Dec. 21.

That's all for now. I'm not worried—are you? Why?

Love,
Greg

* * *

December 21, 1969

Dear Folks,

There will be visiting hours Christmas Day, at which time I expect my girl friend from Univ. of Hawaii to come out (she's on Xmas vacation, her home being in NYC). That would leave Sunday, Dec. 28 available if you insist on coming out here.

On Friday, Dec. 19, 36 days after my court-martial, I was notified that my sentence had been approved. That delay in approval is what has kept me from going to Riley. Now that it's official, I expect to be shipped to Riley on Jan. 6, 1970. As for Dan, rather than direct to him, how about making a contribution to the National Emergency Civil Liberties Committee? ASU will give you the address.

I just recovered from the "flu"; otherwise everything's okay. Until next time,

Love,
Greg

When I reviewed these letters for inclusion here, frankly I was astounded that I had agreed to have my mother come to Ft. Dix to visit me. But she just wouldn't believe that I was not being mistreated because of my open defiance of the military. I was never physically abused during my stay in the stockade. My description of what a visitor would have to go through, including standing in the winter cold awaiting admission, was totally accurate. The combination of these factors with the stress and the long drive that coming down from Long Island would entail must have finally dissuaded Mom. Thank goodness!

Christmas in "the pound"

Every other week, as I recall, the Army issued a Health and Comfort, or H&C, package to all stockade inmates. This consisted of items like disposable razors, bars of soap, deodorant, and several packs of cigarettes. At that time a majority of military personnel smoked, mirroring the larger society. So even non-smoking inmates received these carcinogenic products, with the taxpayers of America footing the bill. Obviously, one of the giant tobacco companies had a nice little deal with the Pentagon. Having no need to barter for anything, I simply gave my allotment of smokes to guys I liked.

As the weather got colder, I was issued a used field jacket that would stay with me the remainder of my tour of duty. The upper sleeves still showed the outlines of sergeant's stripes and the fabric was exhibiting unmistakable signs of "jungle rot." It was easy to deduce that the jacket had been to Vietnam. I had no way of knowing if its prior possessor had survived his tour. As to myself, I remained determined that the jacket would not make a return to Vietnam now that it was mine.

December 26, 1969

Dear Folks,

This letter probably won't go out till Monday, as the place is just about shut down for a 4-day weekend. I've heard all kinds of stories about Ft. Riley, including that I can get out in 4 weeks because of my prior training. I won't know what the real story is till I get there.

I will soon need more books, but I'm sure you can't get them to me here by Jan. 6, as the mail room will shut down again for a 4-day weekend due to New Year's. So pick up 2 more non-political (to be safe) books and be ready to mail them as soon as you get my Riley address. Here are two new titles which should be out in paperback within a couple of months: The Selling of the President 1968 by Joe McGinniss and The Human Zoo by Desmond Morris.

There ain't much else to be said, so I'll sign off for now.

Love,
Greg

* * *

January 2, 1970

Dear Folks,

Well, once again I have escaped Fort Riley, at least for the time being. It's too early to leap to any concrete conclusions, but I feel that if I were going to be sent, it should have been on the first shipment of the year, Jan. 6, as I have "seniority" (having been scheduled to go twice before). If I stay here, my minimum release date (barring earlier discharge) would be April 12. I've been here 106 days now; time's going pretty quickly for me.

Susan was out to see me yesterday and I asked her to call you and ask you to send a couple of paperback books immediately, as I'll be here long enough to receive 'em. Here are two more books to add to the list (the former is definitely in paperback): 2001: A Space Odyssey by Arthur C. Clarke; Custer Died For Your Sins by Vine Deloria, Jr.

I am largely in the dark relative to current events, although I occasionally catch the news on the radio. If there's anything really important you think I should know, please fill me in on it.

That's about all there is to say for now. If I get any news of what the Army has in store for me, I will of course write immediately. So long for now,

Love,
Greg

It was great to finally have Susan as a visitor, especially to start a new year. Susan's primary mission, really, was to convey the solidarity of my comrades out in the World and bring me internal information on the struggle. We planned one more visit, during regular Sunday hours, before she had to fly back to Hawaii.

January 6, 1970

Dear Folks,

I believe I can state with certainty now that I will not be going to Ft. Riley. Apparently, somewhere in the tangled, confused higher echelons of command, it has been decided that it would serve no purpose. This is not a guarantee of a discharge, however; they might try to return me to duty from here. Only time will tell—the way this bureaucracy functions, I could have been recommended for discharge right after my court-martial, yet might only learn about it a week before release. I must warn that it is foolish to set high hopes on my being discharged, as such hopes are liable to be dashed at any time.

I have written to Dan twice in the past month and heard nothing. If you can contact him, please ask him the status of my appeal, and whether he has any idea about what the Army plans for me.

Susan will be out to see me Sunday, and has to return to Hawaii a few days thereafter. Since I'll be sitting right here and not going "out west," I see no necessity for you to make the trip down here. My sentence, with good behavior time, will expire April 12, and I might be released earlier via discharge or return to duty.

Thanks in advance for additional books, and so long for now,

Love,
Greg

"Rabbit food" again: the incident of the dreaded red star

Despite John Lennon's assertion in the Beatles song "Revolution" that "If you go carryin' pictures of Chairman Mao/You ain't gonna make it with anyone anyhow," Chinese influence on leftist youth in the US was at its peak around 1969 and into the early '70s. Many young people were "making it" with one another wearing Chinese peasant style ("Mao") jackets and caps, adorned with red stars. The image of Ernesto 'Che' Guevara had already become iconic, a couple of years after his murder in Bolivia at the behest of the CIA. He was often depicted wearing a beret adorned with a red star. So it seemed natural to me that, when a red ink pen came into my possession, I should adorn my own Army fatigue cap with such a decoration. Just another act of youthful defiance.

The officer—not Roark, but a lieutenant I'd not encountered previously—whose path I happened to cross on the compound's main Yard was not amused by my fashion statement. "A red star represents *Communism!!*" he declared with horror. "No shit, Sherlock!" I said to myself. Out loud I simply said "Yeah, that's the point!" And off to another round of "rabbit food" I went. I immediately sent a letter to Susan explaining why she must cancel the plan to visit me the following Sunday.

To my surprise, Stockade Commander Major Casey himself made the rounds of Disciplinary Seg on the day before the 1970 Super Bowl. When he stood before my cell, he asked: "Laxer, are you ready to resume soldiering?" I didn't want to violate my oath to not address officers as "Sir," but neither did I wish to miss the Super Bowl needlessly. We inmates had been informed that a TV set would be provided for each cellblock for the broadcast. I said quietly, so my fellow inmates wouldn't hear, "Yes, Major Casey." No "Sir" involved, yet I was released that very afternoon back to the general population. There was no time to alert Susan that she could have visited after all. And my reward for being polite to the major? I got to see the Minnesota Vikings, my favorite NFL team at the time, get their butts kicked Sunday night in that Super Bowl showdown. Can't win 'em all.

I didn't even inform my parents of this third trip to solitary at the time it happened. I didn't want to worry my mother needlessly about another absurd clash with the powers that be, plus it was only a brief stay. My next three letters home were inconsequential; then, finally, I got some concrete news.

The log jam breaks

January 21, 1970

Dear Folks,

Well, the Army has pulled through again. Uncle Sam has decided he's going to send me to Ft. Riley after all, on Jan. 27. Please call the ASU. Tell them I'm going to Riley and when, and that I should be dropping in to see them around April.

Normally, a guy goes to Riley about two weeks after he's sentenced. When I depart Tuesday, I'll have served 76 days (almost <u>11</u> weeks) of my sentence. Normally, a guy with a 6-month sentence is happy to go to Riley, because he'll get out of the program there in ten weeks or less and his sentence will be considered served. (In effect, a 6-month sentence becomes a 2 1/2-month sentence.) Because of the delay in shipping me, if I stay out there 10 weeks, it will save me all of <u>5 days</u> off my sentence. Great benefit to me, right? Was the delay deliberate? Very likely.

Tomorrow I'm going to write to Dan; if you want to call him to tell him, go ahead. I advise that you not write me again at this address. At Riley I will have unlimited mail privileges. I haven't yet received the paperback books, by the way. Until next time,

Love,
Greg

P.S.: Just got notification of arrival of package (paperbacks).

So it was goodbye and good riddance to the lovely surroundings of Fort Dix Stockade at last. I had made the acquaintance of some really good people, of course, but certainly would not miss the strutting assholes who ran the place. I had my Special Court-Martial under my belt and the attendant thorough knowledge of military "justice." The verdict was supposedly under appeal, but I had no confidence of success in that arena. Next stop, "rehabilitation" for my grievous offenses—Fort Riley in middle-of-nowhere Kansas.

CHAPTER IX

"Rehabilitation!"

Fort Riley, Kansas
January 27-March 25, 1970

"Alice's Restaurant" is a brief song** by Arlo Guthrie, introduced by a long, long monologue. Recorded and released in 1967 on the album of the same name, it recounted the tale of how Woody Guthrie's son escaped being drafted into the military by admitting to a criminal conviction in Massachusetts for littering (and creating a public nuisance). Arlo is segregated from the other men being examined to determine their fitness to be conscripted, and told to sit on "the Group W Bench" to await further processing. Eventually, some sergeant appears and hands all the "morally questionable" draftees a piece of paper containing an ocean of bureaucratic drivel. The form culminates in the stunning question: "Kid, have you rehabilitated yourself?" Arlo expresses mock outrage that the authorities at the Induction Center, having been advised of his criminal record, question whether he is "morally fit" to torch villages in Vietnam and butcher the inhabitants. Arlo says the expression of this opinion led to his being dismissed from consideration for military service, and that he was advised the FBI would be establishing a file on him.

By January 1970 my own odyssey was way beyond Arlo's. I had expressed my opposition to the enterprise in Southeast Asia in public and directly to Army authorities, twice refused to report for duty in Vietnam, and my own file at FBI Headquarters was growing. But Uncle Sam was not willing to dismiss me. So here I was at the only Army institution of its kind: the Correctional Training Facility (CTF) at Fort Riley, Kansas. Nowhere else is a prisoner taken to a rifle range and handed an M-16 and live rounds of ammunition!

January 28, 1970

Dear Folks,

Well, here I am at lovely Ft. Riley. Already, I don't like it. The flight out from Philly via Chicago went smoothly, and we (14 of us) had a day's glimpse of the outside world; most enjoyable. They didn't use handcuffs on us.

This place is basic training all over again. There's a fence around us, but it's not very impressive; individual barracks aren't fenced off one from another like Dix stockade. However, I'm not at all happy to be here. If you'll recall my letters from Ft. Jackson during Basic, you'll remember that I laughed my way through it. Well, I intend to do the same thing here, but I'll only be laughing on the outside. Although my plans call for me to return to duty in order to organize for the ASU, after this bullshit is over I might say to hell with it for keeps. At any rate, while I'm here I must go along with the game in order to get out of here in 10 weeks. Supposedly, after the first 4 weeks of basic training-type horseshit, I get to work as a medic the rest of the time till I "graduate" and get orders for some new post.

The intent of this place is to persuade one to return to duty and "soldier." The officers treat us decently, the food is good. Ha, ha! Too bad, Uncle Sam, but at least 60% of these guys will be AWOL again after they graduate, and will have to be discharged as non-rehabilitatable. The weather here is incredible—temp. in the 50s! Next month, I just know we'll be buried in the snow.

Outgoing mail is uncensored; incoming is lightly perused. Now, here's the story: my chances of being allowed political books here are better than at Dix. So here's how I want you to work it—please select one non-political book from the list, and send it with one political book. That way I know I'll at least get one. Also, next time you talk to Dan Pochoda (and ASU) please inform him (and them) that the following is my precise mailing address:

Pvt. Greg Laxer, [**Service Number**]
2nd CTU, 1st CTB, 1204 H St.
Ft. Riley, Kansas 66442 'A' Team

Surprise—and this is the only thing making this preferable to Dix—I'm allowed to grow my mustache back! So that's the present situation. Oh, here is one more political (but non-subversive) book of high priority: <u>Sen. Joe McCarthy</u> by Richard Rovere. So long for now,

Love,
Greg

Vacillation was still evident concerning the question of stomaching Army bullshit for many more months or seeking a way to terminate my relationship with Uncle Sam sooner. This old uncle was showing every sign he was determined to hang onto me no matter how hard I tried to hurt his feelings. I was now in a population that showed no real sympathy to my anti-war stance. Some of these guys were actually lifers (in my unit was a guy who'd been a staff sergeant, E-6) who'd screwed-up and gotten caught. Imagine the humiliation for a former NCO busted back down to private and now being treated like a raw recruit just off the bus, including the privilege of pulling KP. The Army's theory was that CTF would motivate him to reform and tread the straight and narrow path of devoted duty after the experience. I can't quote any official statistics, but rumor had it the Army's success rate with this approach left something to be desired. Lifers were distinctly a minority, but we younger guys couldn't help marveling at their very presence.

The secret of psychic survival in any prison environment is learning to deal with the passage of time. As long as I keep my mind active, I am okay. And so, the quest for reading matter resumed. While waiting for my mom to send me more books, I made the happy discovery of a copy of a novel that a former occupant of my barracks had left behind. This was a very funny social satire about computer intelligence threatening to take control from humans: <u>Mechasm</u>, by John Sladek. It skewered modern mass marketing techniques, among many other aspects of modern life.

February 4, 1970

Dear Folks,

Rec'd yr. letter dated Feb. 2 today; good service, but I don't think it's worth the extra 4 cents to send Air Mail. Also got the book, for which I thank you.

Yes, I knew that this was like basic training, but various people had told me there was little or no harassment—that's bullshit. Theoretically, in another 2 1/2 weeks or so, I can work as a medic and escape this bullshit until final testing and graduation. Please save any literature the Army sends you purporting to explain this place; they'll make amusing reading later on.

I found out yesterday that I can't be stationed at Hawaii (considered overseas) or Dix or Devens (because I was court-martialed there). When confronted with the facts, I decided my chances of being stationed near NYC were slim. Therefore, I am requesting to be stationed in the 6th Army Area (Arizona, California, State of Washington) so I can see the west coast. Where I'll actually go I have no way of knowing; but this is certain: I <u>can't</u> be sent overseas (Europe, VN, Korea, Japan, etc.).

That about wraps it up for now. I await your next letter (and **book**).

Love,
Greg

"Sorry, kid, we can't send you to Vietnam."

If there was one thing stranger about going through CTF than being handed a loaded rifle, it was learning that a certain "guarantee" by the Army was on the level. We'd all been told, before being shipped there from various stockades, that if we successfully completed the program we would get to **choose** a geographical area for our ensuing duty station. This was the one carrot dangled in front of us. And now it had been officially revealed that, due to our "criminal histories," we would not be allowed to serve overseas even if we wanted to!

On another matter I would soon find that I'd again been misinformed. I was <u>not</u> to be spared any of the "joy" of Basic Training redux in order to work on base as a medic. Was I being deliberately misled to frustrate me, or was it just another reflection of a bureaucracy in which the right hand knew not what the left was doing? My suspicion leaned toward the former, though the latter situation was ubiquitous. Ask any veteran for confirmation of that.

Meanwhile, life went on: Drill & Ceremonies, Physical Training, scrubbing latrines, buffing floors, KP, preparing for bullshit inspections. I was still hoping for an early escape from this drudgery. There were enough classroom sessions that dealing with the Kansas winter, once it made its appearance, was not that physically difficult. The weather proved nowhere near as bad as I'd expected.

Life as "the green monkey"

At some point in my reading of Sociology literature, prior to enlisting, I had read the theory of "the green monkey." It was postulated that if you remove a monkey of a certain species from its troop, paint it a vivid shade of green, and then reintroduce it to the group, the other members of that troop will see it as <u>alien</u> and rip it to shreds. Though I have always tried to avoid giving the appearance of "putting on airs," members of the working class sometimes viewed me as alien, somehow fundamentally <u>different</u> from them. My vocabulary and knowledge in many areas, obtained via voracious reading, made me appear "aloof," I suppose. "Goddamn bighead" Sgt. Sampaga had designated me back at Ft. Jackson. There was no one in my barracks to whom I could really relate, or feel close to, politically or philosophically.

One quite cold day on a weekend, I had just emerged from the shower when two or three guys grabbed me and forced me out the end door of the building. I found myself locked out, stark naked. Someone emptied a butt can of dirty water onto me from the fire escape landing of the upper floor. I had done nothing to personally antagonize any of the individuals involved in this incident. Apparently they needed to "blow off some steam," and the perceived alien among them was a convenient scapegoat for the moment. It seems I really was "the green monkey." It was several minutes before I regained access to the building, where of course I had to shower all over again. I sought no retribution for this humiliation. I chalked it up as a learning experience: solidarity is not automatic in a prison situation.

February 21, 1970

Dear Folks,

Received book Wednesday and your letter Thursday. There was no difficulty at all with the book; the envelope was given to me at Mail Call formation unopened. I was supposed to show the contents to an NCO later, for approval, but simply declined to do so. Had the NCO come looking for me later, I had merely to show him another (non-political) book and say that's what had arrived. So you see, there's no basis for fearing trouble over this matter. I'm glad to hear you found other books that have high priority on my list. If only I had time to read them, for . . .

I will not be permitted to work in my MOS (Clinical Specialist) while here. Consequently, next week I have to go on bivouac and play basic training games all the way through the eight weeks. So next week I will be doing no reading and no letter writing. When we get back from the field, I'll be able to write again. At that point, I'll have but 3 weeks of this horseshit left.

As of right now, I have more reading matter than I can use, plenty of stamps and about $34 to my credit (and nothing to spend it on), having received a partial payment from Uncle Sam. Thank you for the cute bookmark.

Concerning the Trespass charges at CCNY, I will have an Army lawyer write a letter explaining the situation to the DA and hope for the best. If they still want to prosecute me, they'll have to wait till I'm out of the Army, which (in the event I fail to get an early discharge) will be around June 7,

1971. To wrap up the legal situation, it appears that I won't be coming East for the suit against the stockade, as I haven't heard a word concerning it. Till next time,

Love,
Greg

Next on the training agenda came bivouac for about a week. No national holiday came up to truncate the experience, as had happened with my Basic Training unit back in July of '67. But the Ft. Riley version was a modified approach to living in the field: rather than sharing two-man tents, we would live in squad-sized tents, take our meals in large tents also, and have permanent latrines at our disposal. The latter weren't heated, of course, but were preferable to having to dig new latrines in the semi-frozen fields of Kansas, though snow cover was virtually absent that particular winter.

My mother had received a letter from Dennis Kirkland (he lacked my current address) and of all places, he was then stationed at Ft. Riley. We hadn't been exceptionally close during our stay at "Happy Valley" for 91C20 training. But given the odds against bumping into any of my former colleagues during my tour of Army prisons, I was up for a reunion. But this would be a tricky thing to pull off. He would not be allowed to visit me at my unit, as a friend. With Mom as intermediary, we tried to figure out how to make this happen.

March 8, 1970

Dear Folks,

To answer questions of 2/27/70: 1.) No, outgoing letters are normally not "perused"; 2.) Incoming mail is opened and inspected for contraband items. The actual contents of a letter are normally not read, though. I have heard not a word from Dan Pochoda. Guess I'll write to him and confirm my suspicion that appealing is pointless.

Relating to your latest letter, some mysterious coincidences have occurred. A guy in this unit returned from the dental clinic one day this past week with a note from Dennis, who just happened to be getting a tooth filled that day and saw that this guy was from my unit. The note gave his address in Manhattan, Kansas; only according to the note he's living with Harry Connell, another old friend from Clin. Spec. school. He made no mention of Bob Crossley! If the three of them are all stationed here, it's incredible. It also indicates a great need for Clinical Specialists at Irwin Army Hospital here. The unfortunate aspect of the situation is that when I'm finally released from here, after a total of 6 months behind barbed wire, I very likely will not have time to see any of these guys.

Bivouac can be summed up like this: eating barely warm chow in semi-darkness; struggling to get the heaters to work inside tents on bitterly cold nights; firing the M-16 again, left-handed of course; marching briskly during warm daytime with warm coat and much equipment wrapped about; using a nasty old latrine (outhouse style); getting an upset stomach and diarrhea after returning from the field; seeing a guy return from the field with lice and breathing a sigh of relief that they didn't penetrate <u>my</u> sleeping bag.

Yes, the mail service at this end is dreadful. That's all for now,

Love,
Greg

What were the odds that <u>three</u> of my fellow students from Valley Forge General Hospital, having done their tours in Vietnam, would be stationed at Ft. Riley while I was there?! That was astounding. 'FUBAR' Connell, it turned out, had just been sent to Germany to finish his Army commitment, and I wasn't able to see Crossley. But Dennis and I did have a brief reunion. I explained to him that I'd become a Marxist revolutionary, to which he characteristically replied "Good grief!" This get-together was possible because I was being treated for a mysterious condition picked up during the bivouac. Neither the Army nor I understood at the time what had actually happened, but I figured it out retroactively.

Attack of the Brown Recluse and . . . California bound!

About midway through the bivouac, I had to make a trip to the latrine in the wee hours of the morning. I sat on the funky wooden toilet seat and did what I needed to. It seemed like a perfectly normal operation except for the chilliness of the environment. I returned to my sleeping bag until reveille came around.

When I got up I found I was a little dizzy and felt mildly feverish. This was very unusual for me, but I declined to go on Sick Call. I felt normal again with the passage of a few more hours. It was only upon returning to the company barracks that I found what appeared to be a large boil on my right buttock. I felt it when running my soapy hands over the area, then visually confirmed it via a mirror. Soon I discovered that a fellow squad member had come back with the same phenomenon. Now I was staring at a medical mystery and sought treatment for the first time since enlisting.

March 17, 1970

Dear Folks,

This will be my last letter from here, most likely. On the 25th, I'll be a "free" man again, after 188 days, heading for my new duty station—Fort Ord, Calif. (about 90 miles south of San Francisco). That's pretty far to go on a weekend pass, but still I am pleased with the location. I'll let you know my new address as soon as I can.

Southwest Kansas had 18 inches of snow Sunday; it's cold here still, but we haven't yet had enough snow to even accumulate. Me? Get a leave? I've had more leave time thus far than I'm entitled to in my whole Army "career."

You can write to anyone you like about how the Army has dealt with me, but it won't accomplish a thing. It's as simple as that. As for newspaper clippings, it's not necessary. I've been keeping up on my current events.

The story on my health is this: somehow (very likely while in the field) I picked up a nasty staph. infection on my right buttock (!) and have been under treatment for it for a week. I'm taking antibiotics and go to the dispensary every morning to have the cavity (where the boil was) cleaned out with hydrogen peroxide. It should be completely healed by the time I head for Calif. At any rate, this situation permitted me to have a short get-together with Dennis yesterday. He had the day off, and working things out with the medics at CTF Dispensary, found out what time I'd be in for treatment; thus the rendezvous was set up. On the 25th I will be loaded on a bus and taken to Kansas City Airport. Another benefit of this infection (aside from permitting reunions) is that it gave me the first lucky break in all 8 weeks here: it kept me out of the dirtiest, most physical activities of the training cycle! Hallelujah! Bivouac, incidentally, if I failed to make this clear in previous letters, was only for that one week. But it was long enough to give me my first medical difficulty in some time.

That's all for now; my next letter will be from Calif.

Love,
Greg

In 1970, neither I nor the Army was aware of the spreading presence in the United States of the Brown Recluse Spider, also known in the Midwest as the Missouri Brown Spider. I have no doubt that my squad mate and I had been bitten by one of these venomous critters while sitting on the commode in that chilly latrine, though I'd felt no bite at the time. The phenomenon that appeared to be a boil was either the after-effect of the venom or an actual bacterial infection of the bite wound. At any rate, it was diagnosed and treated as simply an infection, getting us two victims a week of Casual Duty—mostly lounging around, reading. We were spared having to crawl under live rounds and take the Physical Proficiency Test to conclude the training cycle, and we would not be held over in the facility to make up for that. Again, this speaks to the volume of troops who'd gone AWOL in the war years. My bunk was needed by the next lucky guy. Hallelujah!

Meanwhile, push had come to shove in requesting our next duty stations. I made the Presidio of San Francisco (Letterman General Army Hospital) my first choice. There was no vacancy there for a 91C20 Medic, so I had to settle for Fort Ord on the Monterey Peninsula. "California, here I come!" But before we could board our planes, the Army had scheduled one last stop in Kansas for us.

Before flying to their next duty stations, all graduates of CTF were taken on a brief tour of the United States Disciplinary Barracks at Ft. Leavenworth. This was to deliver the simple message: "If you screw up sufficiently, after we've gone to these great lengths to rehabilitate you, this could end up your home for a long, long time." And the USDB was, in fact, sufficiently grim looking. This was a hardcore facility, built of concrete blocks and steel. During our brief stay within its confines, who should wander into my field of view, on a work detail, but Jeff Russell, one of the Ft. Dix riot defendants! I broke formation to greet him warmly; we had time for only the briefest exchange of words and clenched-fist salutes. It was a good day indeed. Next stop would be The Golden State, for which this East Coast boy had so long yearned. But for how long would I be able to enjoy it as a free—that is, non-incarcerated—man?

CHAPTER X

A tenuous truce

Fort Ord, California
March 25, 1970-July 6, 1971

California at last! Surfers and beach bums, bronzed hippie chicks, Hollywood, endless sunny days, the Haight-Ashbury in San Francisco, the coolest rock bands on the planet, astounding physiques getting pumped-up on Muscle Beach. In the national, even the world imagination, it was the USA writ larger than life.

But there was another side to the coin. Migrant farmworkers living in squalor, riot cops itching to bust heads, Charles Manson and his followers, one activist dead and another blinded in the struggle over People's Park in Berkeley, rabid rightwingers in Orange County. And in the Governor's Mansion sat Ronald Reagan, who had strong ideas about quelling campus unrest: "If it takes a bloodbath, let's get it over with." Yes, it was the USA writ larger than life alright.

Fort Ord was a sprawling base, right on the Pacific Ocean, though too flat to enable a view directly to the water from most locations. The facility was primarily used for Basic Combat Training. My first couple of nights I had to bunk down in the Special Processing Detachment barracks—yet another SPD!—until I was processed-in and assigned my specific duties. When I reported to Hospital Company, First Sergeant Newbern saw that my previous station was CTF at Ft. Riley and grunted: "Oh, one of <u>those</u>, eh?"

The hamlet of Seaside was actually the closest town, decidedly not a tourist draw like Monterey. Like any town adjacent to a military installation, it was home to those personnel permitted to live off base who required affordable rent, as well as ex-lifers working part-time in their retirement years.

March 30, 1970

Dear Folks,

This unit is in sad shape. The barracks are quite cruddy; the First Sergeant is an alcoholic; and guys up to the rank of Spec. 4 pull KP (about once a month). Most hospitals have civilian kitchen crews. Many of the guys in the company have themselves been busted at one time or another. Enclosed you will find money orders for $200 to be deposited in the bank. They still owe me at least another $200 back pay, but it's gonna take time to wring it out of them.

Saturday, I explored the nearest town, Monterey. It's a lovely place, but not much action. Next time I have a two-day pass, I'll spend it in San Francisco, 113 miles to the north. I flew out here via L.A.; the coastline of this state is incredibly mountainous. On the trip from Kansas to L.A., incidentally, we flew right over the Grand Canyon. A stupendous sight, indeed.

Well, that about wraps it up. Anything I do I will be very cool about; I have no intention of getting jailed again in the near future. Until next time,

Love,
Greg
Pvt. Gregory Laxer
[service number]
Hosp. Co., USAHSTF, A.R.D.
Ft. Ord, Calif. 93941

The hospital at Ord was (surprise!) of the good old WW II "temporary" stock. Single story, all wood: a firetrap. We of Hospital Company were housed in former wards with bunks, wall lockers and footlockers crammed into a rather narrow configuration. An exit at one end opened into the wider world, while the other end fed into one of the long, long hospital corridors.

There was one semi-private room, occupied by two Spec. 5s, who were held responsible for the barracks goings-on. At least they had their own TV set for "compensation."

I found myself assigned to the three ARD wards, with an occasional stint in Intensive Care if they were understaffed on a given shift. ARD stood for Acute Respiratory Distress. Our real task was monitoring trainees showing cold or flu symptoms for something potentially more sinister. Primarily that meant meningitis, and occasionally I would assist with a spinal tap to rule that menacing condition out. If there was no Registered Nurse on duty on the ARD wards, I—"Mr. Buck Private"—was in charge! By dint of my advanced training, I would actually supervise medics who outranked me. Naturally, this caused raised eyebrows, not so much out of resentment as curiosity.

Enter the Hoosier

One of the first people I got to know at the hospital was James Frandsen of Waterloo, Indiana. Jim was actually in a different company, housed separately—8th Evacuation Hospital Unit. Those guys were basically killing time, waiting to see who would be shipped overseas, and in the meantime assigned to work in the base hospital. Morale was not good in the 8th, Jim informed me, with a lot of illicit substances being consumed. But what the heck, in my own company we had a guy with a sports car who was openly known to be a marijuana dealer.

Frandsen recalls that when he first encountered me I seemed to be under "a cone of solitude." I was sitting in the Nurses' Station on one of the ARD wards, reading a book by V.I. Lenin. As had been my practice since concluding Basic Training, I hesitated not in the least to make my political views known to those around me, including my supervisors. What could they do about it? I'd been certified "rehabilitated"! During idle times on duty, I seized any chance to read up on the subjects that interested me.

Rather than recoil in horror, Frandsen expressed great curiosity about my personal story. Why was I a 91Charlie (advanced medic) with rank of private? How had I come to harbor my beliefs? I trusted him immediately and shared openly; we were destined to become life-long friends. Some of my new co-workers were decidedly less openminded, of course. Mrs. Davis, who also had Indiana roots, was an older civilian RN who worked our wards. She commuted from her home in Carmel. Mrs. D. was a Daughters of the American Revolution type. The idea that the US government could be in the wrong on any issue was simply anathema for her. Yet at one point she would let slip to Frandsen that, though she hated my beliefs, she "loved my soul," because I'd been willing to go to jail in defense of my ethical code.

Jim Frandsen had wheels of his own, and when our work schedules had us both off duty we would go explore Monterey and its surroundings. We did make the occasional drive all the way to San Francisco. Being able to travel at our own pace was a blessing. It was actually not difficult to hitch-hike to the Bay Area from Ft. Ord in those days, though. Yes, long-haired "freaks" would pick up short-haired GIs. Once arrived in S.F., GIs were easily spotted because of our relatively short hair. But I never personally encountered any hostility from the long-haired crowd based on my military status. Everything was mellow, baby.

Criminal acts of sheer desperation

Claiming that the "Viet Cong" had a command center in Cambodia, the Nixon gang launched an "incursion" into that nation in late April 1970. The president had planned no public announcement; it was members of the press who flushed this information out. Parts of Laos were also bombed, trying to stop traffic on the "Ho Chi Minh Trail." These actions blatantly violated international law. When the news got out there was an unprecedented surge of protest on American college campuses. Having triggered this outburst, the administration could then point to rioting in the streets and say the very fabric of society was at risk of crumbling. How would Nixon and company respond?

The answer came on May 4 at Kent State University, an Ohio college most of us didn't even know existed. Ohio National Guardsmen were issued live ammunition and sent onto the campus. They were ordered to open fire directly at students who reportedly were throwing stones. Some of the troops had the decency to refuse, or to fire into the air, but enough obeyed the order to leave four young people dead on the ground. White American students from "middle-class" homes. One of them, Jeffrey Miller, became the subject of an iconic still photo as he bled out on a campus walkway, a horrified woman kneeling at his side. He happened to hail from Plainview, the town immediately adjacent to Syosset, back on Long Island. These kids had been slain as if they were young Vietnamese demonstrating against the regime in the streets of Saigon.

We in the Regular Army stared in disbelief. The National Guard?! Someone issued live ammo to the NG and sent them against students?! To be sure, some Americans in uniform, and in the civilian realm, approved of the deaths of protesting students, but we all understood in our guts that something was very **peculiar** about this picture. Where did these orders originate? Though the White House vehemently denied it, we couldn't help but suspect that the orders came from the very top. Just days after the event in Ohio, riot police at Jackson State University, in Mississippi, fired into a dormitory and killed two students there. Nixon and his minions were totally out of control.

Though the massacre by US troops of hundreds of civilians in the Vietnamese hamlet of My Lai had taken place in March 1968, Seymour M. Hersh's book detailing the horror there had only recently come out in paperback and I immediately bought a copy (My Lai 4—A Report on the Massacre and Its Aftermath; Vintage Books, New York). The Nixon regime's refusal to really discipline anyone involved just added to the disgust with, and fury at, the US War Machine.

Meanwhile, the unfunny comedy of my attempting to recover all my back pay dragged on. My personnel file had gotten all screwed-up back at Ft. Riley, and temporary paychecks were all I'd be issued for months to come. However, I found the money to buy Dave Mason's debut album as a solo artist, Alone Together. Mason had helped form the band Traffic and was one of the masters of "wah-wah" guitar. The album featured a true all-star lineup. Rock 'n' Roll did not get any better than this. I'd discovered a "progressive" FM radio station based in San Jose, and that kept me abreast of the new music coming out. It was courtesy of their broadcasts that I discovered the existence of Spirit, a West Coast band I hadn't been aware of previously. This year of 1970 would see the release of their astounding album, *Twelve Dreams of Dr. Sardonicus*. As an added morale boost, 'Country Joe' & The Fish performed at Monterey Peninsula Community College. And the show was <u>not</u> truncated by a hockey match.

Armed Forces Day canceled!

Richard Nixon's responses to the escalating opposition to the war ranged from the predictable to the absurd. On the predictable end of the spectrum, he pushed the Pentagon to make an increasingly big deal of Armed Forces Day. Enlisted personnel would be forced to perform in parades down Main Streets across America. Alternatively, the public would be invited to actually enter military bases for similar "entertainment." This included an opportunity to "ooh and ahh" over the newest shiny weapons in the military's arsenal. In short order we, the unlucky stuck on the inside, had rechristened this occasion Armed Farces Day. On the absurd, indeed surreal, end of Nixon's behavior was his appearance in the wee hours of the morning amidst anti-war demonstrators in the nation's capital, seeking to win them over to his point of view through "reasoned dialogue."

Armed Farces Day 1970 did not play out to Nixon's liking. Ft. Ord was one of the bases targeted for anti-war demonstrations. Naturally, I would have liked to participate, or at least observe, whatever might transpire. But there arose the little matter of being assigned to KP that day.

May 25, 1970

Dear Folks,

So what's new? I'm typing this on the ward. I'm working the midnight to 8 AM shift, the only shift on which I have enough spare time to take care of personal business. If I goof a lot, it's because I'm sleepy.

I spent the weekend in San Francisco/Berkeley and saw the filmed version of the Woodstock Festival. Politics now occupy most of my free time. The power structure is definitely aware of my activities; however, the fact that I had KP the day of the demonstration was a genuine coincidence. What's happening is that the pigs are intercepting the literature I've requested be sent to me. There is no doubt about this; I am not prone to paranoid fantasies. Also, I'm being framed on a charge of being late to KP. The Commanding Officer wants to give me an Article 15; I refuse to sign it, of course, since I am innocent. If I can't talk them out of prosecuting me, it will result in my demanding another Summary Court-Martial. The most they can do under that is jail me for 30 days. I don't know for a fact now that they're gonna go through with this.

Yes, everybody under the rank of E-5 has to pull KP. We pull it every 2 1/2 to three weeks. The demonstration on the 16th, incidentally, was quite ambiguous. Only 4,000 of an anticipated 10,000 or more showed up; however, the generals were so frightened they shut the fort down and canceled their Armed Forces Day fun and games, parades, etc. This happened all over the nation, actually. It was 100% peaceful here (the Brass had machine guns mounted on vehicles standing by nevertheless). I know the story was otherwise at Ft. Dix, having seen and read the reports on TV and in the papers.

Well, that's about gonna have to wrap it up for now. Until next time,

Love,
Greg

Day to day anti-war activities

The first thing I had to do upon arriving at any new duty station was to feel out the enlisted personnel around me, to learn who was friendly and who was potentially hostile, to my politics. I couldn't count on the friendlies to become militant backers of the ASU who'd be willing to risk their own freedom. If push came to shove, how many would be gone in a flash? Naturally, I encouraged enlisted personnel to sign up for ASU membership.

I also got to know the civilian anti-war activists in the area when I went off the base. They included some really good people, but there was a problem: they were mostly affiliated with the Bay Area Revolutionary Union (in turn, affiliated with the national Revolutionary Union), "Maoist"-leaning. I employ quotation marks because I'm still not sure what it meant to be "a Maoist" in the USA. [See **APPENDIX 6**: "A Dirty Little Secret."] The best of these civilian activists was Bob Mandel. He was very good at smoothing out differences between individuals who had disparate ideas on how to proceed with the struggle. He always broke things down to the basics: what course can we pursue that's best for the anti-war effort?

I committed to working with the core group of local activists, which eventually morphed into a local chapter of the Movement for a Democratic Military (MDM), modeled after SDS. This included contributing to their newsletter, the Right-On Post. Because I had writing and propaganda skills, I quickly gained a share of editorial control over that publication. Each time a new issue came out, we would distribute it surreptitiously on base. With a rotating work schedule, I was privileged to be able to slip into empty barracks during daytime hours and leave literature on top of bunks. But I confined this activity to the medical barracks, not going into unfamiliar areas. Even so, it was only dumb luck that allowed me to avoid getting caught. Some lifer NCO might have swaggered into one of these buildings at any given time.

July 11, 1970

Dear Folks,

This card testifies to the fact that I am still very much alive. It's 1 o'clock in the morning, I just got off work, and this is literally the first opportunity I've had to write since I ceased writing letters.

I have been unable to write because of time-consuming political work. From June 29-July 6 I spent every spare minute attending and reporting on a kangaroo court-martial here on post. Then I had to convert my notes to an article and help hammer out the latest Ft. Ord MDM newspaper—five of us (civilians and GIs) worked straight on from 7 PM Thursday to 8 AM Friday to assemble the paper. I have had perhaps one decent night of sleep in 10 days. Combined with this work in my free time has been a heavy work load on the wards. Things had been quiet for a week, then bang! Another URI epidemic; sometimes I had to watch over 60 patients.

I've been put in for promotion to PFC and the Commanding Officer will almost certainly turn me down. At that time I will write to Senator Goodell and explain the political persecution I'm suffering. Then I think we'll see some action. If I get back up to PFC, I'll gross about $225 a month.

Yes, the articles you've been sending are quite helpful and are appreciated. You hope I had a good holiday? *Oy vey*. I worked July 3. I worked July 4. I had KP July 5. So much for my "holiday."

I'm gonna hit the sack and when I get up maybe I can get Wednesday's paper read (I'm sort of behind in my reading, you see). That's all for now,

Love,
Greg

Things were going relatively smoothly for me at Ft. Ord and I decreased the frequency of my letters home. When I did write, I was still Mr. Militant and my mother continued to fret about my welfare. Ultimately, I did seek the assistance of liberal US Senator from New York, Charles Goodell and, "miraculously," soon thereafter my way-overdue back pay issues were resolved.

National Headquarters for the Black Panther Party were located in Oakland, across the Bay from San Francisco. It almost became mandatory for a revolutionary to make a pilgrimage, to show solidarity, to BPP HQ. And this a batch of us, MDM activists and GIs, did one weekend. As we were entering the fortified building to take a tour, Ron Dellums, the local US Representative to Congress and outspoken critic of the Vietnam War, was just leaving. It was an honor to get to shake his hand. And that's something I could say about precious few American politicians.

Larry and Mariann . . . and Stalinist Jane!

One of the GIs with whom I worked in the MDM coffeehouse scene was Larry Waterhouse, of Austin, Texas. We collaborated closely to maintain publication of a local anti-war paper for GIs. Larry was very self-assured, college-educated, assigned to be a company clerk. Given the general competence of Army clerks, one would have to say Waterhouse was "grossly over-qualified"! When we first met, Larry admitted right up front to being a member of the Communist Party USA. He was the first and only "open" CPer I met on active duty and his candor was refreshing, with additional merit that he was very easy to get along with. His fiancee, Mariann (pronounced "Marion") Vizard, came up from the Lone Star State to be near him. Noting her surname, I suggested she call herself 'Wizard.'

Waterhouse was always urging me to move to Texas after I got out of the Army. He assured me there was a plentitude of "dope-smoking Commie women" down there who'd go for me! We three were quite close, sharing a goodly number of joints over the months in the off-base apartment Mariann had secured. Larry actually talked me into buying a pair of Frye boots, so I could start acclimatizing to being a future Texan. Given my salary at the time, the $45 price tag made this a true luxury purchase.

August 14, 1970

Dear Folks,

The weather out here is nothing like I expected from California. It's only rained appreciably 2 or 3 times in close to 5 months. The sun shines for 3 or 4 days straight, then vanishes for 10. I always need a blanket at night.

Tuesday I threatened to resign my nursing tasks unless I was promoted. Wednesday I was informed that I was promoted to PFC as of July 9; I simply hadn't been informed of the fact. I can't make Spec. 4 again before October, and it'll be a struggle all the way.

My mail is coming in again from non-political friends, but I've heard nothing from anyone connected with the Union. Foul Post Office play can never be ruled out.

I wonder if the news media out there have picked up the story of the rebellion in SPD here Wednesday night (2 mess halls burned) and the subsequent sealing off of the post (only GIs or civilians on Official Business allowed in)? Have you heard or read anything???

That's about all for now. Until next time,

Love,

Greg

The uprising at the Ft. Ord SPD barracks took me completely by surprise. I didn't know discontent was seething at such intensity down there (those barracks were some distance from the hospital). So much for mellowness on the Monterey Peninsula. You never knew where things could explode next. By this stage of events in Southeast Asia, some enlisted men were essentially calling a local peace treaty, making every effort to avoid contact with the other side, or even flatly refusing to go out on patrol.

During my time at Ft. Ord, the actress Jane Fonda allied herself with the GI coffeehouse crowd. Fellow actor Donald Sutherland joined Fonda and others in "The FTA [Fuck The Army] Show." This was an anti-war revue that performed live at coffeehouses or in legitimate theaters that could be rented in towns near military bases. Pressure was being applied on civilian performance venues by the Brass to try to thwart these performances.

Naturally, I was in favor of this kind of agit-prop (agitation and propaganda) work. However, I couldn't help but harbor residual bitterness over the coffeehouse crowd's hostility to the ASU. As a prominent local anti-war soldier, I was offered a chance to meet Ms. Fonda at someone's private residence when Jane was passing through Monterey. It was to be an intimate gathering of local peace activists. Though I found Ms. Fonda very appealing, and knew her heart was in the right place on the question of the war, I declined this invitation as a matter of principle. Darned Stalinist! **I showed her!!**

Mom's condition deteriorates

My mother's emotional state continued to deteriorate, and I knew she was mixing Valium and booze. Even though I was not in danger of being ordered to duty overseas, she managed to find ways to put the most pessimistic slant on any piece of news I sent home. In a heart-wrenching letter in late September, my mother put forth the theory that my conduct in the Army was intended to make her life a living hell. I again tried to explain to her that I harbored no grudge against her for having pushed me into the service by her threats of suicide. But my honesty compelled me to finally inform her that I was my own man, and would no longer allow her to exert control over my life decisions.

I urged my mother to get off the booze and pills and pleaded that she not do anything drastic. I did this in a letter addressed exclusively to her, rather than both my parents. Her next missive contained unmistakable fresh hints at suicide, so I sent a letter to my dad alerting him to how serious the situation had become. I suggested that institutionalization might be required. But Hetty took advantage of being at home when the mail came daily, and opened and read that letter. It set her back on her heels.

Could things get any worse? The next development entailed a car crash when Mom was driving home from a liquid lunch date with a friend. Fortunately, she escaped major injury and this incident proved a wake-up call. She quit mixing pills and alcohol on a "cold turkey" basis.

Purloined penicillin: a personal humanitarian undertaking

I was finding ways to discretely resist beyond the mere spoken and written word. One night, we had a prisoner from the Post Stockade as a patient on my ward; he was accused of having gone AWOL. He was not deemed a high escape risk, so no MP was positioned to keep an eye on him. He asked me for help in getting out of there. Was I being set up? I went with my gut, which told me the kid was okay. I gave him ten dollars to help with travel expenses and conveniently looked the other way as he slipped out a window.

I had a contact in the Bay Area (not the Mr. Nguyen I'd met in 1969) who regularly sent mail to "north" Vietnam, via Japan. I launched a routine of removing medicines—especially antibiotics—and other supplies, like all manner of bandages, from the ARD wards when inventories were full enough that the depletion would likely not be noticed. In the parlance of the times, I "liberated" these goods. I could only make these collections immediately before a day off when I'd be going up to San Francisco, to minimize the risk of a surprise inspection of wall lockers blowing the lid off my little secret.

If someone wishes to accuse me of thus "aiding the enemy," my reply would be two-fold: first, as should be clear by now, I did not consider the people of Vietnam to be my enemy, nor the enemy of the American people, whom they'd never harmed. And second, I was simply lending humanitarian aid to victims of war, just like the International Red Cross does. In my moral universe, the fact that it was "my own" government inflicting the injuries in an insane, unjustified war made it that much more imperative that I take direct action.

One day, I returned to my living area after work to find my expensive Frye cowboy boots had been "liberated"! Regulations required all our footwear, civilian included, be well polished and displayed under our bunks. I had noticed an individual not assigned to our barracks passing through earlier, but had thought nothing of it. It never crossed my mind that something so personal—footwear into which my feet had sweated profusely on a regular basis—would be in jeopardy of theft in an Army barracks. Who could one trust anymore?

Late in 1970, after 23 straight months in rank of private or PFC, I was finally restored to Spec. 4. It wasn't a matter of ego or status that had fueled my battle to climb back to where I'd been prior to the first AWOL. It was a question of principle . . . and income! The revolution would be a little richer now that I actually had an almost-respectable, by Army standards, monthly salary. Pay rates were actually being upgraded in an early phase of what would become a push for VOLAR—a "volunteer" Army, a professional military designed to avoid the conscription of unwilling, potentially dissident, cannon fodder. As part of VOLAR's enticements, civilians were actually being hired for all Mess Hall duties. An end to KP for enlisted persons! A "beloved" tradition cast aside! But on the very last day that Hospital Company personnel still had to pull KP, guess who was assigned? Coincidence?!

A friend departs for Vietnam

Down in the 8th Evac Unit, the boys had been lulled into a false sense of security. Months had passed with no orders cut for deployment to Vietnam. But in October, Jim Frandsen had gotten the word: 30 days of leave at home, then off you go. We were in full agreement on opposing this accursed war, but Jim decided he would go and take his chances. He took his leave, shipping overseas in early November. We would correspond faithfully his whole stint over there. He found himself assigned to the 575th Medical Detachment, a small facility at Nha Trang, right on the beach about 40 miles north of Cam Ranh Bay. Despite the "Evacuation" aspect of the parent unit, Jim was only occasionally (when staffing was thin) assigned to ride helicopters out into the bush to pick up wounded. These casualties would be flown directly to the medical facilities back at Cam Ranh. Fortunately for Jim, as he related it to me, the Warrant Officers who piloted these choppers knew their stuff.

Most of the guys in my own company were cool. There was no real friction generated by my strange politics. Spec. 4 McCombs, one of few black members of the unit, was listening to saxophonist Joe Henderson's *Power To The People* LP when first I encountered him. And inhaling clouds of marijuana smoke, right there in the barracks! But McCombs soon returned to the World. On the whole, my fellow medics were certainly not gung-ho for the war, but neither were they sufficiently opposed to become really politically active.

One day, a barracks mate was reminiscing about a remarkable NCO he'd encountered at Fort Lewis, Washington. He recounted how this guy, a strapping black man, had gone to Vietnam an Airborne Ranger and returned a Buddhist pacifist. "Wait!" I interjected, "I don't suppose his name was Larry Goodman?" "Damn, how did you know?!" the fellow shot back. Here was proof that human beings <u>are</u> capable of changing for the better.

Intercourse (of a social variety) with Junior Officers

A civilian who had been awarded the title Registered Nurse would enter the Army, receive a crash course in military protocol (who and when to salute, etc.) and receive the gold bar of a 2nd lieutenant, with the privileges of a Commissioned Officer. It was frowned upon for these nurses to socialize with enlisted men but, on a practical level, impossible for the Military Establishment to prevent. Of course, this attitude prevailed throughout the military, not just in the medical arena.

Among the crop of young Army RNs on the ARD wards when I first arrived was J.D. Papp, who'd already served a tour in Vietnam and been promoted to Captain. This was a warm, very appealing individual. She was very proper about being an Army officer, but not unsympathetic to the views of a dangerous radical who opposed the war. I would have pursued J.D. in a heartbeat, but she was already dating one of my fellow enlisted medics.

Capt. Papp and her guy joined me and another RN to see Mike Nichols's brilliant film of Joseph Heller's novel, <u>Catch-22</u>. The movie was still in first-run status and showing right in Monterey. When we emerged from the theater, J.D. remarked: "I served a tour in Vietnam, so why do I want to cry right now?" It was testimony to the power of great filmmaking.

The next crop of RNs arriving to work on the ARD Wards included June McClung and Joan Hines. I found June appealing and went out with her a few times on dinner dates. She, too, was opposed to the war on moral grounds, and feared she would be ordered to be a part of it. I counseled her on routes by which she might get out of her contractual commitment to the Army. When June heard on the grapevine that she was, indeed, going to be sent to 'Nam, she resigned her commission and went back to her home in the east, marrying one of my fellow Ord medics.

Joan Hines, a 1st lieutenant, was about my height and almost painfully thin. She had long, long hair you'd call honey-blonde. When she let her hair down off-duty, one had to wonder how she managed to tuck it all under her white nurse's cap when required. I found Joan to be very attractive, friendly, highly intelligent and not at all appalled by my politics. I wanted her to be "mine," but there was a complication: she said she had a serious beau back home in the Midwest, then serving in the Navy. So we entered into what would, I guess, be called a Platonic relationship. We dated when our schedules permitted, spending as much time off base as possible. But Joan never permitted me to go beyond a little necking in the realm of physical affection. It was good to have feminine companionship, even though the relationship came with limits imposed.

Larry and Mariann write a book

I'd held many discussions with Larry Waterhouse and his fiancee about tactical options for opposing the War Machine from within. I had explained specifically how the ASU operated. Now, it emerged that these two had a contract to write a book about such matters. The book would be published the following year, by Praeger. It was titled <u>Turning the Guns Around: Notes on the GI Movement</u>. A rather dramatic title for a work by someone then on active duty!

Larry and Mariann eventually tied the knot, with the wedding right in Monterey and a very stoned celebration down on the beach. Larry was discharged at the end of 1970, so he and Mariann returned to Texas to finalize their book-in-the-making. They mailed me a personalized, autographed copy of the book as soon as advance copies were available to them. Though they recognized that the American Servicemen's Union was one of the major anti-war GI groups, their criticism far outweighed their praise for the ASU. They even claimed we were "a personality cult" centered around Andy Stapp. What poppycock! Down with the Trotskyists! It never ceased. [See **APPENDIX 6** for a deeper critique of the book.]

Delayed communication from Hanoi

Early in 1971, I got my first authorized leave home in a long time. Only upon arriving home did I discover there'd been an official reply from Hanoi, in response to my statement of solidarity mailed via intermediaries in Japan. My mother had kept me in the dark about this. Though she knew I'd be very eager to see what had arrived, she didn't want to risk the material being confiscated, or just plain lost or damaged traveling through the US Postal System to California. There was a two-page letter on very delicate "onion skin" paper from the Committee for Cultural Relations with Foreign Countries. Ho Chi Minh had passed away in September 1969, before my statement of solidarity could wend its way to Hanoi. But Mrs. N-Thu-Cuc, on behalf of the government, assured me my gesture would be honored. Since it would be difficult to reproduce the actual letter here in an easily read form, I retype it below, slightly edited, correcting the occasional typographical or grammatical error:

Hanoi, November 10, 1969.

Dear Friend,

Unfortunately your letter came when our beloved Ho is no more. We have transmitted your letter to the President's office, it will be kept in our Ho Chi Minh Museum as souvenir of a token of friendship between the American and the Vietnamese peoples, as an expression of sincere feelings of the world's people towards our venerable leader.

Dear friend, set your mind at rest. Your letter is not read by comrade Ho Chi Minh but it will be read by the Vietnamese people because Ho Chi Minh and the Vietnamese people is one.

Our people wholeheartedly welcomed the anti-war movement in America and sincerely hailed the American courageous youths who have been valiantly struggling for a just cause despite all ever increasing repression. (. . .) Why do the young Americans have to go and die in the far off land of Vietnam? For whose interests? The Vietnamese people never did harm to the American people. Therefore there is no reason for the American youth coming to Vietnam to kill the innocent people there. The aggressive war in Vietnam of the Nixon administration has caused not only suffering and mourning to the Vietnamese people, but also difficulties to the American people in all fields, and deaths and injuries to tens of thousands of American youth, affecting the living standards of the American people.

Acting upon the sacred testament of President Ho Chi Minh, and for the sake of their independence and freedom, the Vietnamese people are resolved to struggle to demand that the U.S. Government stop its aggressions against Vietnam, withdraw rapidly and completely the troops of the U.S. and those of its satellites from South Vietnam without posing any conditions, and let the Vietnamese people settle themselves their own affairs.

We are convinced that for the sake of their interests and honour of the U.S., the American people will obtain many new successes in their just struggle to demand "withdrawal of all U.S. troops right now!" Dear friend, the Vietnamese people, as the whole of progressive mankind, with warm sympathy and unreserved approval and support fully stands by your side.

Wishing you as well as all your friends success, with most sincere feelings from your Vietnamese friends. Hoping closer relations, we remain,

Cordially,
Mrs. N-THU-CUC
Information Department of the Committee for Cultural Relations
46 Tran Hung Dao
DR Vietnam—Hanoi

I pictured this tiny woman—a reasonable assumption—reporting to work daily, despite US bombing raids, to handle correspondence with foreign sympathizers, banging out her letter to me on an ancient manual typewriter. I hoped that she would make it through the war uninjured. With her letter she enclosed two photos of Ho Chi Minh. One is a famous shot of 'Uncle Ho' dancing in a circle with children in what appears to be a birthday celebration. The second shows the leader considerably younger, personally at war. This was almost certainly during the campaign for liberation from France, likely at Dien Bien Phu itself, site of the decisive battle in that war. [The latter photo is reproduced later in this book.]

"Working within the system": point proved

It wasn't possible to do anti-war work in the Monterey/Seaside area without bumping into the coffeehouse crowd. I had drifted away from close relations with them, but we still collaborated because they were "the only game in town" for civilian activists. Their newsletter for GIs, The Right-On Post, had gone defunct.

I was one of a small group of active-duty personnel who birthed a new publication: P.O.W. On the masthead, in smaller type, this title was preceded by "Every GI is a..." This was my invention and I considered it to be true: every rank-and-file member of the military not there on a truly voluntary basis served under duress. A peon was not entitled to say "I quit!" and simply walk away.

In response to the unprecedented open resistance to the war from within the ranks, the Pentagon had issued regulations on freedom of speech and association, to present the <u>illusion</u> that they <u>weren't</u> trampling on our rights. One of these provided a mechanism by which one could seek official approval to distribute literature on military bases.

The first issue of P.O.W. was dated March 1971. Having proved to ourselves that our little collective could put the thing together, I suggested that we take the military up on these new "freedoms" and submit that premiere issue for approval to distribute. I was quite confident as to what the decision would be. We had even intentionally moderated the tone of the issue's political content. I personally delivered a copy, with the official application filled out (co-signed by three other low-ranking EM), to Base Headquarters. The decision was to be delivered to us, in writing.

Unsurprisingly, it took several weeks for the bureaucracy to respond. And sure enough, the decision was that allowing P.O.W. on the base would pose "a clear threat to loyalty, discipline and morale" of base personnel. Naturally, we took this as a compliment to our work, and proof positive that the military was not about to tolerate even the mildest, politest criticism from within.

Two long marches

In April, Joan Hines and I participated in a large anti-war demonstration in San Francisco. We marched a long way, hand in hand most of the way. I wasn't wearing a full Army uniform on this occasion, but I did wear my fatigue "jacket" (to civilians, a shirt) from Ft. Dix Stockade, with the white rectangular patch on the left shoulder. I had retained this as a sentimental keepsake. In the evening, Joan and I attended a Judy Collins concert at the Opera House. Ms. Collins had recently released her splendid album, *In My Life.*

Not long after this, I was a participant in an equally long march, under the blazing sun of the Salinas Valley. The area is close to Monterey; in fact, Joan Hines had found a house she could afford to rent in the town of Salinas proper. I'd been recruited by the Monterey activists to be one of several sympathetic GIs to serve as security for an organizing effort by the United Farmworkers Union. As a medic, I brought a makeshift first aid kit along. The area was called "The Salad Bowl of the World," producing most of the lettuce and similar green crops, plus other vegetables and small fruits, consumed in the US. This backbreaking labor, which involved exposure to a plethora of dangerous chemicals, was performed almost exclusively by migrant workers from south of the border. These laborers were fearful of organizing efforts to improve their lives, because their status of being "undocumented" put them at jeopardy of deportation.

We marched along an unpaved secondary road that skirted the vast fields of crops, kicking up clouds of dust. The union organizers would call over the workers—those who weren't too afraid to leave their places briefly, being under the watchful eyes of overseers—and address them in Spanish. After a little while, we would move on to the next farm. We all worked up one hell of a thirst.

The irony in all this is inescapable: about two decades had passed since pioneering TV journalist Edward R. Murrow had presented his expose of conditions in these fields, "Harvest of Shame." Hardly any improvements had been achieved for these migrant laborers, and to this very day the work is still done largely by "undocumented" individuals who receive substandard wages, are exposed to dangerous chemicals, and lack adequate sanitation. In his song, "Deportee (Plane Wreck at Los Gatos)," Woody Guthrie had asked, speaking of these migrant workers, "Is this the best way we can grow our good fruit"? Sadly, it is still largely the way it is done.

Sweet Sweetback's Baadasssss Song

An astonishing piece of news arrived from Jim Frandsen, writing from Vietnam. He had put in a request to be discharged from the Army a few months early, on a promise that he would start some college classes that summer. To our mutual amazement, the request was granted. The leadership of the US Army had become worried about troops returning from Vietnam with months still to serve "contaminating" others with "bad attitudes" and perhaps drug habits. Jim would process out of the Army at Fort Lewis, Washington at the end of May. I had the weekend off, so I rented a compact car locally and drove up to S.F. to rendezvous with him at the airport.

It so happened that Melvin Van Peebles's groundbreaking movie, *Sweet Sweetback's Baadasssss Song*, was opening in the city that Memorial Day weekend, and I simply had to see it. Written, directed, edited by and starring MVP, and featuring music he'd written and performed on the soundtrack (backed by the band Earth, Wind & Fire), the movie is the story of a ghetto hustler in the Los Angeles area who rebels against police brutality. The character 'Sweetback' is not a conscious revolutionary; he is a marginalized member of the community who simply has had all the abuse from "the Man" he can take. There had never been an American film quite like this one. Huey P. Newton, co-founder of the Black Panthers, reportedly declared this movie mandatory viewing for all members and would-be members.

Jim and I indulged in a "luxurious" afternoon meal at Tad's Steakhouse, downtown, then pushed on to a mid-afternoon screening of the movie. The atmosphere in the theater was electric, and it was a memorable occasion indeed. We topped off the day at Fillmore West, where we saw Cold Blood, Joy of Cooking, and Sweathog. Jim accompanied me back to Ord and spent a night or two in an unoccupied bunk, catching up with some old friends. Then we found a way to get him to Monterey Airport and thence back to Indiana. It wouldn't be too many more weeks before I, too, would get to ride that "freedom bird."

With my time in the Army counting down—I was a bona fide "short-timer" at last—I spent as much time with Joan Hines as our schedules allowed. We had learned she was going to get orders to ship out to the war. Of course Joan did not support the war, but I couldn't persuade her to quit the Army in protest. We could only hope for the best for her in the near future.

"For My Still-Imprisoned Comrades"

As I approached my own freedom from military servitude, I couldn't help thinking of Terry Klug, Jeff Russell and Bill Brakefield. Their fates had taken them to the United States Disciplinary Barracks at Ft. Leavenworth, compared to which a stay in a regular stockade was a "walk in the park." Bill—"angel-faced Brakefield," Allen Ginsberg had written of him, discussing the sanctuary of late 1968 in NYC—was especially on my mind. I'd heard that he'd been tormented by prison guards because of his devout pacifism, whereas I had escaped such treatment. I wrote one of my "florid" free-form revolutionary poems for the guys, published in The Bond, Vol. 5, No. 6, dated June 30, 1971.

FOR MY STILL-IMPRISONED COMRADES
dedicated to Bill Brakefield

USDB, USDB—a blight upon the land
what shall we do with these? they would not
join us in our My Lai holy crusade
they would not jump when we yelled "frog!"
what say you, colonel, courageous officer and gentleman?
". . . to be confined at hard labor for a period of three years,

forfeiture of all pay and allowances,
and to be reduced to the lowest enlisted grade,"
"next case!"

cinderblock and iron, cinderblock and iron
how many souls have you tried to crush—
how many young lives have you twisted and perverted?
do you think that you can stand forever, in
defiance of the course of history?
don't you know that the political prisoners you
entomb can see right through you?
and the vision is of the future and the future is of the people

every time a yellow infant explodes forth unto the world,
from the womb-darkness to greet the sun
though besieged on every side by napalm-phosphorus-defoliant
another nail is driven into the coffin lid of capitalism
and though the air stinks of death, baby-
san sucks it in and then bawls
and though the jungle may muffle sounds and
the amerikan jets still roar nearby
one could almost swear that the infant cried
"US imperialism can never win!"

comrades, do not despair, though the lackey-
mindless guards may taunt you unceasingly
for the time is not far off when the bones of the
capitalist shall lie bleaching in the sun
and up through the hollow eye-sockets shall push flowers
and the earth shall again bustle with the joy of life.
most of the weapons will lie rusting, but
some we shall preserve to ensure
that never again does this class of bandits subjugate our beings

[NOTE: A portion of this poem was analyzed by Michael Bibby in
Hearts and Minds: Bodies, Poetry, and Resistance in the Vietnam Era,
Rutgers University Press; New Brunswick, 1996; paperback, pg. 125.]

Final insults, then freedom at last

Processing out of the Army for ETS (Expiration of Term of Service) was a multi-day affair. Paperwork, paperwork, paperwork, that was the military way. But for me, it was streamlined by one step. Standard procedure required a visit to the Re-Enlistment Sergeant, who would try mightily to persuade you that staying in would be the best decision of your life. During the Vietnam years, most GIs would laugh in Sarge's face. This stop on my printed itinerary was crossed out. Make a fella feel unwanted, why don't they? Boo-hoo!

I actually received some unexpected good news: I was informed that I could ETS on July 3 instead of the 6th. After all, why should Uncle Sam pay to house and feed me over a holiday weekend when I wouldn't be doing any work? I had all my paperwork in order and was packed to go on July 3. But when I reported that afternoon to Outprocessing for the very final phase, the clerk was nowhere to be found. He had taken off to start the holiday weekend early. "Bastard!" I fumed internally. "I hope you enjoy your long weekend!"

So it was back to the barracks for a few more nights. Hospital Company had actually started to move its personnel to the new brick buildings that came with Nixon's transition to VOLAR. I opted to keep my belongings in the original quarters, pending my departure. Some of my closest friends joined me in taking a motel room in Monterey one of those nights, to relax away from the base. Some serious wine was consumed as we talked over the times we'd been through, and our plans for the future.

The betrayal by that clerk put me back on my original timetable of getting out on July 6, just shy of 50 months since I began my three-year enlistment. I had fought the Army to a standstill, a tenuous treaty of peace presiding over my stay in California. I had made it through without violating my conscience, and the Army had gotten every last day out of me I'd signed up for. Of course, my parents had paid a heavy emotional toll. Just days prior to my ETS, I'd discovered a little tuft of gray hairs on my head, at the ripe old age of 23! I, too, had paid a toll.

The Army had a final surprise for me. When I was handed my Discharge Certificate, I found it stated I was leaving "Under Honorable Conditions." I had never been informed that I was to be issued anything other than a full Honorable Discharge. But here I'd been handed my thanks for putting up with the bullshit of "rehabilitation" and serving out my last year-plus conscientiously in the Fort Ord Hospital.

On Freedom Day, a friend drove me to Monterey Airport, from whence I took the "hop" to Los Angeles and transferred to the flight east. At the earliest opportunity on that final leg home, I used the cramped quarters of a lavatory to change into civvies. Where there's a will, there's a way. My personal war with the Army was over, but the larger war raged on. Vietnamese and Americans were still being killed or maimed. Not by a long shot was I finished working to oppose the madness and injustice of it all.

The ghosts of Vietnam are marching still

New York City
July 1971-May 1975

Within two weeks of my discharge from the Army, I had moved from home in Syosset to New York City to continue my revolutionary activity, now a full-fledged member of Workers World Party. My ongoing volunteer work on behalf of the American Servicemen's Union saw me stepping up my involvement in publication of The Bond. As long as the US government continued to wage its war against the peoples of Southeast Asia, Americans of conscience were compelled to continue to resist.

I wrote quite a bit of the content for the ASU's publication and learned how to put a newspaper together the old-fashioned way, when layout via cutting and pasting entailed the use of actual scissors and paste, then a small rubber roller to "lock down" the copy. I was awarded the job title of Technical Editor. Of course, this "job" lacked a salary, but someone in the NYC FBI offices thought this was real employment. In a memo full of factual errors about who lived or worked where, it was recommended that I not be approached at that time about becoming a government informant. Thus the FBI was spared the heartbreak of what would have been my vehement rejection of their overtures.

I shared an apartment on the Upper West Side of Manhattan with two of my comrades in Workers World Party. Even with this three-way split of the rent, we weren't living too many notches above squalor. No air-conditioning, cockroaches and mice on the prowl, heating system break-ing down in winter. Ah, the romantic life of a revolutionary.

Since I was residing in the city, I made sure to resolve that bench warrant for failing to appear in the trespass trial stemming from the sanc-tuary at City College. I was sentenced to time served, since my attorney informed the court of my military confinement. I declined to seek any kind of "amnesty" for my anti-war "crimes" under post-Nixon administrations. There are ways to get around being branded with a less than fully Honorable Discharge.

By the time I exited active duty, Susan Steinman was back in the city, active with WWP and in labor union organizing, but not "available." Tragically, she would die of malignant melanoma in her mid-30s. Too much strong Hawaiian sun at a young age, perhaps. I had tried to stay in touch with Joan Hines after she went to Vietnam. When she failed to acknowledge a "CARE package" I'd mailed her, I foolishly gave up on our correspon-dence. It somehow didn't occur to me at the time that my parcel, or a reply she may have mailed, could have been on a helicopter that got shot down, or may have simply been lost by the Army. So much for affairs of the heart. My commitment to political activism was my overriding concern.

The war finally winds down . . . Good riddance, 'Tricky Dick'!

By Christmas season of 1972 Nixon and company had turned, in desper-ation, to bombing Hanoi and other civilian concentrations in the north of Vietnam. The worldwide condemnation this earned the US didn't seem to faze the warmakers at all, but that administration was starting to show cracks that would soon open into yawning chasms. The following year, with Ho Chi Minh's successors decidedly not defeated, and Nixon shoring up his fortress as the scandal of Watergate became a running sore, the agreement was reached to withdraw US forces from the ground. The end was finally in sight. The president proclaimed that he was bringing the troops "home with honor." To promulgate this notion, a parade was to be staged in March

1973 on Central Park West in Manhattan, with troops supposedly recently back from Vietnam passing in review.

Unemployment among recently discharged military personnel was especially troublesome. And so, on parade day, the ASU and other anti-war militants showed up along the route with banners and chants proclaiming: "Vets need jobs, not parades!" It was a pretty small demo, easily penned by the police on a side street. Squads of NYPD Tactical kept squeezing us from both ends of that street. In due time, push came to shove as a provocateur, or maybe several, started throwing punches at some of our number. What ensued can be seen as the end credits roll in the documentary *Hearts and Minds*, directed by Peter Davis and released in 1974.

I was standing on the sidewalk, discussing the anti-war movement with a German tourist, when the ruckus began. I politely exited the conversation and instinctively joined my menaced comrades. In no time, I had to dodge a police sergeant who'd just pulled a blackjack from inside his leather jacket. Next, a Tactical cop on horseback whacked the top of my skull with his billy club. Fortunately, the fatigue cap I was wearing afforded just enough padding to keep my scalp from being lacerated. Almost no one was arrested at Nixon's happy little parade. The cops' intent was simply to inflict pain and intimidate those in opposition to the Established Order.

As 1973 yielded to '74, Richard Nixon's upper lip had more and more reason to sweat profusely. "I am not a crook" and similar protestations from the man with the perpetual five-o'clock shadow provided a goldmine for stand-up comics. In August, 'Tricky Dick' finally had to go. Over in Vietnam, the liberation forces rapidly approached Saigon in April 1975. What remained of the ARVN melted away in utter panic. The politician known as 'Big Minh' became caretaker head of the southern regime and surrendered to the troops who triumphantly rolled into the capital in their Soviet T-54 tanks. It was a time for rejoicing for those of us who had stood in solidarity with the victims of murderous US aggression. For the first time in many decades, no foreign troops stood arrogantly upon Vietnamese soil. That had been the vision of 'Uncle Ho' all along.

The American Servicemen's Union continued to publish The Bond for a while. The Pentagon continued its transition toward an "all-volunteer" military with some success. With the national economy in an ongoing funk of "stagflation" (stagnant wages being devoured by ever-rising cost of food, fuel and other essentials), young people were actually turning to the military as a lifeline for employment. The Army was using trite recruitment slogans like "Join the people who've joined the Army" (because if ever there was a people-oriented organization, it's the Army, right?!) and "Army: Be all you can be." We called this "the economic draft," and it was getting the job done—once the military lowered its "standards," that is.

Meanwhile, veterans who had recently exited the military were struggling to find employment, and trying to cope with that "stagflation" situation. We turned our attention to their plight and launched an agitation campaign called "$2500 or Fight!" This was something of an echo of the World War I ex-soldiers' campaign for a bonus for their sacrifices as the Great Depression sapped the economy. ASU cadre disrupted "job fairs," which had made empty promises to hire vets on the spot, in New York and Detroit. It looks like an extremely paltry sum in retrospect, but we had roughly calculated that the difference in pay between two years in the military (based on majority of the troops having been conscripts) and private sector employment came to about $2500. The WW I veterans had been met with brutal repression on the streets of the nation's capital. Our demands were simply met by a deafening silence, which hardly came as a surprise.

The ASU understood that the new class of enlistees in the US military would still have grievances about their treatment, but with the draft suspended and combat in Southeast Asia over, enthusiasm for organizing the rank and file waned. And so the organization was mothballed some time in late 1974 or the ensuing year.

Early in my own post-active-duty existence, I encountered the common problem of vets with "less than Honorable" discharges. Answering truthfully the job application question "Have you ever served in the US military?" meant submitting a photocopy of my official Discharge Certificate (Form DD-214). After I was rejected for employment by some major corporations with no explanation, I heard from some fellow veterans that employers looked for codes on one's DD-214 that revealed whether one's term of service had been smooth, or one had been a "troublemaker." Sure enough, upon closer examination, I found my own certificate contained a summary of my "Bad Time" (time spent AWOL and incarcerated), and other stuff I couldn't even decipher. That latter category probably included an indication I'd been barred from re-enlisting. Thanks to the magic of the product called Wite-Out, I obliterated that information and changed my form to read simply HONORABLE rather than UNDER HONORABLE CONDITIONS. Things went more smoothly, thereafter, in the realm of employment.

I took a series of less than glamorous jobs, yielding paltry wages, to support myself while I continued my revolutionary work to try to bring about a more just world. The fulfillment I find in life is derived from activities for which I receive no monetary compensation. My active opposition to the criminal war against the peoples of Southeast Asia had placed me in a crucible which forged the person I became as an adult. *If I have any regret in that sphere of activity, it is that I did not oppose the war still more vigorously.*

A reunion for "Medal of Honor Rag"

Some people have told me they encounter individuals from their distant past, or even celebrities, with some frequency by sheer accident. This happens for me only very, very rarely. But a few years after my official exit from the Army, while I was en route to a movie theater on Manhattan's Upper East Side, I saw someone standing on line to get into a different theater who looked suspiciously like Harry 'FUBAR' Connell. I didn't investigate the matter up close because I didn't want to be late to my own destination, but I checked the Manhattan Telephone Directory shortly thereafter and found the listing. Harry, a.k.a. 'Harvey,' confirmed it had been he in that line. He was attending medical school in the city, it turned out. I proposed we get together for dinner and to take in a performance of the Off-Off-Broadway play, "Medal of Honor Rag," written by Tom Cole.

Harry, his wife, and I met at The Captain's Table, a restaurant in Greenwich Village. When I'd learned of "Medal of Honor Rag," I knew I simply had to see the play. This is because the story is set on a Psychiatric Ward at none other than Valley Forge General Hospital, where Connell and

I had been trained as advanced medics. The lead character (played early on by the very talented Howard Rollins) is an African-American soldier who'd been sent to the ward because he refused to accept the Congressional Medal of Honor offered him. The citation was to be for valiant efforts, under fire, to rescue fellow soldiers in Vietnam. It is basically a two-character play, the other being the white Army Psychiatrist assigned to the case. The "shrink" probes the soldier's psyche to try to determine his reasons for refusing the medal. It emerges, gradually, that the protagonist was horrified by the actions of the US military in that war, and had come to believe that his participation had made him complicit in war crimes. Though basically an all-dialogue production (very little action unfolds on stage), we found it compelling. And that concludes the list, if a single entry can constitute a list, of Army acquaintances—other than fellow protesters against the war—I have encountered later in life.

A modest proposal for a painful, but definitive, experiment

Of the myths that arose out of the Vietnam Era, I find none more pernicious and irritating than this: "Our troops weren't able to win because their hands were tied by politicians back home. They weren't allowed to really fight." This sentiment was famously espoused by President Reagan in the 1980s. It is time to put this myth well under the ground; it has been stinking up the nation for far too long. Fortunately, I have devised a way we can resolve this matter once and for all. We just need a volunteer for a brief experiment, someone who wholeheartedly subscribes to this belief.

This brave soul will play the role of a Vietnamese citizen, and I will play the role of the US military. First, I will spatter the subject with white phosphorus. This charming chemical burns right through skin and keeps going toward the bones beneath. It had been used in previous wars, and was definitely part of the US arsenal in Southeast Asia. In phase two of our trial, a 500-pound bomb will be dropped on the volunteer. This is quite modest, given that more explosives than that were distributed per capita in this theater of war. To wrap things up, a healthy dose of napalm will be delivered on target, in case any little bits of flesh remain. By this time you have doubtless surmised that our volunteer won't be in any condition to answer my simple post-experiment question. And that is a pity. For I wanted to ask: "Did it feel like I was trying to kill you? Or was I just going through the motions with my hands tied?" Before you condemn me as some incorrigible ghoul, I remind you: I was merely playing the role of the US military in this thought experiment, acting in your name, spending your tax dollars. *Better dead than Red, right?*

To hell with the Conventional Wisdom!

Please review the iconic images from this, "the first televised war": the body of a "suspected VC" being dragged by a rope behind an armored personnel carrier. Thatched huts being torched by US troops in a village that had been declared "hostile." The bodies of the women and children massacred at My Lai strewn on the ground. The dying US Marine, smoking his last cigarette as he awaits medical evacuation. A Buddhist monk engulfed in flames as he immolates himself in protest of the "south" Vietnamese regime. The little girl running down the road naked, her clothes having been incinerated by napalm. That summary execution, at point blank range, of a "VC suspect" on a street in Saigon. The inert bodies of four young American college students at Kent State University, the crimson life running out of them, pooling on the ground. The bloodied victims of the police riot in Chicago during the 1968 Democratic National Convention—they thought they had a Constitutional right to express themselves in public. The "Tiger Cages" in which the "south" Vietnamese regime tortured and starved Prisoners of War. The collaborators with that despised regime clinging desperately to the helicopters evacuating the last US personnel in April 1975. The amputees in long-term care in VA hospitals. The homeless, drug-addled, nightmare-haunted veterans of this war, on the streets, under the bridges, in the parks, of America. The bombs falling from the B-52s over the north, over the south, over Cambodia, over Laos. And always the napalm explosions, with their terrible perverse beauty—seen from the air, at least.

Now tell me, what did America gain from all this? What supposed principle could possibly justify all this suffering? Sages have declared that "One should never say 'never'" and that "Only fools are certain." But that's the conventional wisdom, and I say to hell with the conventional wisdom. And I say to you now, with certainty: you will *never* persuade me that my country was in the right in this sordid episode. *And I will never apologize for the actions I took in opposition to this war.*

* * *

More considerations of the Vietnam War: Rights or wrongs aside?!

After completing the first draft of this memoir, I allowed myself to finally read two revered books about the Vietnam War. These were <u>Matterhorn—A Novel of the Vietnam War</u> (El Leon Literary Arts/The Grove Press, New York; paperback, 2010) and <u>A Rumor of War</u> (Ballantine Books; first paperback edition, 1978). [All page references will be to these editions] The former, by Karl Marlantes, is said to closely parallel the author's real experiences; the latter is a memoir by Philip Caputo. Both men volunteered for service and were junior Commissioned Officers in combat operations.

In the back of <u>Matterhorn</u> (page 603) is a reproduction of an interview with Marlantes by Anthony Loyd that appeared in The Times of London August 20, 2010. The author explains it was beyond his control that he was born in a small logging town in Oregon and grew up absorbing values that compelled him to volunteer for war. "Once you accept that . . . you just have to do what has been assigned to you with as much heart as you can. Throw everything into it. But try not to get the emotions too tangled up. Your job is to do the killing **for your country** without getting too involved in it, and it's very difficult" [emphasis added].

Philip Caputo wrote (page 218): "I cannot deny that the front still held a fascination for me. **The rights or wrongs of the war aside**, there was a magnetism about combat" [emphasis added]. Both these authors admit that, beyond concern number one—personal survival—they sought to **test their manhood in combat,** and desired promotion up the ranks.

If ever I meet these gentlemen face to face, I will be compelled to inform them that they definitely <u>weren't</u> fighting for me, and I don't believe they were fighting for their/our country. Did the Vietnamese people exist only to provide them **a test of their manhood?** Is it that easy to toss aside the question of which nation was waging aggression and which defending itself? True, we have no choice to whom we are born, in what nation and into what socio-economic circumstances. But I will maintain until I draw my final breath that we *can* **choose** to refuse to participate in unjust, unwarranted wars. That is the main thrust of this memoir.

There is a risk that I appear to be placing myself high on a pedestal of self-righteousness. I must take that risk. I don't offer myself as a candidate for sainthood. In my life and times, as I have stated previously, people have tended to find me "different." But how "different" am I, really? I don't fancy myself some comic book Superhero with Super Powers. Last I checked, I had but two arms, two legs, and one head perched above my shoulders. If you prick me I will bleed, I assure you, if I may paraphrase Shakespeare. I have recounted here how I, a college drop-out, acquired the skill to penetrate the smokescreen of "Patriotism," to understand the real motives of the state. But before I learned how to analyze things from a class-conscious perspective, **my "gut"** told me, while I was still a teenager, that this particular war, with which I was on a collision course due to the circumstances of my own birth, *could not possibly be justified.*

"Duties of a Law-Abiding Citizen"

That is the title of Chapter VIII of Hannah Arendt's <u>Eichmann in Jerusalem—A Report on the Banality of Evil</u> (The Viking Press, New York 1963; quotations to follow are from the revised and enlarged paperback edition; Penguin Books, 1977). Briefly, Adolf Eichmann, an architect in the Nazi "Final Solution to the Jewish Question," was abducted from his hiding place in Argentina by Israeli secret agents in 1960, transported to Israel, tried for and convicted of crimes against humanity, and duly executed. In his own defense, he would claim he was a mere pencil-pusher, a bureaucrat of no great distinction or importance. Thus the famous subtitle of Arendt's book.

Eichmann testified that upon being tasked by his superiors with working out the logistics of the Final Solution—mustering sufficient railroad freight cars, for instance, to accommodate the increased traffic of Jews and other "inferiors" and political opponents of the state to the death camps—he "thought that he no longer 'was master of his own deeds,' that he was unable 'to change anything'" (pg. 136). "This was the way things were, this was the new law of the land. (. . .) He did his *duty*, as he told the police and the court over and over again; he not only obeyed *orders*, he also obeyed the *law*" (pg. 135, emphasis in original). Again: "[A] law was a law, there could be no exceptions" (pg. 137). Inside the reality bubble of the Third Reich, you see, the state could <u>not</u>, by definition, issue an <u>illegal order</u>. Every order, no matter how heinous and inhumane its end result, was perfectly legal and had to be carried out down to the finest detail. Recall now the US Army's statement, in the Fort Devens Prisoners Handbook (see **CHAPTER VI**), that we inmates had been ordered confined "by competent authority." A competence certified by who or by what? That very self-same authority, of course.

Here are brief excerpts from the court's ruling in the Eichmann trial, addressed to the defendant: "You also said that your role in the Final Solution was an accident and that almost anybody could have taken your place. (. . .) What you meant to say was that where all, or almost all, are guilty, nobody is. (. . .) You told your story in terms of a hard-luck story. (. . .) Let us assume, for the sake of argument, that it was nothing more than misfortune that made you a willing instrument in the organization of mass murder; there still remains the fact that you have carried out, and therefore actively supported, a policy of mass murder. For politics is not like the nursery; in politics **obedience and support are the same**" [emphasis added—GL] (pgs. 278-279). Are you paying attention, you surviving architects of the American War in Vietnam?

Could Adolf Eichmann, as an individual, or any other member of the Nazi apparatus, have refused the orders they were handed? Of course. (A handful of conspirators tried to say *"Nein!"* to Hitler with a bomb, but failed.) Undoubtedly, such an action would have resulted in their being bustled off to the hangman or firing squad. And so, unsurprisingly, the overwhelming majority chose self-preservation over obeying an innate conscience. Human nature, yes? And therein lies a great flaw in what passes for human nature in the Modern Age. Please understand that I am not placing an equal sign between German troops of World War II and American soldiers in Vietnam on the whole. However, the latter committed no shortage of atrocities, and in particular instances a Nazi parallel **is** applicable. Recall that no civilian in My Lai was spared, regardless of age. Conscription into the military is **coercion** by the state. Unquestionably, the average draftee and enlistee of my generation chose to avoid the pain of the consequences of trying to rock the boat. That said, I certainly did not stand alone in my opposition. Enough of us rebelled to give the US Military Establishment severe concern (see next section, plus **APPENDIX 6**). But all the while, the architects of the war lived out their comfortable, cushioned lives.

In my own situation, placed by circumstance in a crucible where my conscience was absolutely at odds with the policies of the government, I would not allow myself to be blinded by "the flag that magically obliterates reason" (see **ESSAY:** "The human condition—a blunt assessment" on following pages). You may put me in solitary and starve me, you may flog me hourly, you may break my bones, but you cannot force me to violate my own conscience.

"The Collapse of the Armed Forces"

An article bearing the above title, penned by a Lieutenant Colonel Robert Heinl, Jr. appeared in The Armed Forces Journal dated 7 June 1971, only about a month before my own departure from active duty. It opened with the following two paragraphs:

"The morale, discipline and battle-worthiness of the U.S. Armed Forces are, with a few salient exceptions, lower and worse than at any time in this century and possibly in the history of the United States.

"By every conceivable indicator, our army that now remains in Vietnam is in a state approaching collapse, with individual units avoiding or having refused combat, murdering their officers and non-commissioned officers, drug-ridden, and dispirited where not near mutinous."

The colonel's tone grows rather hysterical as he proceeds to whine about high rates of AWOL and desertion, battlefield "mutinies," disrespect of officers of superior rank, use of illicit drugs, fraggings, etc. The word appearing most frequently is good old **"sedition,"** with active efforts afoot to diminish the discipline, morale and so on and so on, of the US military. He complains of sympathetic Federal Judges intervening in military matters, and specifically criticizes Andy Stapp's court triumph in getting his less than Honorable discharge reversed.

Lt. Col. Heinl exemplifies the true military mindset that can't even conceive of a war waged by the United States being anything but just. Like Germany under Nazi rule, his ideal military world would be one in which there was no such thing as a war crime committed by his side, and no such thing as an illegal order that military personnel could refuse to obey. He pretty well states openly that his favored means of restoring proper discipline in the ranks would be *summary execution* of dissident GIs. What would he make of my own record of four appearances in public in full uniform at anti-war protests?! Please, Colonel, go share some weed with an Enlisted Man and mellow down, man, mellow down! [Two full-length books addressing the "collapse" of the Armed Forces would appear a couple of years later. See: **APPENDIX 6.**]

Burns and Novick on the war: 10 years, $30 million, no truth found!

In September 2017 a public television series, "The Vietnam War," produced and directed by Ken Burns and his partner at Florentine Films, Lynn Novick, debuted. The narration was written by historian Geoffrey Ward. Ten years in the making, at a reported cost of $30 million, the film (in ten parts) ran 18 hours. In a guest opinion article in the New York Times of May 29, 2017, Burns and Novick declared their project would "offer no answers, only a series of questions about what actually happened." "Wait a bloody minute!" I declared to myself upon reading the Times article. "You're going to expend 18 hours to *offer no answers*?!" The very notion so astonished me that I wrote "An Open Letter to Ken Burns," and a later follow-up, which were published on the Internet at a social commentary blog site called The Contrary Perspective (see **APPENDIX 8** for full texts).

This documentary project had the associated tagline, "There is no single truth in war." I have presented my argument in this book that there was, in fact, one overarching, indeed overwhelming fundamental truth of the US war against the peoples of Indochina: **It was never justified in the first place.** Mr. Burns and Ms. Novick are considered "liberals," or at least middle of the road politically, not raving rightwingers. So what are we to make of their expenditure of ten years of their lives and tens of millions of dollars, only to produce an end product that cannot—or willfully refuses to—grasp this fundamental truth? All we need do is examine the list of sponsors of their project. Most prominently listed, and thanked most effusively by the Public Broadcasting System and the filmmakers themselves, is Bank of America. And right behind that entity we find the David Koch Foundation. The brothers Koch, David (now deceased) and Charles, have in recent years been exerting more and more rightwing influence on public media in the United States. It is obvious to me that, having tethered themselves to such funding entities, Burns and Novick deemed it wise to not try to bite the hands feeding them. And so, we get "no answers." Millions of human beings killed, or maimed for life, with the damage from Agent Orange being passed on genetically to future generations, and . . . no lessons to be learned. Those who praised it hope that this documentary will be considered the definitive history of the war for decades to come. I find that prospect infuriating, and outright **tragic**.

A 3-pronged plan to heal the wounds of the Vietnam War

The participation of US troops in the genocidal campaign against the peoples of Southeast Asia has left us with a festering wound for a half-century. The ghosts of Vietnam are marching still. This kind of pain requires *catharsis* to resolve, and it has long been said that "Sunshine is the best disinfectant." Here is my prescription for healing:

1.) On behalf of the government and the people of the United States of America, it must be **admitted** that the war was a massive crime against humanity;

2.) An official **apology** must be issued to all the victims of these crimes and their progeny. This includes all US military personnel who were involved in the war, the great majority of whom, of course, did not participate "voluntarily";

3.) Full **reparation** must be made to all victims. This means assistance to Vietnam, Cambodia and Laos—the latter is said to have been even more heavily bombed than Vietnam, relative to its land area—in neutralizing unexploded ordnance and rehabilitating the land so damaged by explosive and chemical devices. And, certainly, this must include proper care for the surviving US veterans of the conflict.

As a realist, I assuredly do not expect to see such a program enacted. The very first plank, admission of massive war crimes by the United States, throws up a high enough barrier to render the following planks virtually inconceivable. And that is yet another tragic element in the whole story of the war. Empires are not in the habit of behaving in such a manner. And so, we will be condemned to suffer the ongoing festering of this wound until the last veteran is dead and buried. But even that will not be the terminus of the matter, as a certain segment of the population will continue to believe that US participation was a "noble" effort to "save" people from "Communist aggression." And wounded veterans will continue to be produced in ongoing, utterly unjustified wars. The psychosis I have termed **"the American Disease"** (see **ESSAY** on following pages) has deadly consequences, you see. Will you *ever* be capable of looking at yourself in the mirror and dealing with it, America?

The human condition—
a blunt assessment

The history of man is simply the history of slavery, of injustice
and brutality, together with the means by which he has, slowly
and painfully, advanced. He has been the sport and prey of
priest and king, the food of superstition and cruel might...
. Reading, writing, thinking and investigating have all been
crimes.... Our fathers reasoned with instruments of torture..
.. There has never been upon the earth a generation of free men
and women. It is not yet time to write a creed. Wait until the
chains are broken—until dungeons are not regarded as temples.

—The Liberty of Man, Woman and Child (pamphlet), by 19th
Century American freethinker and orator Robert Greene Ingersoll

As I write, more than 50 years have passed since my first public
expression of anti-war dissent. In these decades, I must report, the
United States has not launched a single military operation that I could
find justified, that I could approve of. The economy remains dependent
on perpetual war for its sustenance. The cost of this military activity gets
folded into the national debt, which will burden taxpayers for literally
decades to come, or bring the economy to eventual collapse. The US military
is essentially a mercenary force now, augmented by civilian "security
contractors"—more profit opportunities for the private sector. The armed
services have had to lower their standards for recruitment, but the civilian
economy is shaky enough (for those of us not in the uppermost percentiles
of income) that young men and women are still being steered into the ranks
by necessity of earning a salary.

Not far into the opening episode of Dr. Jacob Bronowski's 1973 television series, "The Ascent of Man" (a BBC/Time-Life Films coproduction), we are presented the concept that war is fundamentally a highly organized form of **theft**. And the prize to be seized by force of arms, I will add, is not so much the territory being invaded as its inherent resources. In the modern world, these resources are not merely those rudimentary materials provided by Nature, but the very output of human labor power. The French were the first "Western" exploiters of Vietnamese labor power, having discovered an environment conducive to growing rubber trees. The United States of America expended billions of dollars and untold millions of human lives— Vietnamese, Cambodian, Laotian and American—in its furious but futile effort to become the new exploiters.

Mothers and fathers are still blinded by that magical red, white and blue flag and delude themselves that their precious progeny are "serving their country." In truth, they are serving the interests of the last of the emperors, the plutocrats who feel entitled to rule the world. These are creatures of such an ilk that there is no amount of destruction that can be wreaked on the planet's environment, no amount of blood that can be spilled, no magnitude of human suffering inflicted on their behalf that will induce them to discover within themselves a little tickle of guilty conscience or shame.

More on the class nature of modern society

As explained in **CHAPTER VII**, I started to acquire **the Forbidden Knowledge** via associating with the leadership of the American Servicemen's Union. In our school years, we had been taught that the USA was a democracy, and that government's three branches had been brilliantly designed in a system of checks and balances so that none had excessive power. We were decidedly **not** taught that the state, i.e. government, is instituted fundamentally to defend the privileges of a tiny minority, the Ruling Class. The members of this self-appointed elite come from already extremely wealthy family dynasties, are sent to elite universities, join secret societies (e.g. Skull & Bones at Yale), virtually never put themselves at bodily risk in the wars from which they profit, socialize as members of exclusive private clubs and sit on boards of directors of numerous inter-related corporations. It is almost easier for a camel to pass through the eye of a needle than for a woman, a person of color, a Jew, Catholic or Muslim to be accepted as a member of this elite. The term WASP describes the elite succinctly: White Anglo-Saxon Protestants . . . to which must be added the qualifier, male.

The world that Man has fashioned has long been divided into the exploiters and the exploited. The classic Marxist writers explored the roots of rule by the few, tracing its origin to the implementation of agriculture and its ability to produce what they called surplus value. Once vast numbers of people had given up the earlier mode of existence, hunting-gathering, they lost their independence in the struggle with Nature for survival. They became dependent on those who controlled the supply of foodstuffs, and the latter gained profit from this. As someone interested since childhood in studying human origins, I devoured this knowledge eagerly and it made perfect sense. The privileges (<u>class</u> privileges, as we Socialists say) of the tiny minority are protected by armed police and a large military. The class relationship between workers and bosses wasn't even a very modern phenomenon; it was human technology that had evolved to give the appearance of complexity in society.

In his monumental three-volume work <u>Das Kapital</u> ("Capital"), Marx quoted British economist and trade unionist T.J. Dunning: "Capital eschews no profit, or very small profit, just as Nature was formerly said to abhor a vacuum. With adequate profit, capital is very bold. A certain 10 percent will ensure its employment anywhere; 20 percent certain will produce eagerness; 50 percent, positive audacity; 100 percent will make it ready to trample on all human laws; 300 percent, and there is not a crime at which it will scruple, nor a risk it will not run, even to the chance of its owner being hanged."

Absorbing the "ABCs of Marxism," I felt as if I'd been raised wearing blinders, awash in the Establishment's propaganda, and now I'd shaken my head and the blinders had fallen to the floor. I could penetrate the fog of deceit concerning the motives of US involvement in foreign lands, discarding the preposterous lie that our military was "defending freedom and democracy" (ours or anyone else's). Of course, to espouse these views in public led one to be instantly branded a Commie. It was not difficult for me to shed the fear of being branded a Communist. If the price for standing in solidarity with the poor and downtrodden—"the wretched of the Earth"—was to be reviled as a Commie, so be it. That would be a badge of honor.

Having rejected the conventional wisdom of going through college and the opportunity for a higher income a degree would presumably have offered, I had cast my lot with the working class. My parents were of the working class; was this some dishonor? But we were raised in a society that <u>denies</u> it is divided into classes. We were spoon-fed the myth that we all have an equal chance to grow up and be prosperous if we work hard enough. Our nation had emerged from World War II as the dominant military power on the planet. Any threat to the economic dominance this military might enabled, i.e. the desire of peoples abroad to control their own resources, would henceforth be deemed the Communist or Red Menace. This produced the anti-communist hysteria here at home, following so closely on the heels of the defeat of Hitlerism. But Socialist ideology taught me that the poor laborers in other lands had a common bond with me: we were being exploited by the same corporations, making us <u>working class</u> brothers and sisters. Capital crosses national borders with great ease in the modern world. This is precisely how V.I. Lenin defined modern imperialism, as opposed to the classical style of the Roman Empire. The military is sent to quell "restless natives," but it is primarily <u>capital</u> that invades to fund the establishment of new models of production. Small farmer-peasants are driven from the land they've worked for centuries and become concentrated in cities, where they become the laborers (proletarians) in industrial operations.

Did US military learn anything studying Nazi anti-guerrilla tactics?

When the American Servicemen's Union was mothballed, I took into my personal possession, for safekeeping, four pamphlets ("Historical Studies") that had been published by the US Army in the early 1950s. Someone on active duty, in sympathy with the anti-war movement, had made these available to the ASU. As explained in each pamphlet's Introduction, these studies were written by actual former German officers, in the wake of their World War II experiences combatting Soviet Red Army forces and anti-Nazi partisans in occupied territories. Two of the studies were rated "RESTRICTED Security Information." ASU had brought these pamphlets' existence to the public's attention in an article in The Bond, December 1970.

The pamphlet published in 1954, German Antiguerrilla Operations in the Balkans, 1941-1944, is the most enlightening one for us to examine, since the US military was trying to exterminate guerrilla forces in Southeast Asia. From page 22: ". . . the shooting of hostages or burning of homes of suspects and whole communities suspected of sheltering the guerrillas [failed to] achieve the desired results." Now cut, in your mind, to the many instances documented on film of US troops torching whole villages in Vietnam. On page 38 we find: "The readiness of the Bulgarians [home-grown Fascists collaborating with the Nazis] to shoot suspects without investigation of any kind finally prompted the German Commander in Serbia to request a careful preliminary investigation of each case before an execution was carried out." Now cut to Colonel Mike Kirby, John Wayne's character in The Green Berets (released in 1968), declaring "Out here, mister, due process is a bullet." Then cut to the famous documentary footage of the instant execution, on a Saigon street, of a captured "VC guerrilla."

The Germans designated captured partisans "illegal combatants" (page 53) to deny them protection as official Prisoners of War. Sixty years later, another imperial military/intelligence apparatus would take to kidnapping foreign nationals abroad, designating them "enemy combatants," torturing some of them and/or imprisoning them indefinitely without trial. True military logic at work: troops invade a foreign country without justification, and claim the right to declare "illegal" any resistance by the local population. Despite claiming kill ratios of five- to more than 20-to-one over their opponents in Greece and Yugoslavia, the Germans withdrew in autumn 1944, **having never defeated the guerrilla forces.**

The US military interviewed German ex-commanders of World War II, seeking advice on how to combat guerrilla forces. The Germans had failed in their efforts, as would the US in Southeast Asia.

(Image source: the author's personal archive, via the American Servicemen's Union.)

The epitome of People's War: The Viet Minh hauled artillery pieces, part by part, on foot and by bicycle, up into the hills overlooking the French Army encampment at Dien Bien Phu in 1954. The French were taken totally by surprise, and soon surrendered. Ho Chi Minh is here seen coordinating the Vietnamese effort.
(Photo credit: Government of the Democratic Republic of Vietnam, a gift to the author in late 1969.)

Does this not prove the merit of the doctrine of People's War? With his superior technology, essentially unlimited resources for re-supply of weapons and ammunition, and ability to deliver terror from the skies, Uncle Sam arrogantly went about destroying Vietnam "in order to save it." In the end, General Giap emerged the victor—at a terrible, terrible cost—and nearly 60,000 American lives had been thrown away permanently, with many more disabled for life, or taking their own lives in later years. From this, did the United States take away any lessons? It would be hard to argue an affirmative answer, looking at its record of invasion/occupation in the intervening decades. The changeover from a largely conscripted military to a "volunteer, professional" one does present itself as the one exception to the preceding statement. It is all the more difficult to disobey orders when the commanding authority's response will be: "But, this is what you signed up for! This is the military, after all." Fortunately, there is still some resistance to US military aggression going on within the ranks.

The flag that magically obliterates reason

What magical properties this cloth, with the red and white horizontal stripes and the white stars on a blue field, possesses! It is a wonder, to be sure. The citizenry will dutifully salute whatever it's draped upon, no matter how venal and corrupt. No wonder politicians wrap themselves in it when they spout lies and hypocrisy of indescribable magnitude. When they tell the lies that lay the foundations for unjustified and unjust wars. And when they tell the ongoing lies that sustain the wars. As soon as US bombs start falling on the people of another land, the blood starts coursing with greater vigor through the veins of Americans. The flags appear, fluttering from motor vehicles, proudly displayed on front lawns, utility poles, places of business. "Support Our Troops" command the bumperstickers and car magnets. *Don't think, don't question the claims that this is necessary and righteous,* just give your unconditional approval for what the state is doing in your name. Don't dare to wave a banner of dissent or opposition if you want to avoid being ignored, isolated, ostracized, or very possibly beaten to a pulp.

This is nothing new, of course. The heads of state, the politicians, the generals, the mass media have used these techniques to try to justify military aggression since the modern nation-state arose. But in the United States of America, this disease of "Patriotism" has grown like a cancer, into a malignant obsession. Since Richard Nixon and Spiro Agnew started wearing lapel-pin US flags, it has become essentially mandatory for an aspirant to public office, whether Democrat or Republican, to ape this practice. The flag now appears on uniforms of every conceivable stripe: your local police, your state police, private security personnel, athletic teams at all levels (grade school through professional), the delivery person who brings you clean diapers, and on and on. Apparently, one is to fear **not** associating him or herself with the flag. The national anthem is played before the start of the most petty sports event. Someone must be concerned I might forget that I live in the USA, "the greatest nation in the history of the world," if I'm not constantly reminded where I am.

On his debut album of 1971, John Prine brilliantly expressed his own queasiness stemming from this phenomenon. The narrator of "Your Flag Decal (Won't Get You Into Heaven Anymore)" finds a free US flag decal included with an issue of Readers Digest. He proudly sticks it onto the windshield of his car. Then he gets ten more of them, for opening a new bank account, and puts them in place. This leads to trouble, to be followed by a rude awakening: with his windshield so adorned with flag decals, the narrator crashes into a tree. Upon arriving at the Pearly Gates for judgment of his eligibility for admission to Heaven, our narrator is informed that the house is full up—"We're already overcrowded from your dirty little war."

"Don't give yourselves to these *unnatural* men . . . "

While World War II was on the brink of expanding across Europe, Charles Chaplin made a movie called *The Great Dictator* (1940). In it he plays dual roles: Adenoid Hynkel, fascist dictator of an imperial Central European nation (unmistakably representing Nazi Germany), and a humble little barber who is a *doppelganger* for the dictator. In an absurd mix-up, the barber, mistaken for the dictator, is thrust to a microphone to address the aggressor nation's populace in a radio speech broadcast to the whole world. Seizing the opportunity, the barber pleads: "Soldiers! Don't give yourselves to brutes, men who despise you, enslave you . . . who treat you like cattle, use you as cannon fodder! Don't give yourselves to these **unnatural** men [emphasis in original delivery of the dialogue], machine-men with machine-minds and machine-hearts! You are not machines! You are not cattle!"

Chaplin recognized the dehumanization of the individual soldier by those in authority above him—men "with machine-minds and machine-hearts!" So, what can we say are the proclivities of a <u>natural</u> man? A natural man wants to live unmolested by government oppression (which includes conscription into the military), to prosper, to make love, to enjoy the physical pleasures of a bountiful planet, to bring the next generation into a peaceful world. As the little barber says, "We want to live by each other's happiness, not by each other's misery." This speech is a call for world peace and human solidarity, and is reviled by fascist minds to this day. Germany had turned to military conquest, in the name of a fictitious "master race," to benefit a tiny ruling elite. The regime created an internal terror operation called the Gestapo, whose official emblem was a human skull, representing death. A natural man would be repulsed by such activities. It took millions of natural men, the Allied Forces, which included the Soviet Red Army, to put a halt to the Nazi madness.

America, why are you still offering up your sons and daughters to risk their lives and limbs, to perpetrate crimes against civilians in far distant lands, to come home to be haunted forever-after by nightmares? How much longer will you swallow the lies of "Patriotism," and take flags in exchange for your precious children? Is that a fair trade-off? When will you start questioning the claims made by government to justify its military adventures at the outset, instead of ten years into, a war? When will you lift that flag that covers your eyes and see that these wars are not waged in the interest of us, the majority? They are waged for the benefit of the Ruling Class, society's self-anointed elite. When will you stop offering your sons and daughters to "these **unnatural** men"?

Dalton Trumbo's Johnny Got His Gun

In 1939, as European civilization was already slipping over the cliff-edge into the madness of war—in fact, in the very month Nazi Germany invaded Czechoslovakia—the American writer Dalton Trumbo published a groundbreaking cry against this insanity in the form of a novel. Johnny Got His Gun is the story of an American combatant in the First World War who is so maimed, so physically destroyed, that only a miracle allowed his mind to survive. All four limbs were blown off and his face so disfigured that he has no mouth left with which to verbally express his feelings; nor nose, nor eyes, nor ears. The tale is narrated from within the protagonist's mind. He tries to communicate with those caring for him by tapping his head on his pillow in Morse Code.

Johnny regrets, with burning resentment, that he and his fellows were duped into marching off to war on another continent in the name of "Patriotism." His expressed realization that he is one of "the little people," manipulated and exploited by society's "elites," is just one aspect that would bring grief to the author during the McCarthyist witch hunts in the US starting in the late 1940s. Trumbo was blacklisted from screenwriting for Hollywood, though he got some work on screen using pseudonyms and later enjoyed a comeback of sorts with the help of liberal elements in the movie industry. (Kirk Douglas insisted he get on-screen writing credit for *Spartacus*, the film completed by Stanley Kubrick in 1960 after other directors had failed with the epic project.)

Following are excerpts from the final pages of this novel, Bantam Books paperback edition, 1970, second printing. Note that Mr. Trumbo omitted all punctuation except periods, to present a stream of consciousness presentation of the protagonist's thoughts. I have chosen to not use an ellipse (...) to represent my edits of the material quoted, to avoid excessive appearance of that device.

"Already they [society's rulers—GL] were looking ahead they were figuring the future and somewhere in the future they saw war. They knew that if all the little people all the little guys saw the future they would begin to ask questions. They would say to the guys who wanted them to fight they would say you lying thieving sons-of-bitches we won't fight we won't be dead we will live we are the world we are the future and we will not let you butcher us no matter what speeches you make no matter what slogans you write.

"If you make a war if there are guns to be aimed if there are bullets to be fired if there are men to be killed they will not be us. Oh no it will not be us who die. It will be you.

"Remember this well you people who plan for war. Remember this you patriots you fierce ones you spawners of hate you inventors of slogans.

"We are men of peace we are men who work and we want no quarrel. We will use the guns you force upon us we will use them to defend our very lives and the menace to our lives does not lie on the other side of a nomansland that was set apart without our consent it lies within our own boundaries here and now we have seen it and we know it.

"Put the guns into our hands and we will use them. You plan the wars you masters of men plan the wars and point the way and we will point the gun."

If these words helped inspire Bob Dylan to pen "Masters of War," I am not aware he ever publicly acknowledged it. Surely they did inspire the slogan "Turn the guns around!" at the height of the struggle within the US Military to oppose the American War in Vietnam, and the titles of two books about that movement cited elsewhere in this work.

In 1971, with the VN War still raging, Dalton Trumbo's "rehabilitation" reached the point that he was able to adapt his novel for the screen and direct the movie himself. Timothy Bottoms starred as the protagonist with the gruesome injuries. Unfortunately, it being a Hollywood production, Trumbo was not allowed to express the strong class consciousness conveyed in the excerpt above. The American Servicemen's Union made note of this watering down in a review of the movie published in The Bond. We said it was a worthwhile project, but urged readers to obtain a copy of the original book. Now let's take a further look at this business—oh, and a business it is!—of "Patriotism."

Patriotism: It's strictly for suckers

The bankers and the diplomats are going in the army,
It seemed too bad to keep them from the wars they love to plan.
We're all of us contented that they'll fight a dandy war,
They don't need propaganda, they know what they're fighting for.
They'll march away with dignity and in the best of form,
And we'll just keep the laddies here to keep the lassies warm.
Chorus:
Oh, oh, we hate to see them go,
The gentlemen of distinction in the army.

—We Hate to See Them Go, *by Malvina Reynolds*

As I approached my majority, New York State instituted a lottery to raise revenue for government. My father wisely advised me to not dabble in that kind of game of chance. "It's strictly for suckers" he declared. The standard appeal to "Patriotism" is old news. It was going on long before George Orwell wrote his brilliant novel on the perversion of language, 1984. The Ruling Class of one nation-state has been sending its armies, drawn from the ranks of the working class, to slaughter the armies—and, increasingly, the civilians—of other nation-states for what seems like an eternity. And always the big lie is told that this is necessary for the *defense of*, and the betterment of, the Nation. But when heads of state and other politicians speak of the Nation, they are speaking in code. They are winking at the Ruling Class ("Rest assured, we're at your service"), and suckering the working class into believing they really *must* march off to war or the Nation—*their* understanding of the term—may perish. As citizens, you have been raised to believe this; you've been taught this in the schools; it's drummed into your heads daily by the corporate mass media; it's reinforced by what passes for popular culture in the USA.

In the late stage of preparation of this book, I encountered for the first time marvelous words of wisdom from Mark Twain, confirming again that he'd thought these matters through nearly a half-century before my birth. The context here is as follows: Twain pretended to have discovered diaries written by Biblical figures such as Methuselah, Adam, Eve, and even Satan himself, which he personally translated. These are among the works Twain insisted not be published for 50 or even 100 years following his death, due to the potential controversy and backlash against his family. These particular observations on "patriotism" appear in "Passage From 'Glances at History' (suppressed)." Here we find what we might call an alternative biblical universe. Here, not only writing, but newspapers and other strangely modern phenomena, already exist in the ninth century since the creation of Adam and Eve. A "great republic" has been constructed, but a figure known as The Prodigy is pushing it toward a monarchy, which he will rule unopposed. The ensuing discussion of war was commentary on the US military's crushing of Filipino freedom fighters, after having used them as allies to wrest possession of the islands from Spain in the War of 1898 (more on this shortly). Twain writes:

"I pray you to pause and consider. Against our traditions we are now entering upon an unjust and trivial war, a war against a helpless people, and for a base object—robbery. At first our citizens spoke out against this thing, by an impulse natural to their training. Today they have turned, and their voice is the other way. What caused the change? Merely a politician's trick—a high-sounding phrase, a blood-stirring phrase which turned their uncritical heads: *Our Country, right or wrong!* An empty phrase, a silly phrase. It was shouted by every newspaper, it was thundered from the pulpit, the Superintendent of Public Instruction placarded it in every schoolhouse in the land, the War Department inscribed it upon the flag. And every man who failed to shout it or who was silent, was proclaimed a traitor—none but those others were patriots. To be a patriot, one had to say, and keep on saying, 'Our Country, right or wrong,' and urge on the little war" [italics employed in the original].

A little later, Twain adds: "The stupid phrase needed help, and it got another one: 'Even if the war be wrong, we are in it and must fight it out: *we cannot retire from it without dishonor.*' Why, not even a burglar could have said it better" [again, italics in original]. Twain emphasizes that each citizen must decide for himself whether the regime's claim that the republic is in danger, if such and such an "enemy" is not defeated, holds water. If the government's claim is found wanting, how can a citizen, in good conscience, support such a war? [Excerpted from The Bible According to Mark Twain, edited by Howard G. Baetzhold and Joseph B. McCullough; Simon & Schuster, New York; Touchstone paperback edition 1996; pages 87-88.] The US effort to conquer the peoples of Vietnam, Cambodia and Laos, to be sure, was no "little" or "trivial" war. But the relentless pressure, by every outlet for propaganda available, on the citizenry today to wave the flag and support every military expedition, utterly unjustified though it may be, has reached a level Twain could not possibly have imagined in his wildest flight of fancy. But George Orwell would likely be sickened to discover how far the perversion of language has proceeded.

Here in the 21st Century, in this age of technological wonders, raw natural resources are still necessary to run the world. Unfortunately for the planet's environment and inhabitants, crude oil is still king. Modern society cannot operate without it. To obtain it, to control its flow, nations will launch wars of aggression. And leaders of aggressor nations will concoct preposterous lies to conceal their real motivation. It will be stated that such and such an action was necessary "to protect this nation's vital national interests." **Vital national interests.** Translation: "We will take whatever measures we deem necessary to ensure the profitability of our corporations, and the well-being of the plutocrats who control them." When these well-rehearsed liars say "the Nation," they're not talking about you and me, our loved ones, our communities, our "amber waves of grain." They're talking about the *narrow economic interests* of the tiny fraction of society that rules. As long as this situation prevails, as long as society is organized this way, if these liars come to me and say "In the name of the Nation, you must take up arms and march off to war," I will answer them just as I did in 1968: "GO TO HELL!" If you wish to deem this treason, that is your prerogative. But I ask you to bear in mind that treason entails *betrayal.* Since I refuse to pledge loyalty to the parasitic minority that runs The System, who am I betraying?

The Conventional Wisdom needs to be discarded

By now it should be clear that I am an unrepentant Socialist. "But," you object, "Socialism has proved a failure anywhere, anytime it's been tried! It goes against human nature!" I will reply as concisely as I can. To the first objection, I say Socialism has never had a fair, practical trial. Any regime attempting it has been assaulted militarily and/or economically by the dominant Capitalist powers. To the second, I say that human nature—social relations, the way people interact—has been distorted under the rule of capital by society's class distinctions. Your notion of "human nature"—a dog-eat-dog environment where success requires selfish personal conduct, your socio-economic advancement only possible at the expense of your fellows—has been drummed into your head so subtly that you very rarely even question its morality. "Socialism can never work!" is the conventional wisdom, and I believe nothing is more unwise than to unquestioningly accept the conventional wisdom. It saddens me today to encounter young people whose minds have already been tightly compressed to fit inside the "little boxes" Malvina Reynolds so well described in her marvelous song. They have been stripped of the ability to even *imagine* a different way to organize human society.

We are incredibly fortuitous to live on a planet hospitable to life, but its resources are finite. This world cannot benignly absorb an infinite quantity of poison dumped into the ocean, buried in the ground, spewed into the atmosphere. How could this not be obvious? Well, **the Conventional Wisdom** was that this is how the economy works, this is what gives people employment, this is what leads to progress. If we are to survive as a species, we need to <u>cooperate</u>, not slaughter one another in a quest to seize the remaining resources, or to dispute artificial lines on a map defining nations. This whole concept of "Patriotism" needs to be **discarded**, for our world has become one where *cooperation is our only hope for survival*, so immense have the problems of the impact of human activity on the environment become. When I started this memoir, I contemplated defending the actions of those of us in the anti-war movement as the acts of "winter soldiers," the true patriots. But I have come to realize I do not wish to be thought of as **any** brand of "patriot" at all. "Patriotism"—if I may be allowed to update Samuel Johnson—has become the <u>first</u> and last refuge, and all levels of refuge betwixt and between, of scoundrels.

The American Disease

> **Loyalty to petrified opinions never yet broke a chain or freed a human soul in this world—and never will.**
>
> —Mark Twain, 1884 speech in Hartford, Connecticut; published 1923 as an essay titled "Consistency"

The original thirteen British colonies on the North American continent (south of Canada) were expanded by brute force, practically exterminating the indigenous dwellers, until the United States of America stretched "from sea to shining sea." This is indisputable history. This expansion was said to be the new nation's "manifest destiny." In the mid-19th Century, a large swath of Mexico was seized by brute force and incorporated into the USA. But I consider the War of 1898, or Spanish-American War, to mark the start of Modern Imperialist Aggression by our so-called republic. With the mysterious and convenient sinking of the US battleship Maine in Havana Harbor, the US military was off to the races, seizing not only Cuba, Puerto Rico and other Caribbean entities, but also territories on the vast Pacific that Spain had originally conquered and colonized. In the Philippine Islands, the US military massacred their former allies in the fight against Spain. Those guerrillas had gotten into their heads the foolish notion that they might be allowed to become a genuinely independent nation. US business interests thought otherwise and, unsurprisingly, they got their way. Mark Twain published a scathing essay, "In Defense of General Funston," revealing our nation's gross and murderous treachery in the islands.

But prior to the action up north, Imperial Spain had committed widespread genocidal acts against the indigenous populations of South and Central America. In his wide-ranging examination of how the modern world came to be as it is (Guns, Germs and Steel: The Fate of Human Societies, W.W. Norton; paperback edition, 1999), Jared Diamond tells the story of the "Collision at Cajamarca." The site is Ecuador, the year 1532. The *conquistador* Pizarro, with 168 troops, captures Atahuallpa, Emperor of the Incas, despite the latter reportedly being defended by an army of tens of thousands. Pizarro sends Friar de Valverde to offer the grace of the Christian God to the heathens (and I mean no offense by that term). The Emperor is handed a bible. Never having seen a book of any kind, Atahuallpa is puzzled at first. Then, unimpressed, he tosses the book aside. "The Friar returned to Pizarro, shouting 'Come out! Come out, Christians! Come at these enemy dogs who reject the things of God . . . '" (pgs. 69-72). The Spaniards had sturdy body armor, steel swords, firearms and horses. The Inca had never seen large, powerful animals like these, and they shrunk in terror. This process of inflicting terror with bible in hand was alluded to in a largely forgotten song written by Richard Farina

(1937-1966) and recorded by him, with wife Mimi (sister of Joan Baez), titled "Bold Marauder." The chorus includes the phrase "I am the white destroyer." Nearly a decade later, Neil Young would touch on a similar theme with his song, "Cortez the Killer."

What followed was one of numerous massacres of inadequately-armed indigenous peoples by representatives of the "advanced" Western cultures, bearing bibles and superior weaponry. Though the Spaniards may have exaggerated the size of the army opposing them, their military victory at Cajamarca cannot be doubted. The toxic combination of religion as a cover for conquest in the interest of economic exploitation, and weapons honed for inflicting maximum damage on human flesh is, unfortunately, the story of the Modern Age. The post-script to the tale of Atahuallpa's defeat is sad, and telling. He was held for ransom for about eight months. His people finally delivered to the Spaniards an enormous amount of gold. The *conquistadores*, nonetheless, executed the former Emperor of all the Inca.

Now let us advance this delusion of innate, "God-given" racial superiority several centuries. The British author Rudyard Kipling is credited with giving birth to the notion of "the white man's burden." This foul attempt to give moral cover to the looting of the West Indies, Africa, India and the Far East posited that Britain was <u>obliged</u> to spread its knowledge, cultural traditions and language—the glorious tongue of Shakespeare, Donne, et al.—to "less fortunate" peoples. (And Mark Twain was once again on the scene to counter such nonsense, with essays like "To the Person Sitting in Darkness" and "King Leopold's Soliloquy.")

"Rudyard Kipling proclaimed Britain uniquely fitted to rule '**lesser breeds** without the law.' The **responsibility** for governing India had been 'placed by the **inscrutable design of providence** upon the shoulders of the British race.' . . . An unnamed British civil servant in a Parliamentary debate c. 1900 speaks of 'the conviction in every [English] man [in India] that he belongs to **a race which God has destined to govern and subdue**'" [emphases added] —<u>Freedom At Midnight</u>, by Larry Collins & Dominique LaPierre (Avon Books; paperback edition, 1976, pgs. 14 and 21).

Advancing a few decades into the 20th Century from Kipling's time, we find the British Empire in tatters and the United States of America the most powerful nation on Earth. The latter's weaponry is arrayed against a modest-sized nation called Vietnam. The attempted justification for the military behemoth's presence halfway around the world from its home soil is not to spread "enlightenment." It is to save the world from the spread of the Communist Menace. The Communist Menace! The domino of Vietnam, with its neighboring states in Southeast Asia, must not be allowed to topple! The following statement by US President Richard Nixon, speaking around the time that some Americans were awakening to the reality that military victory was not to be achieved, is heard in the 1983 public television documentary series produced by Stanley Karnow, titled "Vietnam: A Television History." I have placed in boldface the words emphasized by the original speaker. "If the United States **now** were to throw in the towel, and come home, and the **communists** took over South Vietnam, then, all over Southeast Asia, all over the Pacific, in the Mideast, in Europe, in the world—the United States would suffer a blow. And **peace**—because we are the great peacekeeping nation in the world today, because of our power— would suffer a blow, from which it might not recover." Richard Nixon, Apostle of World Peace! Imagine that!

Some years ago, a global public opinion poll revealed that outside the borders of the US, people understand that the pre-eminent threat to world peace today is, precisely, the United States of America, with its military expenditures vastly outstripping the combined war budgets of major powers Russia, China, and the US's principal allies *combined*.

After the internal collapse of the Soviet Union in the early 1990s, there was talk of a "peace dividend" for workaday Americans, since military spending could presumably be scaled back. Predictably—and I did predict it at the time—no such dividend appeared. Always yearning to expand its tentacles of economic dominance, the US turned its focus to the crude oil beneath the sands of the Middle East. Despite the public anti-science bias of Republicans, the level-headed real directors of government, meeting behind closed doors, understood that fossil fuels are a finite resource.

Enter the "Neo-Conservative" cabal of advisers to President George W. Bush. They drew up a list of nations (all in the predominantly Muslim world) where they wished to install new regimes, compliant to their desires. The doctrine of "regime change" was born. Now, stir into this pot of toxic ideology the notion that the United States was created as "a Christian nation." (A majority of "the Founding Fathers" would be outraged at this assertion, by the way.) A nation ordained by God to exert its will anywhere, anytime, by military means, regardless of the cost in lives lost and damage to the environment. Bush's apologists loved to employ the phrase **"American exceptionalism."** None other than Barack Obama, constantly vilified by racist elements in the United States from his first to last day (and beyond) in the office of the President, would end his tenure declaring that his greatest honor had been to serve as Commander-in-Chief of the Armed Forces and that the USA is **"the indispensable nation"** on Earth. The mild-mannered professor of Constitutional Law, who came to office with a brave promise of "Change we can believe in," emerged from the anus of The System a full-fledged advocate for imperial domination of the globe.

And so, have we traveled very far from Mr. Kipling and his "white man's burden"? This notion that the USA somehow has a right to impose its will on other nations as it sees fit, and damn world public opinion and even agreements on humane treatment of prisoners of war signed by relatively civilized nations, is what I call **the American Disease**. It is a fantastic self-imposed delusion of colossal proportions, and it can only guarantee perpetual war and suffering, planet-wide. Our country's rulers have designated shadowy "Islamic terrorist" groups as the current enemy to be dreaded. These are stateless organizations that seemingly arise from the mist one day to menace the Western world. I am not a "conspiracy theorist" by any stretch of the imagination, but it seems to me legitimate to suspect that at least some of these operators are creatures of the CIA. (Osama bin-Laden, accused of masterminding the terrorist attacks on US soil on September 11, 2001, was certainly such a creature, by US government admission.) In the absence of the good old Communist Menace, they provide ever so convenient a "justification" for keeping the war corporations rolling in juicy contracts. As I finalize this essay in 2021, thousands of US troops are roaming numerous nations on the African continent, supposedly to search for, and try to "neutralize," these ectoplasmic phantoms.

Having essentially failed to learn anything from the Vietnam quagmire, the US has engaged in military campaigns without clearly drawn battle lines or objectives, campaigns that seem practically designed to fail. Concurrently, the mainstream media are jamming down our throats, 24 hours a day, 7 days a week, compulsory worship of the Military Beast. Uniformed personnel are on display almost universally at sports events, with fighter jets flying over the biggest events. Sideline personnel (coaches, trainers, etc.) at games in the National Football League and Major League Baseball are dressed in pseudo-military camouflage outfits. Actors portraying military personnel appear in numerous advertisements. And just in one recent (2018/19) network television season, three new programs glorifying the activities of US Special Forces personnel debuted. Needless to say, you'd have to put a gun to my head to make me watch any of that drivel. This constant worship of the military, I believe, is a sure sign that the termination of what civil liberties we still can exercise in the USA is drawing near. Were not the Roman Legions the great pride of <u>that</u> empire, lo those many centuries ago? One day, the citizens awoke and found that their republic had become a dictatorship. Mark my words, the citizenry here will not be able to evade indefinitely the suffering I've here written of.

* * *

The worst idea ever concocted

Man is the Religious Animal. He is the only Religious Animal. He is the only animal that has the True Religion—several of them. He is the only animal that loves his neighbor as himself, and cuts his throat if his theology isn't straight. He has made a graveyard of the world in trying his honest best to smooth his brother's path to happiness and heaven.

—Mark Twain, <u>Letters from the Earth</u>

If I have learned but one thing in this life, it is this: *The worst, most wrong-headed, most harmful idea ever concocted by the mind of Man is the notion that he stands above, separate from, and superior to, Nature.* My beloved Mark Twain expressed this idea as Man fancying himself "the Creator's pet." Let it not be forgotten that voices of warning about humanity's impact on the environment were raised decades ago, but no significant action was taken to avert calamity. Why? Because Man has come to be governed by servants of corporations, and politicians are not elected for wisdom in general, and knowledge of ecological matters in particular. Indeed, no few have been elected precisely to reward their <u>disdain</u> for Science. As a species, we have utterly discarded the ancient wisdom of living in harmony with Nature, and the price to be paid is unimaginable—but the bill is coming, interest on it accruing, absolutely inevitable and unavoidable. **The Conventional Wisdom** still says keep your mouth shut, don't try to rock the boat. The human race is in need of a revolution of consciousness that will turn it inside out and upside down. But the clock keeps ticking mercilessly and time is short, very short. Therefore, I have felt compelled to offer an updated version of The Pledge of Allegiance I was made to recite in childhood:

PLEDGE OF ALLEGIANCE FOR AN ENDANGERED PLANET

**I pledge allegiance to no flag,
but to Earth's glorious diversity,
the preservation of which is our sacred duty:
one great web of life, Nature's love, one planet,
one choice—share it or perish.**

Astronomer/educator Carl Sagan (1934-1996) famously observed that "We are made of star-stuff": all the elements essential to the origin of life on Earth were manufactured in the cores of stars that exploded eons ago, disgorging these materials toward their neighbors. He said that the evolution of human consciousness represented a little chunk of the Universe attaining the ability to behold and ponder itself, to seek the details of its own origin. Henry David Thoreau observed that "The great majority of men lead lives of quiet desperation." Man flees the gift of consciousness, dulling it at every opportunity. For it is a double-edged sword, making Man the only animal that can grasp the concept of mortality . . . and keeping him busy furiously trying to deny that reality.

* * *

From misanthropy to Buddhism: a mutual attraction

If you take your deepest questions into the core of your being, into your very blood and marrow, one day, quite naturally, you will understand the connection between thought and action.

—venerable Vietnamese Buddhist teacher Thich Nhat Hanh, Fragrant Palm Leaves: Journals 1962-1966

I told you in **CHAPTER I** that, as a twelve-year-old, having assessed the state of the world around me, I would have been perfectly content had the human race vanished overnight. Despite the occasional victory for progress and enlightenment in the intervening decades, the human race has not persuaded me that it has righted its course of determined self-annihilation. But this has not driven me to embrace nihilism. I have taken responsibility for my actions in the world and I have fought for peace and justice to the best of my ability.

It seems I was moving toward Buddhism long before I began even a rudimentary investigation into that school of thought/action. And forgive me for what can only sound like a mystical statement from someone very scientifically minded, but I now feel like Buddhism was "moving toward me." Buddhism can actually be described in just five words, I have learned: The training of the mind. From Buddhist teachings, I discovered a new way of looking at "the damned human race" (Mark Twain again): Behold these wretched, pathetic beings whose failure to grasp reality causes them to suffer so, and to inflict so much suffering on others. They are fixated on the illusion that they are separate from the Universe, and they go stumbling about in search of their own individual happiness. They understand not that true happiness is only achieved by being of service to others. They stagger along weighed-down by the load of the suffering they create. Therefore, *they must be treated with compassion!*

Buddhism and War

My personal view is that no war of aggression, no invasion of another territory with the intent to conquer its inhabitants and exploit its resources, can possibly be considered a "just war." Thus, the American War in Vietnam was utterly unjustifiable. The Vietnamese people did not long for war, they had no desire for war, but the United States—and the French and the Japanese before this—forced them into a defensive posture. Many, though not all, Vietnamese identify as being Buddhist. So what is the Buddhist view of war?

Fundamental Buddhist doctrine prescribes The Noble Eight-Fold Path as the only road to "salvation" from the otherwise endless cycle of *Samsara*: rebirth into a world of suffering, suffering which is our lot simply by dint of being human beings. The Path is essentially a code of conduct, the closest to perfect that this author has ever encountered. Walking the Path requires right view (substitute "thinking"), right resolve (substitute "intention"), right speech, right conduct, right livelihood, right effort, right mindfulness, right *samadhi* ("meditative absorption or union") [as summarized at Wikipedia January 2021]. To willingly participate in an unjust war is to violate pretty well all these ideas (expressing hatred for someone you've never seen before and a desire to kill that person, swallowing the hateful propaganda of the state, is certainly not right speech, for example, to say nothing of carrying out the act of killing or injuring). Buddhists generally seek to live in pacifist mode. But there was Buddhist participation in the National Liberation Front resisting the US invaders of Vietnam. What about the Japanese military in World War II? Many Japanese profess to adhere to Buddhism (though Shinto is actually dominant in that society), but troops of that nation committed grave atrocities. The overwhelming majority of soldiers in any war waged by a major nation are in uniform against their wishes; they are conscripted combatants. The state ensures that they will suffer miserably if they deny their bodies to the War Machine. This yields the clash of the individual's conscience with the wishes of the state which has been the focus of this book.

Buffy Sainte-Marie, Native American human rights activist who gained attention in the Vietnam War years, wrote a song called "Universal Soldier." Donovan, the former Scottish tailor with the lovely, lilting voice, recorded a popular version of this work. The song lists various "faiths" to which a soldier might adhere while engaging in war, including Buddhism. But Sainte-Marie erred by trying to blame the common soldiery for the never-ending wars of Mankind. "He's the Universal Soldier, and he really is to blame" she wrote. Are we to hold blameless, then, those who instigate the wars and reap the profits from a safe position thousands of miles from any combat? ("The bankers and the diplomats are going in the army" indeed! The extreme unlikelihood of this happening, of course, is what gives the song its delicious irony.) As I have made clear, the likes of Mark Twain, Malvina Reynolds, Ernest Hemingway, Dalton Trumbo and I had very different perspectives.

* * *

Permit me to conclude with a Universal Buddhist prayer:

May all beings everywhere be safe from harm,
and free from fear;
May they learn to refrain from doing harm to others,
as well as to themselves.

A Condensed History of the Vietnam War

In war, truth is the first casualty.

—attributed to Aeschylus, Ancient Greek playwright

[**Author's Note:** I here concentrate on the origins of what Americans call the Vietnam War. The Vietnamese still refer to it as the American War, waged on their soil. I am grateful for historian Christian G. Appy's book <u>American Reckoning—The Vietnam War and Our National Identity</u> (The Viking Press; New York, 2015), which brought me new information on an episode of history I thought I knew very well.]

I quoted in **CHAPTER I** H. Rap Brown's observation that "Violence is as American as cherry pie." Of course, the Establishment raised a terrific ruckus over this statement. But long before this period in our history, it had been observed that a nation's foreign policy reflects its domestic policy projected outside its borders. Blood was running in the streets of America's poor communities. Impossible to ignore was the even greater violence being unleashed against a nation of slender rice farmers halfway around the world. This war was being waged on **a complete fiction** (and wouldn't be the last US war so concocted, to be sure)—*the notion that a nation can commit aggression against itself.*

The people of Vietnam had a very long tradition of fighting off attempted foreign domination. At different times the area was known as "Tonkin China" and "Cochin China," but the inhabitants always strove to maintain their own identity, culturally as well as geopolitically. They threw off the yoke of Chinese domination almost a millennium before the arrival of white colonists. In the 19th Century, European powers, by force of superior arms, made an "opening" in Asia to gain access to its vast natural resources and plentiful cheap labor pool. Vietnam and neighboring Cambodia were "blessed" with falling into France's "civilizing" hands. Right after the First World War, during the peace negotiations at Versailles in France, a young Ho Chi Minh (1890-1969) had beseeched the US for aid in becoming independent from European powers, only to be brushed off by the Woodrow Wilson administration. It is little known that Ho had actually spent some years in the USA, working at "menial" jobs in the kitchens of hotels. The United States would establish a remarkable record of betrayal of the peoples of Indochina as the 20th Century proceeded. After his rebuff in Versailles, Ho's interest in other means—revolutionary means—of seeking national sovereignty sharpened. He attended the founding sessions of the COMINTERN (the Third, or Communist International) in Moscow in the young Soviet Union, while V.I. Lenin (1870-1924) was still alive.

Vietnamese nationalist sentiment in those prepared to fight the French colonialists to regain independence congealed around Ho Chi Minh's leadership. The struggle against French domination was sidetracked by World War II, when the Japanese Imperial Army invaded and occupied Indochina. The leadership of the anti-Japanese armed resistance remained under Ho and provided a training ground for the brilliant military strategist, Vo Nguyen Giap. During the Japanese occupation, the US actually supplied war materiel to the guerrilla forces of Ho and Giap, and the Vietnamese helped rescue downed American pilots. At the conclusion of the world war, Ho's forces were still concentrated in the northern part of Vietnam. British forces, in the name of the Allies, occupied the southern part.

In August 1945, the very month the war in the Pacific ended with the surrender of Japan, General (and future President of France) Charles de Gaulle paid a visit to Harry S. Truman. Hat in hand before the US President, the tall general pleaded for assistance in regaining and maintaining French dominance in Indochina. Since the revolutionary army of Mao Tse Tung [now called Mao Zedong in an attempted simplification for readers of English] was fighting for control of mainland China, leaving that immense country's future in question, de Gaulle argued that France's presence in Indochina would provide the only beachhead for the "Western powers" on the Asian mainland. (The island nation of Japan was under direct occupation by US troops.) The loss of such a beachhead would mean the loss of the ability to economically exploit that part of the world. At this time, Britain still "possessed" India (though that situation would change by the end of 1947), but India was considered a "subcontinent," and was divided from China by the Himalaya Mountains, and so left out of discussions of Asia proper. The first wave of France's renewed aggression employed members of the notorious Foreign Legion and re-armed Japanese POWs. The latter aspect of the situation so offended members of the US Merchant Marine and active-duty US Navy personnel—who had been ordered to transport these Japanese soldiers—that they launched a protest movement, thousands signing petitions to their commanders and President Truman. Likewise, there was agitation among US military personnel in Europe and the Pacific Theater, calling for faster rotation back to the States, and their demobilization from active duty since, in theory, peace had been attained. [For wider historical context on troop rebellions through the centuries, see Turn the Guns Around: Mutinies, Soldier Revolts and Revolutions, by John Catalinotto, World View Forum, New York 2017; paperback. I also address this matter in **APPENDIX 6** of this book. Catalinotto's study encompasses the story of the American Servicemen's Union, to which he was a civilian adviser in its early years, and other GI resistance during the Vietnam War.]

Undeterred by the French attempt to regain control, Ho Chi Minh declared an independent nation in September 1945, the Democratic Republic of Viet Nam (DRVN), to be governed by a constitution modeled largely after that of none other than the United States of America. Ho believed that any reasonably impartial international body examining the Vietnam situation would recognize his government as legitimate. The "Western powers," of course, were anything but impartial. The French began reintroducing an increasing number of their own troops into the region.

Again, the people of Vietnam were forced to fight for the principle of self-rule, and fight they did. At the urging of US Secretary of State John Foster Dulles, his brother Allen at CIA, and other anti-Communist fanatics, the USA started funding a growing portion of the French military effort, providing weaponry directly, as well. Toward the end of the French effort at re-conquest, the US taxpayer was footing up to 80% of the pricetag of that war. It would be learned in later years that when things took a bad turn for French forces, US President Dwight D. Eisenhower even considered offering de Gaulle's side atomic bombs. Despite all this, with material aid from the USSR, Ho and Giap's Viet Minh fighters inflicted a stunning defeat upon French forces at Dien Bien Phu, in northern Vietnam, in 1954. France quickly surrendered, and an independent Vietnam seemed within arm's reach.

'Uncle' Ho took his case to the United Nations and a comprehensive democratic election was scheduled for 1956. A completely artificial border had been decreed at the 17th Parallel, with "north Vietnam" having Hanoi as its capital, and "south Vietnam" ruled by a succession of puppets based in Saigon. Eisenhower would later admit he had no doubt Ho would have been elected leader of the whole nation in a fair and open process. And that is precisely why the "Western powers" maneuvered behind the scenes to scuttle the 1956 elections. The National Front for the Liberation of South Vietnam—called the "Viet Cong" by the US—waged resistance to puppet rule in the south of the nation, with aid from the Hanoi government in the north. (Though the leadership came from seasoned Communists, this front was an alliance of numerous groups, including pacifist Buddhists, committed to the struggle for independence.) And so, in two easy steps, the US tried to justify its presence in the former French colony: 1.) artificially divide Vietnam into "two nations," north and south; then 2.) cry, "Look! The North is waging aggression against the South!" The United States of America, born of a struggle against British colonial domination, now vowed to crush a small nation's aspiration for freedom from colonial domination.

In 1983, the Public Broadcasting Service aired a multi-part documentary series titled "Vietnam: A Television History." The program was produced by Stanley Karnow, with different writers and directors for the various installments. I had never viewed this program until 2017, when I rented it on DVD. The first episode begins with a montage of US presidents spouting "Domino Theory" nonsense, as follows. (I transcribed these statements verbatim from the video; the words I have emphasized were stressed by the original speakers.)

Eisenhower, while US was funding the French attempt to regain Indochina: "So when the United States votes $400 million to help that war, we're not voting for a giveaway program. We are voting for the **cheapest** way that we can prevent the occurrence of something that would be of the most **terrible** significance for the United States of America."

John F. Kennedy: "If we withdrew from Vietnam, the communists would control Vietnam. Pretty soon Thailand, Cambodia, Laos, Malaya, would go."

Lyndon Johnson, with big smirks: "If this little nation goes down the drain, and can't maintain her independence, ask yourself what's gonna happen to all the other little nations."

Richard Nixon: "If the United States **now** were to throw in the towel, and come home, and the **communists** took over South Vietnam, then, all over Southeast Asia, all over the Pacific, in the Mideast, in Europe, in the world—the United States would suffer a blow."

But American presidents came and went, and still the war ground on. Weekly claims of "enemy" killed grew into the thousands; whistleblowers pointed out that the US obsession with body counts led not only to civilian casualties being lumped into the "enemy" statistic but even body <u>parts</u> being toted up. When the official count of Americans killed grew to multiple hundreds some weeks, more folks on the home front started questioning the war. The daily Official Press Briefing by US military officials in Saigon became known in the press corps as the "Five O'clock Follies." Credibility was ebbing away as one supposedly brilliant strategy after another failed to turn the tide against the liberation forces: "Strategic Hamlets," "Pacification," "Vietnamization." Richard Nixon, who'd built his political career on anti-Communist crusading, was elected on his promise of "a plan to end the war." It was on his watch that US troop strength in Southeast Asia reached its maximum, about 600,000 if we include the crews of naval vessels deployed in the area and personnel at air bases in US-occupied southern Korea, Thailand, the Philippines, Guam, Japan. Additionally, there were many thousands of troops from allied nations whose leaders bought into Domino Theory, not wishing to defy the US superpower, notably from "south" Korea, the Philippines (these first two essentially outright puppets of the US), Australia and New Zealand.

In the years since US forces ceased active combat roles in 1973, per the Paris Peace Agreement, with the last personnel evacuated hurriedly in spring 1975, we have learned much about the cynical maneuvering of American politicians. Their intentional bogging down of negotiations—which initially were kept secret from the American public—to avoid having a president admit defeat with an election looming, cost an untold number of lives, of US military personnel and Southeast Asians. As the colossal, overwhelming technological advantage of the USA, with its immense expenditure on weaponry, failed year after year to break the will of the liberation forces, morale on the American side decayed to the point that the Pentagon commissioned its own internal studies of the problem. [Again, see **APPENDIX 6** of this book.] Ultimately, conscription would be suspended and the US military declared a volunteer, career-oriented organization. As I recounted in **CHAPTER X,** this process had already begun when I completed my stint in the Army in July 1971. Recent deployments of, and conditions for enlisted personnel within, the updated US Military are discussed later in this book.

Music with a Social Conscience

Is it fair to say that my generation was the first to grow up immersed in popular music, and to often be influenced by same? Hardly. Long before Beatlemania erupted, clarinetist and bandleader Benny Goodman and singer Francis Albert Sinatra whipped crowds of young, predominantly white kids into frenzies. "Hep cats" and "bobby-soxers." Black folk had their own entertainment (recordings of which were designated "race records"), virtually unheard and unknown by members of mainstream society except for the few who had been initiated into the Jazz scene. Eventually, the biggest names would "cross over" into the wider society—**Louis Armstrong**, the 'Duke' Ellington and 'Count' Basie big bands, Ella Fitzgerald, Lionel Hampton, Nat 'King' Cole, Dinah Washington, etc. But many years before 'Pops' (Mr. Armstrong) would have a huge hit with "Hello Dolly," he'd recorded "Black and Blue," a subtle comment on racism, and Blues legend **'Big Bill' Broonzy** had recorded "Black, Brown & White," featuring these lyrics:

> *If you white, you alright;*
> *If you brown, stick around;*
> *But as you is black, oh brother*
> *Get back, get back, get back . . .*

(Copyright ownership information not obtainable;
Fair Use Doctrine asserted.)

Racism and segregation take a heavy toll on all aspects of a society. **Billie Holiday** recorded "Strange Fruit," about victims of lynching, for Commodore Records in 1939, but I would not become aware of this song until I became an activist for social change. The roots of Rock 'n' Roll largely grew in the soil of Blues, "jump" Jazz and what came to be called Rhythm and Blues, and somewhat later, Soul music. I passed through adolescence in virtually lily-white Syosset, New York, taking a portable battery-powered transistor radio with me wherever I could. My constant companions were the WMCA 'Good Guys' (disc jockeys) and their arch-rivals on WINS, led by Murray Kaufman, a.k.a. 'Murray the K.' These were the archetypal New York City Top 40 stations on the AM radio band.

Despite the dominance of white performers on the pop music scene, the mix heard on radio airwaves began to change as the Sixties decade progressed. I was sold on James Brown from the moment I heard "Please, Please, Please," "Try Me" and "This is a Man's World." Then Motown arrived—"The Sound of Young America": a brilliant marketing slogan, for it didn't specify just young "black America"—bringing a whole slew of artists. I had a towering crush on Diana Ross of The Supremes, and I'm certain I wasn't the only "white boy" so smitten. The Four Tops, The Temptations, **Stevie Wonder** ("12-year-old musical genius!"), **Marvin Gaye**—hit after hit came flowing from that Detroit songwriting/publishing/recording power-house. Outside the Motown stable, Aretha Franklin ruled as 'The Queen of Soul' and the likes of Ray Charles, **Sam Cooke**, Jackie Wilson and Otis Redding had big mainstream hits. Mr. Cooke's "A Change Is Gonna Come" was popular in 1964. Harry Belafonte was very popular; it would be some time, as he became increasingly outspoken, before we would find out the depth of his feelings about societal ills. Trini Lopez, Ritchie Valens, and soon Jose Feliciano were stars representing the country's Hispanic heritage. Gradually, my generation acquired the opportunity to expand our musical horizons as the larger society became a bit more integrated.

Social commentary began to be documented fairly early in the history of recorded music. The father and son team of John and Alan Lomax had their field recording gear on the road, documenting chain gangs singing work songs, "field hollers," tales of farmers in distress during the Dust Bowl of the 1930s, etc. This is how the world discovered the existence of performers like Huddie Ledbetter, a.k.a. '**Lead Belly.**' Too, there were trade union ballads and combative labor anthems. I was aware of the talent of **Paul Robeson** when I was growing up, but only later would I learn of the degree of grief laid at his door by the Establishment, punishment for his public praise of the Soviet Union in addition to his criticism of US racism. It was actually Steve Allen, hosting "The Tonight Show" in its early years, who made me aware of **Oscar Brown, Jr.** The latter's lyrics for trumpeter Nat Adderley's "Work Song," appearing on Oscar's 1960 debut LP *Sin & Soul*, were inspired by the chain gang song tradition documented by the Lomaxes. In 1992, I had the great honor to interview Mr. Brown when I was a Jazz radio broadcaster in Connecticut.

Jazz bassist/composer **Charles Mingus** did not hesitate to slam the racism of the Establishment; his "Original Faubus Fables," about a certain governor of Arkansas resistant to integration of public schools, still exemplifies brilliant social commentary. At the end of the Sixties decade, Jazz artists **Les McCann** and **Eddie Harris** recorded what would become a classic version of "Compared to What," penned by **Gene McDaniels**. That version was done in concert at the 1969 Montreux Jazz Festival in Switzerland. The lyrics touched on various social issues and made an unmistakable reference to a certain war that was raging in Southeast Asia. ("Havin' one doubt [about the war], They call it treason!") And of course, people like **Woody Guthrie** and **Pete Seeger** had long been writing, singing and recording their own contributions to the musical literature of social protest. But with the exceptions of the young **Bob Dylan**, Oscar Brown, Jr. and Pete Seeger—the latter, a survivor of McCarthyism, actually could occasionally get material played on commercial radio stations—I remained unaware of many of these figures until my own commitment to social change brought me into new circles of knowledgeable friends.

Pete Seeger's anti-war ballad "Where Have All the Flowers Gone?" was on the airwaves while I was still in junior high school. (The version by The Kingston Trio had been a hit record in 1962.) The very year I entered the Army, Seeger released *Waist Deep in the Big Muddy and Other Love Songs* on the Columbia Records label. The title song of the album told of an incident on a Marines Basic Training facility during World War II, in the bayous of Louisiana, where the arrogance of an officer led to his own drowning. Cockily proclaiming that the river in front of them can be safely forded, " . . . the big fool says to push on," ordering a platoon of trainees to follow him into the water. Toward the end of the song, Seeger famously states that before long even a tall man will find the water too deep. Lyndon Johnson was surely the tallest US President since Abraham Lincoln, and the reference was plain. Ironically, CBS Inc., owner of Columbia Records, censored Mr. Seeger's attempt to perform "Waist Deep . . . " on its own "Smothers Brothers Comedy Hour" program later in 1967.

Joan Baez, Simon & Garfunkel, Peter, Paul & Mary and others had songs heard by millions. In fact, Peter, Paul & Mary's version of "Blowin' in the Wind," penned by that young fellow from Minnesota who called himself Dylan, reached number two on Billboard magazine's Popular Music chart in August 1963, the month they sang it live at the massive Civil Rights March on Washington. The advent of "progressive" radio on the FM band would soon open the door to greater freedom in questioning the Established Order. The biggest issue of the day was the civil rights struggle here in the US, with the then-escalating war in Southeast Asia starting to gain attention.

There were oddballs, who the music industry had trouble pigeonholing but came to realize it could not ignore; indeed, could even make a buck or two from. They were people who penned lyrics like those of Bob Dylan, addressing the "Masters of War" who reap profits from mass murder, wishing for their deaths and vowing to stand over their graves to make sure we're rid of them. This was serious stuff, issued by one of the world's oldest and most respected record labels, Columbia. This young man had the audacity to challenge the Conventional Wisdom soon after the Cuban Missile Crisis made mutual nuclear annihilation between the US and the USSR all too plausible. In other songs, he employed devastating wit to reveal that the Emperor's new clothes were absent. In "Talkin' World War III Blues," from *The Freewheelin' Bob Dylan* (1963), he even managed to take a swipe at vapid Pop Music lyrics.

Even if Dylan's apparent concern about social issues expressed on the earliest recordings was but half-hearted—that is to say, his only real concern was becoming rich and famous—these albums produced sparkling examples of social criticism possessing seldom-equalled brilliance, I contend. "The Lonesome Death of Hattie Carroll," about an African-American housemaid slain with virtual impunity by her rich employer in Maryland, ranks among the most powerful songs I've ever encountered. It is vastly superior to, say, the muddled politics of P.F. Sloan's "Eve of Destruction" (popularized by Barry McGuire), a number one hit on the radio as I entered my senior year of high school.

It was only after my arrival at Syracuse University that I discovered the outspokenly anti-war and generally anti-Establishment music of **Phil Ochs**, subject of my teaching exercise at Valley Forge General Hospital, as recounted in **CHAPTER 4**. Phil's song "Outside of a Small Circle of Friends" is a catalog of social phenomena we really should be concerned about—the Kitty Genovese case, where multiple citizens were aware a woman was being stabbed within their eyesight or hearing range but failed to call the police; a black man sentenced to 30 years in prison for possession of a single marijuana joint; the plight of the very poor, "sweating in the ghetto"; a publisher on trial for printing "obscene" literature. Shouldn't we all get off our asses and do something? But "demonstrations are a drag" and we're having too much fun playing Monopoly. And anyway, it wouldn't really interest anyone "outside of a small circle of friends." Complacency and apathy seemed to be winning the day. By this time, too, I was fully aware of Joan Baez. By the time I would report for induction into the Army, I owned all but one of the LPs issued up to that time by Oscar Brown, Jr.; all of Dylan's early works; Phil Ochs's *I Ain't Marching Anymore* and *Phil Ochs In Concert* albums (the latter contained "Cops of the World"); the early Beatles records; some Baez; and, of course, some James Brown. I had also discovered the magnificent (and sadly under-appreciated) voice of Leon Bibb, the splendid singing duo of Joe & Eddie, and an assortment of other "American roots music" items.

Space does not permit a truly comprehensive essay here on songs of protest and other social commentary. That would require a separate book, and indeed, whole books on the subject have been published. I do want to make clear, though, that this music did not evaporate when the 1960s came to an end. Since oppression, bigotry and injustice are very much still alive and well—indeed, thriving—in today's world, singer-songwriters are still commenting on our plight. Witness just these few gems that followed on the heels of the pinnacle of the movement to end the Vietnam War, from artists better known for love songs and bouncy Pop music: Marvin Gaye's 1971 album *What's Goin' On* featured, in the title tune, an exquisite commentary on the events of the times, with its references to police brutality and protests against same, demands for equality, and the declaration that "war is not the answer." The album, featuring additional songs like "Inner City Blues" and "Mercy Mercy Me (The Ecology)," sold a huge number of copies. The very next year appeared Stevie Wonder's *Talking Book*. A perhaps under-appreciated selection on this album was "Big Brother." The narrator is a poor resident of a ghetto, barely getting by economically (" . . . my name is nobody . . ."). He condemns Big Brother for having " . . . killed all our leaders . . . " and ends with a warning: "I don't even have to do nothin' to you/You'll cause your own country to fall."

The late **Gil Scott-Heron** (1949-2011) was an extremely gifted commentator on our times, with a deep, rich singing voice and ability to deliver his own poetry with dynamic rhythm. In the early 1970s, with Nixon's Watergate scandal on everyone's mind, Gil's music even "crossed over" to receive airplay on mainstream "progressive" Rock radio stations—or, at least, in New York City, where I was residing at the time. No one, but no one, was recording commentaries on contemporary events like his "Pardon Our Analysis (We Beg Your Pardon, America)," a spoken-word piece too long for radio airplay, except on some open-minded non-commercial stations. Scott-Heron's song "Winter in America" was probably the composition that would gain most radio play in his career. Like Stevie Wonder's "Big Brother," he spoke of the murders of leaders of the Civil Rights Movement, and furthermore he questioned rhetorically if there was anything left of our society worth trying to save. I had the pleasure and honor to meet Gil in person once, in Detroit, Michigan in 1981. Gil authored a memoir, The Last Holiday (The Grove Press; New York, 2012), which recounts his efforts, with Stevie Wonder, among others, to have the Dr. Martin Luther King, Jr. national holiday enacted into law. At the time of this writing, several volumes of Gil's poetry/lyrics are also available in print.

The rise of environmental consciousness

With the war in Southeast Asia being questioned openly like no previous conflict, other societal issues were no longer taboo. Equal treatment for women, American "Indians" (Buffy Ste.-Marie's career got underway in the 1960s), homosexuals, the physically or mentally challenged—everything was fair game for analysis, demands for change, agitation, action. It was really the Civil Rights Movement of the 1950s into the '60s that had blown the doors open. But there was one overriding issue that affected everyone, regardless of skin color, sex, religion or politics: the planet's environment was deteriorating due to the impact of human industrial activity.

Awareness of this issue was not brand new to popular music, as the folksingers had been addressing the threat of nuclear armageddon and industrial pollution for some time. But in 1970, the year Earth Day was first observed, there appeared two major rock anthems touching on this subject. One was performed by **Spirit** on their astounding LP *Twelve Dreams of Dr. Sardonicus* (brilliantly produced by David Briggs); the other was by legendary British bluesman and finder of new talent, **John Mayall**, on his *USA Union* album. But before exploring those songs, let us examine the work of a songwriter not quoted in the body of this book, **Dino Valenti** (birth name Chester Powers, Jr.), of the band Quicksilver Messenger Service. His "What About Me?" (on album of same name) was a virtual anthem of youthful rebellion. The song was considered too long for most commercial radio stations to play, and when released as a single in 1971 it barely grabbed the bottom rung of Billboard magazine's Top 100 Pop Chart for that year. It touched on the destruction of the natural world and urged like-minded concerned people to do something about it, though this would make them virtual "outlaws" within the larger society. The narrator is defiantly asking those in power what they're going to do about a youth rebellion, with the "me" a stand-in for the many. As we know, the Establishment's answer was repression, repression and more repression.

"Nature's Way," credited to **Randy California**, appeared on the Spirit album mentioned above. The "dying trees" are " . . . nature's way of telling you . . . " that something is wrong, very wrong. Mr. Mayall's song "Nature's

Disappearing" pulls no punches in laying blame for the damaged environment. "Man's a filthy creature . . . " he declares, and we are collectively guilty
of a massive crime against Creation. Future generations will pay a dear
price for our present indifference. Focused only on short-term economic
gain, those running the world casually dismissed all these concerns and
the Global Climate Catastrophe we are now experiencing is the bitter fruit
of generations of failed leadership. It is likely that even the authors of these
songs from 1970 could not imagine just how prophetic their words would
prove to be. This music impinged upon my consciousness courtesy of the
"Progressive FM" radio station in San Jose that had become the only source
I needed for what was new and worthwhile during my lengthy stay at Fort
Ord, California.

Official Government Documents

General Introduction: The United States Congress had instituted the legislation creating the Freedom of Information Act (FOIA) in response to the corrupt and unconstitutional conduct of the Nixon administration. These practices, these abuses of the power of the Executive branch, had started to come to light during and in the wake of the Watergate scandal. Many political activists/opponents of the Vietnam War took advantage of the opportunity to examine what the Federal Government had been doing to try to counter opposition to the war. I was but one of many to do this initiating the process in the late 1970s. I had originally planned to publish images of the actual documents, but this would have resulted in poor quality reproduction and forced the reader to employ a magnifying glass to examine them. Therefore, I have opted to retype the relevant segments of select documents. If you are familiar with the history of "COINTELPRO" and other government operations to spy on American citizens, and actively attempt to disrupt movements for social justice in this country, you will have no doubt of the authenticity of what appears below. Though military personnel being Absent Without Official Leave (AWOL) is strictly a matter for military "justice" to address, it is clear that the FBI was working closely with the military. The accuracy of the information being exchanged was less than unimpeachable. Also, note that when the FBI refers to an informant, this is not necessarily an undercover agent conducting surveillance of anti-war activities. It can simply be a clerk at an Information Desk at a newspaper or a petty bureaucrat in a local government office. I have "translated" FBI abbreviations in what follows to best of my ability. Finally, I note that nine pages of my FBI file were deemed too "sensitive" to be released to me. We Americans have been living in a National Security State for decades now, it should be clear.

FBI Report of Boston University Teach-In, November 1968 (CHAPTER V)

Dated November 23, 1968, this report was sent by teletype from FBI Boston office to Bureau HQ in Washington, D.C.

re: **The Resistance—teach-in, Boston University, eleven twenty two last, VIDEM, possible FUDE. [Vietnam Demonstrators; Fugitive Deserter]**
Provost Marshal's Office, Ft. Devens, Mass., advised Boston FBI today that two individuals who participated in captioned matter might surrender themselves at Ft. Devens today.

Provost Marshal's Office, Ft. Devens, later advised Gregory G. Laxer, AWOL ten twenty two last, from Medical Student Detachment, Valley Forge General Hospital, Phoenixville, PA, and [**REDACTED, but this was clearly Martin Gross, as recounted in CHAPTER V of this book—GL**], AWOL from Overseas Replacement Station, Ft. Dix, N.J., as of six twenty eight last. Both due for reassignment to Vietnam. Both voluntarily surrendered themselves to MP at Ft. Devens this date.

Both individuals arrived at Ft. Devens in a bus with approximately twenty five to thirty civilians. These civilians, not further identified, photographed surrender to MPs. No incident. Both individuals now in confinement at Ft. Devens.

Bureau is requested to advise Boston if subjects are fugitive deserters so that appropriate FD two twenties can be submitted. Local agencies advised.

FBI Documents relating to Hawaii Sanctuary (CHAPTER VII)

In a memo sent by encoded teletype to FBI Headquarters on August 21, 1969, and initially marked "Confidential" for the next 20 years, the Hawaiian FBI Office reported as follows:

TO: Director (encoded)

FROM: Honolulu

ATTENTION Deserter Desk and Division Five

re: Servicemen in sanctuary at the Church of the Crossroads, Honolulu, Hawaii, Deserter Matter, **Sedition [emphasis added--GL]**; SDS-TR **[Students for a Democratic Society--The Resistance]**

re: Honolulu radiogram, August 20 last, and Bureau teletype, August 20 last.

[REDACTED], Honolulu, advised on August 21 instant that an additional serviceman had taken sanctuary at the Church of the Crossroads during the morning hours of August twenty one instant. This individual is identified as Greg Laxer, E-one, U.S. Army, age twenty one, no Serial Number or date of birth available, whose home is Long Island, New York, who has reportedly been AWOL for over 50 days from Fort Devens Massachusetts. **[Technically, I was AWOL from Oakland.]**

The next document, dated August 30, 1969, refers undoubtedly to Major Geary (though his name is redacted), the obnoxious Army Chaplain who had visited us at the sanctuary. The issue under discussion--the possibility of relocating the AWOLs to The Wesley Foundation in Honolulu--never came to my attention during the sanctuary. I can only surmise that a plan had been hatched for Armed Services Police to arrest everyone the moment we stepped off the church grounds.

re: Servicemen in sanctuary at the Church of the Crossroads.

On August twenty-nine instant **[REDACTED]**, U.S. Army Chaplain, was interviewed by bureau agent concerning previously reported contact had by him with **[REDACTED]**, Wesley Foundation, Honolulu. **[REDACTED]** advised that he has never had a contact with **[REDACTED]**. However, on the afternoon of August twenty-seven last he received a telephone call from a member of the board of officers of the Wesley Foundation, whose name he could not recall, who invited him to attend a meeting of that board on the night of August twenty-seven. **[REDACTED]** said that this individual stated that at this meeting discussion was to be held concerning the feasibility of inviting the servicemen in sanctuary at the Church of the Crossroads to continue their sanctuary at the Wesley Foundation, University Avenue, Honolulu. This individual informed **[REDACTED]** that he desired him to be present at this meeting to give arguments **opposing [emphasis added--GL]** the action of inviting the servicemen to take sanctuary at the Wesley Foundation. **[REDACTED]** advised that because of the adverse publicity he has received in the past in connection with his removal **[at request of the church directors--GL]** from the Church of the Crossroads, he has been instructed by his superiors that he should not participate in any discussion at the Wesley Foundation at this time.

[REDACTED] stated that from this conversation with the aforementioned board member, he was of the impression that the Wesley Foundation is seriously considering inviting the AWOL servicemen to take sanctuary there.

[REDACTED], Honolulu Police Department, advised instant date that he learned from the office of Barry Chung, Prosecuting Attorney, City and County of Honolulu, that on August thirty next inspectors of the County Health Department will again check the premises of the Church of the Crossroads and note any changes made in attempt to conform with building codes. Upon completion of the inspection a report will be made on the findings and subsequently submitted to the Prosecuting Attorney's office. **[REDACTED]** intimated that this action would probably take somewhere in the neighborhood of three weeks.

On August twenty-nine instant sources who have furnished reliable information in the past advised they learned this date that the Students for a Democratic Society--The Resistance are seriously considering fighting in a court of law any attempt by the City and County of Honolulu to evict them from the Church of the Crossroads, and that the SDS-TR have no present plans to move the AWOL servicemen from sanctuary at the Church of the Crossroads to any other location.

[final page:] **Classify Confidential to protect sources.**

Identifying data concerning **[REDACTED]** and Greg Laxer, previously reported as entering sanctuary, has not as of this date been received. Bureau will be advised when such info is received. Military intelligence agencies advised.

END

Here is a memo dated September 11, 1969. I am listed as a deserter because I had been AWOL in excess of the magic 30 days, but this status ultimately had to be determined by military authorities in court-martial. The FBI here reminds the Army that apprehending and trying AWOLs is their responsibility, not that of Mr. Hoover's agency. The only point on which I could ever agree with J. Edgar!

To: The Adjutant General
Department of the Army
The Pentagon
Washington, D.C. 20310

From: John Edgar Hoover, Director
Subject: **[first individual's identity REDACTED]**
Gregory G. Laxer
Deserter

Enclosed are seven copies each of Department of Defense Form 553 (DD-553) on the above-captioned subjects.

These DD-553s are being returned and no action is being taken by this Bureau inasmuch as both individuals were reported to be in the Church of the Crossroads in Honolulu, Hawaii, and their presence is well known to the military. It is the military's responsibility to apprehend these men in accordance with the memorandum from the Assistant Secretary of Defense for Assistant Secretaries of Military Departments, dated December 23, 1968. NOTE: The two deserters are in the Church of the Crossroads in Honolulu and this information is set forth by the Army on the DD-553 concerning Gregory G. Laxer. In the memorandum from the Assistant Secretary of Defense, referred to above, it is the responsibility for the military to apprehend military personnel **in sanctuary situations [emphasis added— GL]** where there are servicemen in absent without leave status as well as others in a deserter status.

The next document, dated September 25, 1969 lists the final 12 military personnel in sanctuary, arrested at Church of the Crossroads on September 12, by which time I was long gone from Honolulu. All their names were redacted by the FBI, though this information would have been published in local newspapers. A second page of the memo states:

The following servicemen who were in sanctuary have not been returned to military control to date:
[REDACTED—I cannot be sure who this was—GL]

Gregory G. Laxer, PVT (E-1), U.S. Army
AWOL July 1, 1969, en route from Ft. Devens, Massachusetts to Oakland, California then Vietnam
Entered Church August 20, 1969

Another FBI document, also dated September 25, 1969, was generated in New York City and sent via teletype to Headquarters. It refers to an earlier report on the September 18 demonstration that led to my being returned to military control. The subject is the sponsoring organization of the demo, Youth Against War & Fascism (YAWF), the "youth arm" of Workers World Party (WWP).

Subject: Youth Against War and Fascism/WWP
Enclosed for the Bureau are 10 copies of an LHM **[letterhead memorandum, an FBI document to be shared with other intel or law enforcement agencies—GL]** concerning activities of captioned group. Copies of this LHM are being furnished locally to the 108th MI **["Military Intelligence"]** Group **[other agencies' abbreviations follow, including the Secret Service—GL].**
[A list of REDACTED official memo recipients follows. GL]

A characterization of the WWP appears in the appendix hereto.

On September 22, 1969, [REDACTED] New York City Police Dept. advised that the following described persons had been arrested on disorderly conduct charges, as an outgrowth of the above described demonstration: [**All names but mine REDACTED—GL**]

Gregory Laxer, white male, attired in United States Army Enlisted Uniform, residing 109 Candy Lane, Syosset, New York.

✳ ✳ ✳

FBI Documents from my post-Army life (see: EPILOGUE)

The following document, dated November 28, 1972 is a summary of an FBI investigation of my political activities—that is to say, my exercising freedoms provided by the First Amendment to the Constitution of the United States— conducted between September 1 and November 20, 1972. This was the work of FBI offices in New York City and in New York State's capital, Albany. The report is marked classified Confidential for the following 20 years. I now had the honor of being an FBI "Case," justified as "SM-WWP": Security Matter—Workers World Party.

A suitable photograph of the subject is available in the New York office. [REDACTED] was by Special Agent [REDACTED] who attempted to contact the subject [**date and place apparently REDACTED**].

Attached are two copies of a FD-376 and one photograph of the subject which are for transmittal to Secret Service, Washington, D.C. [**Secret Service? Was I a threat to the President? This is addressed several pages later. —GL**]

While stationed at Fort Devens, Massachusetts, as a medic, the subject applied for a discharge as a conscientious objector in January of 1969. It should also be noted that on his army application the subject stated that a security clearance was necessary for his employment in 1967, at Amperex Electronics, 230 Duffy Avenue, Hicksville, New York.

It is felt that the subject's activities do not warrant his inclusion of the ADEX **[an index of subjects under active surveillance —GL]** of the NY office; however, NY will follow his activities and make further recommendation.

INFORMANT
Identity of Source/File Where Located
[all REDACTED]

The following sources of the New York office were contacted regarding the subject in October, 1972, and November, 1972, and were unable to provide any information:
[a short list, REDACTED; possibly infiltrators of leftist groups, but I can't be sure —GL]

LEADS
ALBANY
AT ALBANY, NEW YORK. Will cover leads as set out in referenced letter.
NEW YORK
AT NEW YORK, NEW YORK. Will follow the subject's activities and advise the Bureau of any pertinent information and will attempt to verify subject's arrest by reviewing NYCPD records.

Next comes the memo from FBI to Director, United States Secret Service, Department of the Treasury, Washington, D.C. 20220, with a copy to NYC office of same. Observe the checklist of potential justifications for the Secret Service to keep an eye on a citizen.

Dear Sir:
The information furnished herewith concerns an individual or organization believed to be covered by the agreement between the FBI and Secret Service

concerning protective responsibilities, and to fall within the category or categories checked.

1. ___ Threats or actions against persons protected by Secret Service.
2. ___ Attempts or threats to redress grievances.
3. ___ Threatening or abusive statement about U.S. or foreign official.
4. ___ Participation in civil disturbances, anti-U.S. demonstrations or hostile incidents against foreign diplomatic establishments.
5. ___ Illegal bombing, bomb-making or other terrorist activity.
6. ___ Defection from U.S. or indicates desire to defect.
7. _X_ Potentially dangerous because of background, emotional instability or activity in groups engaged in activities inimical to U.S.

Photograph enclosed.

Very truly yours,
L. Patrick Gray, III
Acting Director

[Necessary comments: The First Amendment to the United States Constitution states that "Congress shall make no law . . . (prohibiting) the right of the people peaceably to assemble, and to petition the Government for a redress of grievances." Now we see that the Executive Branch nevertheless authorized the Secret Service to conduct surveillance on citizens seeking a redress of grievances. As to the third item above, yes, I plead guilty to having made unkind statements about any number of U.S. officials! Concerning item four, this potentially covers every citizen who ever took part in a demonstration calling for an end to the American War in Vietnam, and/or protesting lack of protection for members of racial minorities, etc. The implication is that to express these sentiments makes one a potential threat against the lives of government officials. Item five, illegal bombing or terrorist activity? Millions of people around the globe considered the US government itself massively guilty of these crimes. Item six indicates that merely expressing a "desire" to renounce one's citizenship is a virtual crime. Finally, item seven is the only one checked for my case, since I was an active member of the American Servicemen's Union and Workers World Party.]

The FBI report continues:

Copy to: Secret Service, NYC

Character: Security Matter—Workers World Party

Synopsis: **[REDACTED TOTALLY. Presumably this is background explanation of why FBI was keeping a file on me—GL]**

DETAILS:

This report is predicated upon information that in the March 31, 1972, issue
of "The Bond," self-identified as the voice of the American Servicemen's
Union, the subject was listed as the Technical Editor of this paper.

BACKGROUND

Birth

[REDACTED] advised that the subject was born _____ **[redacted
by GL]**, at Jackson Heights, New York.

Citizenship

The subject is a citizen of the United States by reason of his birth.

Residence

On November 20, 1972, it was determined by **[REDACTED]**, Special Agent
of the Federal Bureau of Investigation (FBI) that the subject resides at 22
West 21st Street, New York City, New York. *[Necessary comments: Here
are your tax dollars at work, fellow citizens. Workers World Party for many
years maintained its national office at 46 West 21st Street. However, I never
resided at 22 West 21st Street, I never entered such a building (which was
likely a commercial, not a residential, address anyway), and I'm not aware
any member of WWP ever resided at such an address. Great job of sleuth-
ing, FBI!]*

Employment

The March 31, 1972, issue of "The Bond," self-identified as the voice of the American Servicemen's Union, 58 West 25th Street, New York, New York, listed the subject as being on "The Bond" staff as the Technical Editor. *[More inaccuracy, since all my political activity was strictly voluntary and in no way constituted "employment." The following summaries of revolutionary organizations are essentially historically accurate—score one for the FBI!]*

The American Servicemen's Union (ASU) was founded in 1968, by the Workers World Party (WWP). Its objective is to cause discontent among military enlisted personnel and call for the establishment of a servicemen's union. *[I must point out here that the military itself was the cause of discontent; ASU was merely trying to take advantage of it to help end the criminal American War in Vietnam.]* Its main propaganda weapon is the publication, "The Bond—The Servicemen's Newspaper."

The WWP was founded in 1959 by individuals who disagreed with policies of the Socialist Workers Party (SWP). The WWP dissidents advocated unconditional support of the Soviet Union and the building of a revolutionary party geared to the overthrow of Capitalism. More recently, the WWP has called for peaceful solutions to Sino-Soviet disputes; however, the WWP generally supports the Peoples Republic of China in its ideological differences with the Soviet Union. *[This stance was evolving, with Mao in declining health and his successors-in-waiting embracing Nixon and Capitalism.]*

The SWP has been designated [**as meriting surveillance—GL**] pursuant to Executive Order 10450.

Army Service

[**REDACTED**] advised that the subject enlisted in the United States Army on May 12, 1967, and was discharged under honorable conditions on July 6, 1971, and transferred to the United States Army Reserve until March 6, 1974.

[REDACTED] was advised that the subject had been trained in basic combat, medical corpsman clinical specialist, and was awarded the National Defense Service Medal—Sharp Shooter.

Education

[REDACTED] advised that the subject had attended Syracuse University, Syracuse, New York, as of 1966.

[Next appears a notice that the next page is entirely withheld from me, then comes the following:]

[Two fairly brief entries at top of page REDACTED]

MISCELLANEOUS

During October, 1972, and November, 1972, various confidential sources in the New York City area who are familiar with New Left and Communist activities were contacted regarding the subject and they advised they were not familiar with the subject or his activities. [**The benefit of not associating with stoolpigeons!—GL**]

The report concludes with some "fine print":

All sources (except any listed below) whose identities are concealed in referenced communication have furnished reliable information in the past.

This document contains neither recommendations nor conclusions of the FBI. It is the property of the FBI and is loaned to your agency [**Secret Service in this case—GL**]; it and its contents are not to be distributed outside your agency nor duplicated within your agency.

The memo concludes with two brief paragraphs:

The subject's activities do not warrant his inclusion on the ADEX of the New York Office, and in view of his occupation as a Technical Editor of "The Bond," it is not felt an interview should be conducted at this time.

In the event further pertinent information comes to the attention of the New York Office, the Bureau will be advised.

[Comments: So here is a reference to "an interview." If I was not to be taken into custody and interrogated, would this interview be voluntary on my part, accepting an invitation from the NY Office to come in for a friendly chat with a Special Agent? Would the first thing out of the questioner's mouth be "We know you reside at 22 West 21st Street in Manhattan"?! If someone in the Bureau thought I might be willing to become an informant on their behalf, someone didn't have his head screwed on properly!]

Application for Conscientious Objector Status

Following is my Statement in support of my Application for Separation by reason of Conscientious Objection, per Army Regulation 635-200 [see CHAPTER VI]. I have re-typed the text verbatim, with correction of the numerous slip-ups by the Army clerk-typist who transcribed it originally from my handwritten original. This document was appended to the Trial Record of my Special Court-Martial in November 1969 [see APPENDIX 5]. The letters 'a,' 'b,' etc. correspond to questions posed on the application form.

a.) I believe in non-violence as the only sane, moral, constructive way for human beings to deal with and relate to one another. Although I lack conventional religious beliefs, I feel that I qualify for Conscientious Objection status just as fully as an orthodoxly religious person. Below I will explain how my beliefs may be considered as essentially religious.

b.) I am applying for discharge as a Conscientious Objector despite lack of conventional religious beliefs. Although as an absolute moral law, this [**principle of non-violence**] has unquestionably been true since before Jesus Christ's time, it is especially relevant at the present time. Richard M. Nixon is obsessed with the insanity of nuclear overkill. Enough nuclear weapons have been stockpiled to destroy the Earth's population many times over. Violence only leads to more violence; Christian love begets forgiveness, humility, selflessness, understanding, peace. Christian love, in my belief, must embody non-violence. An explanation of my view of Christ is appropriate here. When I speak of Jesus, I speak of Christ the man. Not maintaining a conventional belief in God, I do not conceive of a divine Christ; I do not believe in "immaculate conception" or the "Resurrection."

I believe simply that Christ was a man who made of his life a great force for goodness, truth and love. It is in such a sense that I feel justified in calling myself a Christian. In recent years the religious community, in the "God is Dead" movement, has found members in its midst proclaiming themselves "Christian Atheists." I am an agnostic practicing Christian love.

I was raised in an atmosphere conducive to free-thinking; religious beliefs were not forced upon me, neither were atheistic dogmas. My parents are agnostic and so am I, by choice. I feel that Man is incapable of having certain knowledge of either the existence or non-existence of a Supreme Being. In support of my claim, I quote from the precedent-setting Supreme Court decision in the case of U.S. v. Seeger, March 8, 1965. The court ruled that Mr. Seeger, a self-professed agnostic, must be recognized as a Conscientious Objector and deferred from military service: "[T]he test of belief 'in relation to a Supreme Being' is whether a given belief that is sincere and meaningful occupies a place in the life of its possessor parallel to that filled by the orthodox belief in God of one who clearly qualifies for the exemption. Where such beliefs have parallel positions in the lives of their respective holders, we cannot say that one is 'in a relation to a Supreme Being' and the other is not. The test might be stated in these words: a sincere and meaningful belief which occupies in the life of its possessor a place parallel to that filled by God of those admittedly qualifying for the exemption comes within the statutory definition; while the applicant's words may differ, the test is simple of application. It is essentially an objective one, namely does the claimed belief occupy the same place in the life of the objector as an orthodox belief in God holds in the life of one clearly qualified for exemption. We believe this construction embraces the ever-broadening understanding of the modern religious community." It may be argued that the Seeger decision, since it involved the Selective Service System, has no bearing on the military. However, since the military bases its decisions on the same criteria, asking questions very similar to those on Selective Service System Form 150, I think this decision by the interpreters of the laws of our land is very relevant to my predicament in the Army. It is my contention that my belief in non-violence as my way of life (and is this not what a religion should be, a way of life?) holds a position in my life parallel to the beliefs of a religious pacifist. The previously mentioned "Christian Atheists" have not been tried as heretics. The definitions and boundaries of religion have been broadening over the years. In my devotion to non-violence I think that I fit within these boundaries.

Though lacking belief in the personification of truth, love and perfection as a white-bearded Supreme Being called God, I nevertheless do conceive of some sort of mystical life force. It is difficult to speak of such concepts in lucid, pragmatic language because of the limits of the human mind in understanding the Universe and Man's role in it.

I have developed a reverence for life in all its myriad forms. I believe that each and every human life is sacred and "lower" forms of life deserve all the respect possible. I literally do not step on an ant if I can avoid doing so. I have often thought of becoming a vegetarian. Although it is Nature's way for predators to slaughter other animals for food, I object to the cruel methods used in the slaughterhouses. I totally oppose hunting for "sport." To take the life of a beautiful, wild, free animal and hang its head on a wall to glut the ego of the hunter is an utterly despicable act.

All one need do is dwell on the wonder of the natural world to be awe-inspired and realize that there must be some organizing, driving force behind our presence here on the third planet from the sun. So much our greatest scientists do not yet understand. Can animals reason? How does Man learn? How do salmon find their way back to their spawning place after traversing thousands of miles of ocean? How does the cocoon of some species of butterflies assume for camouflage the color of the tree trunk to which it is attached? Or, more basic and mind boggling, what is the origin of the Universe? And the greatest miracle of all is the growth of a human being from a single fertilized egg, under the direction of the genetic code. The beauty and magnificence of the phenomenon is staggering.

There are natural laws in the Universe which seem to have "a goal"; life on our planet has evolved and progressed for millions of years, seemingly "aiming" for stability and a balance of nature, peace and tranquillity. Yes, peace and tranquillity: all other creatures kill only out of necessity; only man commits wanton, senseless murder. His capacity for destruction, particularly in this, the Nuclear Age, is staggering. His violent, aggressive

tendencies are not natural—they are virtually psychotic and must be subli-
mated with the help of men of reason and goodwill. This must be my role
on Earth, as it must be for all Christians, be they members of the church or
not. I cannot in good conscience participate in activities to the contrary; I
cannot and will not participate in the military any further.

I have acquired these beliefs over a period of several years. My interest
in natural science began when I was still in elementary school; I devoured
voraciously book after book on astronomy, evolution, paleontology, etc. As I
grew older, I broadened my diet to include philosophical works. I have read
much of Thoreau and essays by Tolstoi on non-violence. I have not yet gotten
around to Gandhi but I am greatly interested [in] and in admiration of his
way of life. I recently read several works of the late Martin Luther King, Jr.
During my short stay in college, I spent my time reading serious studies of
pacifism, most of them by religious objectors. I saw no great gulf between
their opinions and mine except their reference to God, in the conventional
sense. With this background I enlisted in the Army on May 12, 1967. I did
not want to be drafted and placed in something like Infantry or Artillery.
I chose and was given a Medical MOS. It had not occurred to me to apply
to Selective Service for Conscientious Objector status because I felt I could
serve in the Army without violating my beliefs and principles.

As the months went by, however, a growing realization chafed my
conscience. I came to see that merely by wearing the uniform and cooperating with the military machine I was helping to spread the climate of
violence that threatens to tear civilization asunder. I have come to believe
after more than 17 months in the Army that every man in uniform has on
his hands the blood of his brothers, American as well as Vietnamese. The
Vietnamese are my brothers; in the eyes of a Christian, all men are brothers.
Churchgoers who preach this on Sunday but fail to practice it during the
week are hypocrites, not Christians.

I will not participate in the war in Vietnam in any capacity. Although
as a medic I could be a force for goodness, I believe it is more important to
resist the evils of militarism which are creating the casualties. The preceding holds for all wars, but I stress Vietnam because that is the war I have
been ordered to participate in. I intend to continue in the medical field as a

civilian, but will not do so in the military. I will not compromise my beliefs in this matter. I seek to be discharged under honorable conditions, but the rejection of this application would not stop me from wanting to separate myself from the service. I hope that in this statement I have shown myself to fall within the bounds of the definition of Conscientious Objector.

c.) There is no individual upon whom I rely for guidance, due to the fact that I do not participate in organized religion.

d.) **I must make it clear that I am not an absolute pacifist [emphasis added for this book].** Applicants for Conscientious Objector status are often asked questions such as: "What would you do if a thug or maniac was attacking your wife (or mother, sister, etc.)?" My reply is that I would attempt to restrain the assailant by grabbing and pinning his arms, and disarming him. I would try to keep him so restrained until help could arrive; I would not restrain him by smashing his skull with a club, unless I lost my sense of reason in a fit of blind anger. No Conscientious Objector applicant can claim to have perfect self-control at all times. Further, I feel that an applicant who states that he would not use any force at all in such a situation is not being perfectly honest; to stand by helplessly and inert would be cruel and callous. I think that Christ himself would view the situation similarly. One must bear in mind that the previously mentioned hypothetical situation is not analogous to military service. The former is defense of a victim of aggression; the latter is participation in aggression.

e.) Prior to my enlistment, I participated in one peace demonstration. Since enlisting, I have participated in others, in civilian clothing of course. I have worked in the offices of anti-war organizations at such tasks as printing and mailing leaflets. I have never participated in a violent demonstration, nor have I worked in conjunction with anyone seeking the violent over-throw of the government. The last time I deliberately hurt another living being was when I was only 15 years old and hadn't yet acquired my current beliefs. At that time I administered a slightly bloody nose. I have tried to convince others to adopt my beliefs and have done my best to make my life a model for them. I have clung to my belief in non-violence and feel that it qualifies me for status as a Conscientious Objector. My refusal to go to Vietnam or serve further in the Army is in keeping with my beliefs.

f.) I have expressed my beliefs and convictions concerning non-violence and participation in war in writing in letters to my friends and parents. I have expressed my feelings openly and honestly to fellow members of the Army, from Private through Lt. Colonel. I have also expressed them often to sympathetic, as well as hostile, civilians since my enlistment.

* * *

1.) Prior to my enlistment in the US Army I was never associated in any manner with a military organization;
2.) I am not a member of a religious sect or organization;
3.) I have never been a member of any organization not related to labor or politics.

[Application concludes with a list of military and civilian persons who can testify to the sincerity of my beliefs.]

NOTES: 1.) My claim to consider myself, essentially, a "Christian" was a bit of a stretch. To be sure, I had studied considerations of non-violence from a Christian perspective written by the likes of Martin Luther King, Jr., but I considered the authors more humanists than Christians. And I despised then, and still despise, the gross hypocrisy of most of those who proclaim themselves Christians. In today's American politics, the more loudly someone proclaims him- or herself to be a Christian, the more suspect are they of failing to practice what they preach; 2.) the US Supreme Court case I cited above should have served me well in appealing the Army's rejection of my application, and the ruling of the Federal Court in Boston, in June 1969, in favor of the Army, but I opted to avoid treading the long road of legal brambles that process would have set me on. Though I was still vacillating somewhat over the question of refusing to serve any further in uniform in any capacity, my increasing militancy suggested I should continue to resist the war vigorously if I was destined to remain on active duty. What was absolutely sure was that I would not set foot on Vietnamese soil as a member of the US military; 3.) my admission that I was not an "absolute pacifist"—jeopardizing my chance to be approved as a CO—was simply a demonstration of the depth of my honesty; 4.) in contrast, my claim to have only demonstrated against the war in civilian garb since enlisting was, obviously, a lie. Recall my participation in the Boston University teach-in, November 1968 [**CHAPTER V**]. The question to which I was responding was essentially "Explain what actions you have taken to demonstrate the sincerity of your beliefs." I guess we may designate this tactic on my part a "strategic untruth." Or, as Oscar Brown, Jr. proclaimed in one of his songs: "I may be crazy, but I ain't no fool!"

Special Court-Martial Trial Record

NOTE: Due to the technical difficulty of reproducing directly the pages of the Trial Record of my Special Court-Martial held at Fort Dix, New Jersey in late 1969, and the deteriorating condition of pages that were merely photocopies to begin with 50 years ago, I have re-typed the most pertinent sections for inclusion in this appendix. I have excluded superfluous information as seemed prudent. You will note that participants in military legal proceedings are not required to be trained lawyers. The Prosecutor, indeed, was an Infantry Officer assigned to the unit responsible for the base stockade, and had likely tried innumerable soldiers for AWOL by this time. Explanatory notes to liken the proceedings more to a civilian trial appear in [ ], as well as my "sidebar comments" to the reader where I can't resist illuminating certain points. An ellipse (…) indicates that more material followed, but has been deleted by me as superfluous. This record is not a verbatim one of everything said in the proceedings, by the way, but does accurately reflect the arguments of both sides for the most part, with my factual corrections appearing enclosed in brackets.

As explained in **CHAPTER VIII**, the Army initially offered me a jury consisting of all Commissioned Officers, hardly my peers. In a pre-trial hearing (Article 39B Hearing) on November 6, 1969 the Defense challenged this fact and formally requested the presence of enlisted personnel on the jury. Excerpts from those proceedings are directly below.

* * *

Defense counsel moved to dismiss the charges against the accused on the grounds that he was denied his right to a speedy trial as guaranteed by the 6th Amendment to the Constitution of the United States and by Article

10 of the Uniform Code of Military Justice. Counsel further stated that the accused had been held in pre-trial confinement since the 19th of September, 1969 and that this was too long a period of pre-trial confinement.

Trial counsel offered into evidence a Chronology of Delay and a Copy of the Charge Sheet dated 5 November 69 and 3 October 69 respectively, requesting that they be admitted and marked as Appellate Exhibit Number One and Appellate Exhibit Number Two. [I have opted to not include these documents here. —GL] The Chronology and Charge Sheet was [sic] admitted and marked as requested, there being no objection.

Defense counsel argued that the accused was informed of the charges when he first got to SPD and that there was no need for the preparation of 2 Charge Sheets as they already had all the evidence they needed to draw charges against the accused.

The accused elected to make a sworn statement and testified in substance as follows:

DIRECT EXAMINATION

I am GREGORY G. LAXER, PRIVATE E-1, SPD, Fort Dix, New Jersey, a member of the US Army. I AM THE ACCUSED.

I first arrived at SPD on 19 September 69. I was aware of the charges against me. Armed Forces Police Department had the correct information on me when I went AWOL from Oakland on or about 1 July 69. I told them at SPD that I had gone AWOL on 1 July 69. I was placed in the stockade on 19 September 69. I think that I was put in the stockade because when I arrived at SPD I refused to salute an officer. I knew that I was going to the stockade and I knew that I would be charged with being AWOL. I put my correct AWOL dates on a form at SPD.

CROSS EXAMINATION

When I was interviewed I was told that I was being charged with being AWOL.

Defense counsel argued that he had made the motion because of the length of time that it took SPD to prepare the charges against the accused. This time would not have been as long if the charges were drawn from the information that the accused had given to SPD. When SPD went to verify the charges they came up with incorrect charges. This reflects negligence on the part of the government in verifying the charges.

Trial counsel argued that the accused was aware of the charges against him. Counsel further argued that the administrative problems were not the result of negligence or unreasonable delay. There was a continuous effort made to verify these charges. The word of the accused is not enough to base the charges on and expect that they be correct. There were problems in preparing the charge sheet and the charges had to be re-referred and re-verified.

Defense counsel argued that SPD had all the information necessary to draw up correct charges against the accused and that the accused was completely cooperative in helping to prepare these charges.

The military judge announced that the motion was denied.

MOTION: DENIED

Defense counsel moved to dismiss the charges against the accused on the grounds that the jury that had been selected was not a jury of the accused's peers, as guaranteed by Article 6 of the Constitution of the United States. Defense counsel again requested a continuance so that both counsel might submit briefs. Defense counsel stated that he also needed more time so that he might submit further evidence.

Defense counsel stated that his motion was based on the method of selecting the members of the court and the ranks of the various members.

Defense counsel further stated that he would like a continuance in order to get some witnesses from distant localities.

The military judge stated that the court would be closed and that the case would be continued until 13 November 69. Court was closed at 1135 hours, 6 November 69.

*   *   *

Court was called to order at 0945 hours, 13 November 69 and trial counsel stated that all persons who were present when court was closed were again present.

[Court was then closed, i.e. the Jury dismissed from the room, for consideration of the Defense argument from 6 November re: constitution of the Jury. —GL]

The military judge stated that court had been closed to give counsel time to prepare briefs concerning a motion to dismiss the charges based on the composition of the jury.

Defense counsel stated that the jury that had been selected was illegal and unlawful in that it was not a jury of the peers of the accused as guaranteed by the Constitution and the manual [Manual for Courts-Martial, or MCM].

Defense counsel offered into evidence a Stipulation of Expected Testimony dated 13 November 69 requesting that it be entered and marked as Appellate Exhibit Number Three. The Stipulation was admitted and marked as requested, there being no objection.

Defense counsel asked the military judge to note that the stipulation indicates that the enlisted members of the court were limited to those men of a rank of E-6 [Staff Sergeant] or more. It is obvious that there was only to be 3 names submitted and that this eliminated the possibility of the selection being made from a cross section of potential members. The fact that there were to be only 3 members of the enlisted ranks on the court also represents the bare minimum required. Counsel contended that the method of selecting enlisted members of the court violated the accused's constitutional rights. The accused is entitled to a trial by a jury of his peers and it is not possible to consider any of the members of this court as the peer of the accused.

The manual states that we must look to the age, education and length of service of a member of the court to use him as an enlisted member. It seems that it is necessary to look to the decisions in order to get a closer definition of what is necessary for an enlisted man to be qualified to sit on a court. The Federal cases that were checked seem to indicate that the enlisted members of the court ought to be at least equal in grade to the man being tried. It is also clear from the legislative history of this provision that enlisted members of the court were not to be limited to the higher ranks.

Defense counsel concluded that the court should be dissolved and that a new court should be selected by such means as to allow for a proper cross section of prospective members.

Trial counsel argued that the enlisted members of this court were selected by using their reasonable availability as a guideline. The manual gives the convening authority the right to detail members of a court-martial board as he chooses. The convening authority is not required to detail members of any specific rank nor is he required to detail members of the accused's rank. The convening authority has the discretion of determining who is to sit on the board. The members of this court-martial board were duly selected and they were selected with no prejudice to the accused.

Defense counsel stated that he did not really disagree with this but the manual does not clearly set out the standards to be used in selecting the enlisted members of a court-martial board. Counsel further argued that it was unfair to rule out all the members of the accused's rank.

The military judge stated that the manual states, concerning selection of enlisted members of a court-martial board, that any deliberate exclusion of certain people from sitting on the board violates the Constitution of the United States and the Army Regulations. The MCM para 36c,2,a states that the convening authority shall detail members best suited and qualified under Article 25 of the code. It further states that it is up to the discretion of the convening authority to detail such members. Any evidence of deliberate exclusion or inclusion [of] any specific people would violate the accused's rights but the defense evidence in this case is insufficient to prove this. The 3 enlisted members sitting with the board is more than the one-third required under Article 25 of the manual.

The military judge further stated that he specifically found that there was no deliberate exclusion of any particular people from sitting on the board. The military judge further stated that the motion was denied.

MOTION: DENIED.

* * *

STIPULATION OF FACT
UNITED STATES VS LAXER

13 November 1969

It is stipulated by and between the prosecution and the defense with the expressed consent of the accused that if Sergeant First Class Anthony Costantino, Headquarters, Special Troops were present in court and were sworn as a witness, he would testify in substance as follows:

I called three companies and asked them for the names of an E-6, an E-7, or an E-8 [highest-ranking NCOs shy of a Master Sergeant, E-9 — GL] to sit on a Special Court Martial. The reason I asked for an E-6, E-7 or an E-8 was because the note on my desk said to do that. I don't know who wrote the note. [It could have been a practical joke, then, for all he knew! —GL]

Also it is stipulated between Trial Counsel and Defense Counsel with expressed consent of the accused that the enlisted members of the court were selected as they were reasonably available in the companies concerned and were either E-6, E-7, or E-8 as directed by Headquarters, Special Troops. [If you've been paying attention, you can see how the military judge blatantly swept under the rug the fact that all persons <u>below</u> rank of E-6 had, indeed, been specifically **<u>excluded</u>**! But that's military "justice" in action. This ruling should have served as grounds to overturn my conviction, had we pursued an appeal later. —GL]

✳ ✳ ✳

The court met at Fort Dix, New Jersey at 1015 hours, 13 November 1969, pursuant to the following orders:

PROCEEDINGS OF A SPECIAL COURT-MARTIAL

COURT-MARTIAL CONVENING ORDER 13   November 1969
NUMBER 257

A special court-martial is hereby convened. It may proceed at this Headquarters to try the case of United States v. Private E-1 GREGORY G. LAXER, US Army, Special Processing Detachment, Special Troops, US Army Training Center, Infantry, Fort Dix, New Jersey, only. The Court will be constituted as follows:

MILITARY JUDGE

Captain JEFFREY A. WEINER, Judge Advocate General Corps, US Army Judiciary, Office of the Judge Advocate General, Washington, D.C., certified [to act as a judge —GL] in accordance with Article 26(b) . . .

MEMBERS [Jury]

[Here are named a Lieutenant Colonel, two Captains, a Second Lieutenant, two Sergeants First Class (E-7), and one Staff Sergeant (E-6). One of the Captains was assigned to G-2, Army "Intelligence," at Ft. Dix. —GL]

COUNSEL

Captain MICHAEL E. HUDSON, Special Processing Detachment, Special Troops, TRIAL COUNSEL, not a lawyer in the sense of Article 27(c).

First Lieutenant THEODORE W. VOLCKHAUSEN, Command Group, DEFENSE COUNSEL, certified [as a lawyer] in accordance with Article 27(b).

[In the pre-trial hearing, the military Defense Counsel introduced to the Court Mr. Daniel Pochoda, lawyer and member of the Bar of the State of New York, to assist in the defense. The Court had no objection. Mr. Pochoda was also present for the proceedings of November 13. —GL]

CHARLES E. WEDDLE, COLONEL was in command on the date of the reference for trial.

Charge: Violation of the Uniform Code of Military Justice, Article 86.

Specification: In that Private E-1 Gregory G. Laxer, then of US Army Over Seas Replacement Station, Oakland, California, did, on or about 1 July 1969, without authority absent himself from his unit (. . .) and did remain so absent until on or about 18 September 1969.

The accused pleaded as follows:
To the Specification and the Charge: NOT GUILTY.

PRESENTATION OF PROSECUTION CASE

The trial counsel made no opening statement.

The following witnesses for the prosecution were sworn and testified in substance as follows:

NONE.

Trial counsel offered into evidence Two Extract Copies of Morning Reports [documents discussed earlier in this book —GL] dated 22 October 69 [should state "68," my original reporting date for shipment to Vietnam; this is a vestige of the Army's original erroneous idea that I'd been AWOL for nearly a year continuously —GL] and 14 October 69 requesting that they be entered and marked as Prosecution Exhibit Number One and Prosecution Exhibit Number Two. The Morning Reports were admitted and marked as requested, there being no objection.

Trial counsel stated that the government had presented a prima facia case of AWOL against the accused and that the government rested.

PRESENTATION OF DEFENSE CASE

The accused was advised by the president [i.e. the Military Judge] of his right to testify or remain silent. The following witnesses for the defense were sworn and testified in substance as follows:

NONE.

Defense counsel offered into evidence an Extract Copy of Special Orders Number 187 dated 6 September 68 requesting that they be entered and marked as Defense Exhibit A. The Orders were admitted and marked as requested, there being no objection.

Defense counsel stated that he was introducing these orders into evidence because he wanted to question the legality of the orders sending the accused to Viet Nam [that is, the second set of orders —GL]. The accused had received the same orders at a previous date but he had disobeyed his previous orders because of his beliefs as a conscientious objector. The same order was given to him again with the full knowledge that he would disobey it.

Defense counsel offered into evidence an Extract Copy of Summary Court-Martial Order Number 1 dated 10 January 69 requesting that it be entered and marked as Defense Exhibit B. The Order was admitted and marked as requested, there being no objections.

Defense counsel offered into evidence a Statement of Facts Hearing Record dated 27 March 69 [a summary of my views regarding conscientious objection to war; see **APPENDIX 4** —GL] requesting that it be entered and marked as Defense Exhibit C. [This was the statement made by the individual who interviewed me at the seminary in Boston area. —GL]

Trial counsel objected to this evidence on the grounds that it was irrelevant. Trial counsel also objected on the grounds that it appears to be a statement signed by the accused and in the 3rd person which would violate the best evidence rule as it was written by someone other than the accused, who is present in court.

Defense counsel stated that the accused's attempt to get a conscientious objector status is relevant. Counsel further stated that he was trying to prove that the events at Fort Devens did tell all concerned how the accused felt about the war and the Army and the subsequent orders to Viet Nam were given as punishment for these views. It is a question of whether or not these orders were lawful.

In response to a question by the military judge, defense counsel stated that he was not specifically per se contesting the denial of the conscientious objector status at the hearing.

The military judge stated that he would sustain the objection to Defense Exhibit C on the grounds that it is hearsay and the fact that there has been no evidence to show that it was ever considered by anybody as a part of the accused's application for a conscientious objector status. [But, of course, it was incorporated as part of my <u>official</u> application! —GL]

Defense counsel offered into evidence an Application for Conscientious Objector Status dated 27 March 69 requesting that it be entered and marked as Defense Exhibit D. The application was admitted and marked as requested, there being no objection.

Defense counsel offered into evidence an Extract Copy of Special Orders Number 92 and two Stipulations dated 18 April 69 and 12 November 69 respectively, requesting that they be entered and marked as Defense Exhibit E, Defense Exhibit F and Defense Exhibit G. The Orders and the Stipulations were admitted and marked as requested, there being no objection.

* * *

STIPULATION OF FACT
UNITED STATES VS LAXER

12 November 1969

It is stipulated by and between the prosecution and the defense with the expressed consent of the accused that if Private First Class Martin Gross, Casual Holding Detachment, Fort Devens, Massachusetts were present in court and were sworn as a witness, he would testify in substance as follows:

I was the outprocessing clerk at Special Processing Detachment, Fort Devens in April of 1969. I know the accused, Private Laxer. When his Conscientious Objector application was disapproved, I was told to prepare a request for reassignment orders. Before I was finished, I was told to drop it. It was normal procedure to process these reassignments through me. The request for Private Laxer's reassignment did not go through me. It was not processed the usual way, and the orders came through with exceptional speed. Normally they take a month. These came through in two weeks.

* * *

STIPULATION OF FACT
UNITED STATES VS LAXER

12 November 1969

It is stipulated by and between the prosecution and the defense with the expressed consent of the accused that if Mr. Joseph Kelly, Professor of Law at Dickenson School of Law were present in court and were sworn as witness, he would testify in substance as follows:

Prior to August of this year, I was the Staff Judge Advocate at Fort Devens, Massachusetts. I know the accused, Private Laxer.

Private Laxer put in an application to be discharged as a conscientious objector, an application to be classified 1-O. When he put it in, I felt that he probably did not qualify as a 1-O, but he did as a 1-A-O, and I expected that Department of the Army would classify him as such. When the application returned, it was simply denied. I asked why and was told that to be classified as 1-A-O, he would have to apply specifically for that.

I informed Private Laxer of the decision and told him he could apply for 1-A-O, but he said he didn't want to do it. I then told him he would be reassigned. Assignment orders were requested. They came through from Department of the Army and were for Viet Nam. It was felt that he probably would not comply with these orders since he had not complied with a previous set. General Cushman [Commanding Officer, Ft. Devens] then called Washington to find out why the orders were for Viet Nam. **We felt that Private Laxer was a sincere conscientious objector and it would seem that the Army might use him effectively somewhere else [emphasis added by the author —GL].**

I don't remember who General Cushman talked to, probably someone in the enlisted assignment branch. However, they replied that the assignment was to Viet Nam because of Private Laxer's MOS, which was critical in Viet Nam. [This is an indisputable fact. —GL] This assignment was not punishment.

Private Laxer received his orders and signed out [on the unpaid leave, per **CHAPTER VI** —GL]. He then filed suit in Federal District Court for habeas corpus on the grounds that his Conscientious Objector application had been wrongfully denied. By order of the court, his reporting date to Oakland was twice extended. My recollection of the final reporting date was 30 July 1969 [actually, it was 1 July —GL].

When the court finally denied Private Laxer's suit, I called him at his home and informed him that his last reporting date remained valid. I told him he could come back to Fort Devens and we would ship him from there. I didn't order him to come back. I was concerned mainly for the great amount of time he was on leave. Coming back to Fort Devens would have shortened his leave time. We at Fort Devens did everything possible to help Laxer.

* * *

The accused elected to continue his sworn testimony and took the stand. Trial counsel reminded the accused that he was still under oath.

DIRECT EXAMINATION

I enlisted in the Army on 12 May 67.

I'm opposed to war in general based on morality and ethics. I enlisted in order to get my choice of MOS rather than be drafted. Prior to entering the Army I had considered applying for a conscientious objector deferment but I didn't because I'm not a member of any conventional religion. I felt that I wouldn't have a chance to get the deferment. I can see no alternative to the service unless I could be recognized as a conscientious objector.

I was given a combat medic MOS and I felt that I could serve in this capacity without violating my beliefs [provided, that is, that I **not** be ordered to participate in the Vietnam atrocity —GL]. I found that I was wrong and that I could not serve. [That is, my stance was evolving toward refusal to continue to serve in any capacity. —GL]

(. . .) On 13 September 68 I was given orders to go to Oakland and then to Viet Nam. I went AWOL rather than go to Oakland. I was tried for this offense and I received a Summary Court-Martial.

Before I received this court-martial I had decided to get a discharge on the grounds that I was a conscientious objector. I applied for a 1-O discharge. I turned in a statement of beliefs and a summary of my personal background and then I went to a hearing. My Commanding Officer and my chaplain [i.e., one assigned to my case —GL] both made recommendations to the hearing board.

My beliefs are not part of any conventional religious beliefs. They are based on the belief that all life forms are sacred. It has been held by the Supreme Court that such beliefs are acceptable in order to get this classification. I wanted at least a 1-A-O classification [willing to serve, but in non-combat setting —GL] if I could not get the 1-O classification. My application was denied.

My beliefs were well known within my own unit at Fort Devens. My Commanding Officer and Executive Officer were both fully aware of my beliefs.

At this time I became politically active against the war and I was picked up 3 times for distributing anti-war literature. [Actually, twice: the harassment at Devens PX and the confiscation of literature from my wall locker there. —GL] No charges were ever brought against me for this. I knew Colonel Kelly at Fort Devens.

I got my next set of orders for Oakland on 18 April 69. I was to report on 12 May 69. On 9 May 69 I began a suit in Federal Court in Boston alleging that I had been wrongfully denied a conscientious objector status. The judge issued an injunction which moved my reporting date up to 1 July 69.

I felt that since disobeying an order in the presence of my Commanding Officer, for example, would really jeopardize things, I decided to go AWOL rather than to report to Oakland. I refused to go to Viet Nam because of moral and political beliefs.

I never intend to go to Viet Nam. After I entered the Army I decided that I couldn't serve the Army in any capacity in Viet Nam. These views have been consistent throughout my tour in the Army. [More accurately, as recounted in this memoir, I knew while in high school I could never be a participant in the American War in Vietnam. —GL]

CROSS EXAMINATION

I know of no ruling on the question of whether or not the war in Viet Nam is illegal. I was never told that I got these orders as a form of punishment for my beliefs [as if the Army would make such an admission! —GL]. I felt that the only alternative to reporting was to go AWOL. I know of several men that were forced [that is, physically abducted from US soil —GL] to report to Viet Nam. I knew that I would be apprehended and that I would be punished.

EXAMINATION BY THE MILITARY JUDGE

My suit in Federal Court was denied. It was denied first because I had not exhausted all the remedies the Army offered and because I was selective in that I only opposed the war in Viet Nam.

The members of the court were excused so that the military judge could hear argument on proposed instructions from counsel. The members were excused at 1145 hours, 13 November 69.

The military judge stated that he intended to instruct the court generally on their duties (. . .).

Defense counsel requested that an instruction be given on the illegality of the second set of orders that were given to the accused.

The military judge denied this request.

Defense counsel objected to this denial by the military judge because there had been evidence introduced that could lead the court to the reasonable inference that these orders were illegal in that they were given as punishment for the accused. Counsel further argued that intent is a state of mind that is rarely subject to any direct evidence. The court might find this intent because the orders were not going to serve any need for the Army but that they were punishment [in the form —GL] of an inducement to commit another crime. Counsel argued that an instruction on the illegality of the second set of orders ought to be given for these reasons.

The military judge stated that the objection was noted but that as a matter of law the orders were legal, not illegal [see discussion of law under Nazi rule in **EPILOGUE** of this book —GL], and that defense counsel had previously stated that he was not contesting the fact that the accused had been denied a conscientious objector status so this cannot be considered in the question of whether or not the orders were legal.

Defense counsel objected to this finding based on the fact that evidence had been introduced from which the court could reasonably infer that the orders were illegal.

The military judge stated that there had been no evidence introduced that could even raise the issue so the court could not consider the question.

Defense counsel stated that the proposed instructions were not for the purpose of contesting the illegality of the orders or the denial of the conscientious objector status but rather for the purpose of showing the effect of the orders in punishing the accused or inducing him to commit another crime that the accused might not otherwise commit and that in cases concerning the disobedience of an order the court should look to the acts ordered and the needs of the Army. The evidence introduced indicates that the orders could serve no valid military service but rather were intended as a punishment. It becomes a question of intent on the part of the Army.

The military judge stated that there were no instructions on intent on the charge of AWOL as there is no specific intent involved here. The military judge stated that in this regard he would only instruct on the elements of the offense.

Defense counsel stated that, from his point of view, the intent in issuing the orders is in question and that the court must look to all the circumstances of the case and that these circumstances should be presented to the court.

The military judge stated that the defense objection was noted but that based on the reasons previously given and the fact that there has been no evidence of an intent to punish the accused entered before the court, the request for instructions is denied.

* * *

[Follows the text of "Defendant's Proposed Instructions," the introduction of which was blocked by the Military Judge —GL]

<u>Affirmative Defenses</u>

An order may be disobeyed if it is illegal or if it is punitive. An order is punitive if its purpose is to punish or if its effect or its result is that of punishment.

The purpose of an order depends upon the reasons which motivated its issuance. If the intent was to force the recipient of the order into the commission of a crime which he would not otherwise commit then the orders stemming from such intent would be illegal.

Intent is a state of mind and as such is rarely the subject of direct proof but ordinarily must be inferred from the circumstances. Often a person knows not what motivates him and his expressions on the subject may be of no value. A person is said to have intended those results which are the natural and foreseeable consequences of his acts. Thus, purpose must be determined by a sensible consideration of all the facts.

In cases concerning the disobedience of an order the Court must look closely to the connection between the personal act required by the order and the needs of the military service.

The Court should consider if there was an immediate military necessity for the issuance of this particular order and if it was required to maintain the morale, discipline or good order of the military. Evidence demonstrating that the recipient of the order would not obey it is relevant to such a determination.

The fact that it is expected that the recipient of an order will not obey it indicates that the order is punitive.

If it is proven beyond a reasonable doubt that an individual refused to obey a particular order, he should not be found guilty of a willful disobedience of the same order when it is repeated by another. A re-issue of the same order that an individual has previously disobeyed would only tend to increase the punishment for his refusal.

If a person willfully disobeys an order to do a certain thing, and persists in his disobedience when the same order is given by the same or other superior, a multiplication of charges should be avoided.

* * *

Defense counsel moved to dismiss the charges against the accused on the grounds that the orders to report to Oakland and then to Viet Nam are illegal due to the unconstitutionality and illegality of the war in Viet Nam. [This motion was to get on the record an argument presented in other trials of the time, as basis for possible future appeal. —GL]

The military judge stated that the motion was denied.

MOTION: DENIED

The hearing was terminated at 1215 hours, 13 November 69.

Court was called to order at 1320 hours, 13 November 69. Trial counsel stated that all parties who were present when court closed were again present.

The prosecution made no argument.

The defense made an argument.

The prosecution made a closing argument.

The military judge instructed the court generally on their duties towards findings, the presumption of innocence, the burden of proof, the elements of proof, reasonable doubt and voting procedures. The military judge further instructed the court that they were not to consider the question of the legality of the orders to report to Oakland or the accused's application for a conscientious objector status.

Trial and defense counsel stated that they had nothing further.

Neither the prosecution nor the defense having anything further to offer, the court was closed. Thereafter, the court opened and the president announced that, in closed session and upon secret written ballot (. . .) the accused was found:

Of the Specification and the Charge: GUILTY.

The trial counsel read the data as to age, pay, service, and restraint of the accused as shown on the charge sheet. The defense counsel stated that the data was correct.

Trial counsel asked the court to note the evidence of previous convictions [which, of course, the accused had had to bring to the prosecution's attention, due to the Army's own bungling! —GL] previously introduced as Defense Exhibit B.

After the accused was advised by the president of his right to present evidence in extenuation or mitigation, including the right to remain silent or to make a sworn or unsworn statement, the defense counsel stated that he had nothing further to offer.

Trial counsel waived opening argument.
Defense counsel made argument.
Trial counsel made closing argument.

Neither the prosecution nor the defense having anything further to offer, the court was closed. Thereafter, the court opened and the president announced that in closed session and, upon secret written ballot (. . .) the accused was sentenced:

To be confined at hard labor for 6 months and to forfeit $75.00 per month for 6 months. (One previous conviction considered.)

The court adjourned at 1435 hours, 13 November 1969.

* * *

[A copy of my transcribed Statement in support of my Application for Separation by reason of Conscientious Objection followed in the Trial Record; see APPENDIX 4.]

The "Collapse" of the Armed Forces—A Look Back

As the American War in Vietnam wound down—that is to say, President Nixon ordered cessation of US offensive operations and the suspension of the draft in 1973—books started to appear that undertook to explain the loss of the world's most massive military machine in the far-off land of rice paddies and tropical forests. Their real intent was not to try to ward off future wars launched by the United States, but to recommend ways to make the military experience more tolerable for enlisted personnel so they could fight from a base of higher morale. The transition to an "all-volunteer military" had been launched by the time of my own exit from active duty in summer 1971, as I recounted in **CHAPTER X**: living conditions were slowly being improved, pay rates raised, civilians hired to do KP duty, etc. In the **EPILOGUE**, I touched on a rather hysterical 1971 article by Lt. Col. Robert Heinl, Jr.

Let us now examine a book by a cooler-headed writer, another career officer, Lt. Col. William L. Hauser: America's Army in Crisis—A Study in Civil-Military Relations (Johns Hopkins University Press, 1973). Reference is made (pg. 53) to "demobilization riots of 1945," when US troops in the Asian and European theaters objected to being held on foreign soil as an occupying force after the Axis Powers had clearly been defeated. Petitions were signed by many thousands of personnel demanding repatriation to home soil, and there were even mass demonstrations by the troops. This is covered in Turn the Guns Around, by John Catalinotto, previously cited. "[T]hey [the 'riots'] also reflected widespread enmity between officers and enlisted men." The Secretary of the Army appointed a commission, headed by the famous General James H. Doolittle, to study officer-enlisted persons relations. The findings, issued in May 1946, " . . . shocked the country and the Army" by recognizing that the Army operated under a **"caste system"** (emphasis added). Members of the working class—people from humble backgrounds, those decidedly not born with mouths full of silver spoon— simply felt a natural and justified resentment at being ordered about by pompous asses, strutting about like little dukes or princes. Recall that among the first demands of the American Servicemen's Union was relief from being required to salute these buffoons and address them as "Sir," with the threat of punitive action looming if one refused to engage in these quasi-feudal customs. Were we men or serfs? The Doolittle Committee recommended "an end to off-duty social segregation, the establishment of a sanction-free complaint system, abolition of the salute off post and off duty, and equal treatment . . . under military law" (pg. 54). These recommended liberalizations were, not surprisingly, wholly rejected by the Brass. Perhaps they looked at the commission's recommendations as a mandate to, indeed, "do little" (sorry, I couldn't resist).

Hauser touches on "Race and Dissent" and "Discipline and Justice" (these are chapter titles), discussing some specific then-recent cases—"the Darmstadt 53" (African-American troops in Germany protesting racist abuses), the Ft. Dix Stockade rebellion, and "mutinies" in Vietnam, among them. I am proud to say the American Servicemen's Union publicized these cases, and helped secure legal assistance for those with grievances where feasible.

Finally, Hauser has some recommendations for improving the military experience without putting dissident troops in front of firing squads. Again, the intent is not to discourage or curb the use of the US military in unjustified aggression. Far from it. Hauser suggested dividing the Army into a **fighting Army** and a **support Army**. The former would encourage the participation of the sociopaths who enjoy killing, the latter would be reasonably assured of remaining far behind the lines. The fighting army he describes is essentially a mercenary force—though the colonel denies this—and resembles the military of today. Improved pay, improved living conditions, improved prospects for a nice pension. "All" one needs do is **not** think about whether the cause in which one has been deployed is just.

The support army, in this fantasy, would actually enjoy looser discipline and a quasi-civilian atmosphere. In the reality of how the US Military Machine "evolved" in the intervening 50 years, we find that within the self-appointed "elite" units, such as Navy SEALs, atrocities are still committed against foreign nationals, with attempted cover-ups standard practice. And there is no shortage of support, given the massive amounts of taxpayer dollars lavished on the corporations only too happy to feed at the public trough; let's not lose any sleep if the goods and services are sometimes rather shabby. How often are contracts awarded on a no-bid basis? Far too often. It seems war really is good business.

But "all's well that ends well," the Bard informed us. So Lt. Col. Hauser concludes with his assurance that the concept of the "elite" fighting force poses no threat to "democratic rule." My fellow Americans, you are now free to breathe a huge collective sigh of relief!

∗   ∗   ∗

Let us now turn to <u>Defeated</u>, by Stuart H. Loory, also published in 1973 (Random House; all page references to first edition). Loory (1932-2015) was a fellow at the Woodrow Wilson Center at Stanford University, and the first Kiplinger Professor of Public Affairs Reporting at Ohio State University. The Wilson Center affiliation explains why the tone of this book is essentially that of a "think tank" report. Part I, "The Assembly Line Generation Goes to War," observes "[O]fficers and men . . . began to mouth the same 'I was only following orders' justification for war crimes that marked the defenses of World War II enemies on trial; drugs became a way of life for thousands who might otherwise have been unexposed; discipline broke down to the point that some superiors began to fear for their safety. . . . The American military machine is defeated" (pg. 10). "Military leaders became so engrossed with their own career progress and with nurturing the seductive growth of the machine that they never realized what was happening in the enlisted ranks. The enlisted men were exploited" (pg. 20). While I agree with the first half of that statement, I have to point out that by the height of the Vietnam War, the officer corps was quite aware of the dissent in the ranks. With AWOL and desertion rates at highs not seen since the US Civil War, I imagine they could not possibly be <u>unaware</u>. The issue is that they didn't give a damn for the welfare of the enlisted ranks. The Uniform Code of Military Justice hung over the heads of enlisted personnel like the dreaded Sword of Damocles; the threat of imprisonment enabled the Brass to maintain enough discipline to avoid complete collapse of discipline.

On to Part II, "A Generation of Yes Men": "'Civilians can scarcely understand or even believe that many ambitious military professionals truly yearn for wars and the opportunities for glory and distinction afforded only in combat.'" —David M. Shoup, former Commandant, United States Marine Corps, 1969 (pg. 41). General Shoup emerged a relative good guy, having publicly criticized the war in Southeast Asia. See my criticism of Karl Marlantes and Philip Caputo in the **EPILOGUE** of this book. From page 73: "[T]he military establishment these days has so many generals and admirals that it sometimes seems as if it does not know what to do with them." Loory presents a table of statistics showing that during World War II, with 12 million Americans in uniform, the personnel rolls carried 38 generals ("full," or 4-star generals) and admirals (the Navy equivalent of that rank); in June 1971, near the peak of number of personnel engaged in the Vietnam War, he shows the figure as 45. The figures for lieutenant colonel (Navy equivalent: commander) are amazing (pg. 77). During WW II we find 51,956; during Vietnam, with far fewer members of the US military, 57,819! "The sublime nightmare [the scramble to advance in rank] corrupted the officer corps, creating a generation of yes men" (pg. 116). The author paints a picture of conditions for enlisted personnel in the 3rd Armored Division, part of the post-WW II occupation forces that were kept in Germany (then "West Germany," of course) . . . and remain there to this day, 75 years after Hitler's defeat. He writes of deplorable housing conditions, rampant drug and alcohol abuse, racial tensions, general demoralization and, very importantly, a smoldering feeling that the troops deserved recognition of some "individual rights." These are precisely the issues the American Servicemen's Union agitated around, of course, within the larger context of asking "Why the hell are we being sent to the other side of the world to try to kill people who've done the USA no harm whatsoever?"

The next section of the book is titled "Part III: A Generation of Exploited Men." We are reminded that the US Marine Corps was compelled to court-martial more than 60 of its Drill Instructors for wanton brutality between 1965 and 1971 (pg. 133). We may be confident that this was only the tip of the iceberg of maltreatment of recruits, cases that had gained the attention of the news media. "Throughout the services, there were stories about broken equipment that had made training impossible or meaningless" (pg. 143). Remarkably, this was one of the grievances of 'Bowe' Bergdahl in the run-up to his deployment to Afghanistan a few years ago. Having enlisted in the Army post-9/11 enthusiastic to go take down "bad guys," Bergdahl was tremendously disappointed with the Military Machine of the 21st Century. *Plus ca change, plus la meme chose*, eh? And here's another anecdote that rings down to us through the decades, though it concerns would-be officers rather than enlisted men: in 1971 President Nixon wanted a monument to Confederate soldiers installed at West Point. Ninety African-American cadets then enrolled, plus 18 of 22 black faculty members at the academy, signed a petition of protest. "Cadet Percy Squire, 21, a black upperclassman from Youngstown, Ohio delivered the petition to [West Point Commandant] Knowlton on a Friday afternoon in November 1971. The meeting lasted 'about ten seconds,' Squire said. 'Knowlton looked at all the signatures and then said, "I have to go watch a football game" or something like that'" (pg. 149). A very Nixonian response!

Discussing grievances of black enlisted personnel, it is reported that in a single year, among the US troops stationed in Germany, there were 54 instances of large groups of African-American personnel organized to protest or present petitions for change (pg. 156).

"In 1945, 95% of all stewards [essentially, valets to commissioned officers —GL] in the Navy were black, the rest being Filipinos, Guamanians, Samoans [etc.] . . . Between 1952 and 1968, 19,468 Filipinos were recruited **for mess duty**" (pg. 157) [emphasis added; recall the testimony of Seaman Kelley at the Honolulu GI Sanctuary]. One wonders how often the Mess crew might have spat or urinated in the admiral's soup?!

"At the 1970 White House Conference on Hunger, it was reported that as many as 50,000 servicemen with large families might be living below the poverty line" (pg. 191). We need to remember that, despite the strong presence (indeed, tradition) of institutionalized racism in the Armed Forces, members of racial/ethnic minorities in the US came to believe that they had a better chance at a decent career in military uniform, or some civilian branch of the Federal Government such as the Post Office.

"A good part of the military's drug problem resulted from a lack of any genuine interest of commanders in morale, troop health and welfare. . . . To live beyond its means, the institution mortgaged its future with drugs, slot machines, alcohol and fancy PX items to maintain a modicum of serenity but not true morale among its troops. It also used sex" (pg. 213). Here we need only recall my own unintended visit to a brothel in Columbia, South Carolina (**CHAPTER II**). I had then, and have no doubt now, that the taxi driver who took us trainees there was a retired lifer (or maybe still active-duty, moonlighting on weekends!), and that the Army was fully aware of what transpired in that "hotel." This was undoubtedly true of towns bordering military installations virtually anywhere the US Machine planted roots. Let's hear from Colonel Frederick W. Best, Jr., Commanding Officer of Camp Humphreys in "south" (occupied) Korea, interviewed after Korean prostitutes reportedly stopped "servicing" black American troops: "'I spend all my time on this and what do I have to show for it?' Best said. 'I have the cleanest center of depravity in all of Korea. . . . I sometimes wonder what I'll be fit to do after I'm finished in the Army. My answer to myself is that I'll be fit to be a madam [!!]'" (pg. 222). One can't help but suspect that the colonel's career came to a close fairly promptly after that interview.

Stuart Loory goes on to discuss the contradiction between the fairy tale (my choice of words) told Americans during the "Cold War"—the United States is the last hope for freedom and democracy in the world—and the totalitarian conditions under which the troops actually lived. "By the 1970s, the disparity of this condition began to rankle, raising issues within the military machine that had seldom been raised before, that had never been raised before with such ferocity. The issues related to the rights of individuals within the system" (pg. 235). Recall the demands of the ASU for granting to GIs the Constitutional rights deemed the birthright of US citizens. This struggle is a historical fact, despite the unfortunate efforts (largely successful) of the American "left" to write the ASU out of existence when recounting the story of GI Resistance. "With the system stacked against the soldier to the extent that defense and prosecution work hand in glove to fulfill the wishes of the command, it is little wonder that the soldiers refuse to believe that military justice is blind" (pg. 263). Tell me about it, brother!

"[T]he result of exploitation and repression was the consolidation of a beachhead within the services by young radicals who did not stop at calling for the mere reform of the institution. They began to press for its overthrow [Amen!] . . . A former serviceman by the name of Andrew Stapp organized the ASU, saying: 'We must band together in the fight for an enlisted men's union and show these brass gods who rule us that we are men and not dumb animals'" (pg. 266).

Next comes "Part IV: A Generation of Deception and Self-Deception." "In 1969, Dr. Henry A. Kissinger ordered a complete review of Vietnam policy . . . [Among his areas of interest was] the question of how effective the B-52s were. . . . " Secretary of Defense Melvin Laird's staff came up with these estimates: "[I]t took about 2 1/2 planeloads of bombs—some 275 five-hundred-pounders in all—to kill one enemy soldier. . . . [T]he rhetoric claimed success, and the highest echelons of the Air Force, publicly at least, were not willing to admit anything else. In that kind of atmosphere, lessons were bound to go unlearned" (pg. 348). And so, the carpet bombing continued, leaving Vietnam and parts of Laos with literally tens of millions of bomb craters. Now think of the recent "Global War on Terror," in which the US experimented with dropping an eleven-ton bomb (that's 22,000 pounds of explosives) on a cave complex in Afghanistan to see if it would collapse as a result. I don't even recall any US claim of a smashing (pardon the expression) success, of how many Taliban or other "insurgents" may have been killed, or whether the caves, in fact, were destroyed. As George Orwell posited in 1984, the purpose of **perpetual war** is to waste resources that otherwise might be employed to improve the general welfare of the worker drones of the warring party.

Discussing pros and cons of an "all-volunteer military"—I continue to employ quotation marks because of "the economic draft" driving many lesser-skilled young people into the ranks of the Machine in search of job security—Loory observes: "The logical extension of the [con] argument is that the [situation] . . . would heighten the danger of military dissatisfaction growing into military disobedience of its civilian masters and eventually of a military takeover of the country" (pg. 360). With the relentless growth of the Machine's weight within our economy, the incessant media propaganda leading cheers for the military, and the 2016 election of a fascistic demagogue named Trump, do you doubt for a second that, if anything, this threat is far more real today than when Mr. Loory penned those thoughts? Next comes a suggestion that the military went overboard in its enthusiasm for the "Cold War" and that engaging in the crusade against an "alien" (my word) ideology—Communism—was not the proper role for an organization that should be representative of the society as a whole. Loory was conjuring the concept of "the citizen-soldier" answering the call to defend the nation when it is genuinely under threat (pg. 363). Was the mighty United States genuinely under threat? Precisely because the US declared Vietnam a mere "proxy" for <u>Soviet "aggression,"</u> rather than a nation of people fiercely determined to be independent, millions of human lives in Southeast Asia were exterminated.

"In the 1960s, Robert S. McNamara . . . mesmerized the nation with his computerized systems-analysis approach to military policy which brought forth the assessment that the US could fight '2 1/2 wars' at once . . . As it turned out, the 'half war' that was Vietnam, in itself, **brought the Army to ruin**" (pg. 364, my emphasis added). McNamara and his successors—with their computers, aircraft carriers and B-52s—**were defeated in Vietnam by People's War.**

On the matter of use of military force to quell domestic unrest: "After that [rebellions by the black communities in Watts and Detroit in the '60s] . . . the civilians in the Department of Defense assigned to the Army the mission of gathering whatever information it might need beforehand to maintain order in any of the nation's 25 largest cities. And that's how the Army got into domestic spying in a big way. . . . [O]verly zealous planners also set out on a hunt for the names of potential troublemakers [which came to include the names of some governors, mayors and legislators]. . . . At the height of the activities, the Army had 350 different records centers around the country where dossiers were stored . . . " (pg. 366).

Part V of <u>Defeated</u> is titled "A Generation for Tomorrow." We read: "It was the military leadership, then, that brought on the machine's defeat—not on the battlefield [you already know how strongly I disagree with <u>that</u> assessment, though there is some truth here —GL] but in the huge bureaucracy it built—by compromising a deeply rooted tradition of loyalty in favor of a less than wholesome concern for individual careers. . . . The military adopted the corporate ethic . . . This shift in outlook helped give the US not a strong military machine but an overbearing one, a machine that threatened to suffocate American Democracy, not protect it" (pg. 374).

On the issue of attempting reform of the military: "Reform of the officer corps, including the reintroduction of a professional ethic, is the key to the reconstitution of the military machine as an effective fighting force." I can assure the reader that if you had a penny for every sheet of paper used by the US military in the succeeding decades to expound and distribute among its personnel its ideas on "professionalism," you would be the wealthiest person on the planet. None of this waste of the pulp of felled forests prevented the use of the Machine in unjustified wars, ginned up by lies like those about Saddam Hussein's "weapons of mass destruction," *ad infinitum,* or the committing of war crimes by US personnel against a demonized, designated enemy of the moment. Doubt not that today's officer corps considers itself highly professional and super-competent, with the good old "Can do!" attitude always on display. With very rare exceptions, any doubts they harbor in private are kept that way. Mr. Loory next predicts the need to lower standards for new recruits, post-conscription, which actually came to pass. "Instead of being disbanded [bear in mind, it has only been suspended, not ended —GL], the draft should be reinstituted and broadened into a program of universal service for all the nation's youth—women as well as men" (pgs. 374-379). As I complete this book, the United States Congress is actually considering legislation to do precisely that; that is, to reinstitute the draft and to include women, with or without options for non-military public service.

Our Woodrow Wilson Institute scholar—let us bear in mind that the Wilson Institute is a thoroughly pro-imperialist organization—has some suggestions for changes within the ranks. Outside of units directly concerned with active combat, Loory suggests some relaxation of discipline—the rules and regulations we enlisted personnel called "Mickey-Mouse" or "chickenshit" back in the day—should be acceptable (pg. 381). This is but one of the reforms suggested in the book that fell on entirely deaf ears. The testimony of the aforementioned 'Bowe' Bergdahl suggested strongly that life in the military for enlisted personnel has essentially not changed in the 50 years since I was in uniform.

"The question of war crimes should be addressed by the military . . ." This is remarkably naive! Let's put the foxes in charge of security for the hen house! Was the professor on a very long coffee break during the entire shameful aftermath of the My Lai massacre, which saw not a single soldier, up or down the chain of command from Lt. William Calley, facing any real punishment? This proposal is followed by one even less rooted in reality: "In keeping with the defensive rationale for the American military machine, the services should abandon all their overseas garrisons and bases" (pg. 383). I'm sure the generals and admirals at the Pentagon split their sides with paroxysms of laughter over that one. As I finalize this memoir in 2021, the US has so many installations on foreign soil—ranging from mere listening posts for gathering intelligence to sprawling bases remaining in Europe, in occupied ("south") Korea, on Japanese/Okinawan soil all these decades after World War II, plus an increasing presence in the "Middle East" and on the continent of Africa—that no one in the civilian world can state with accuracy a number. The figure of 800 has been bandied about of late. The troop presence in the Pacific region and the European mainland is maintained as ever-present threats against China and Russia, respectively. These countries, which have embraced Capitalism with a vengeance, are constantly described by American politicians and mainstream media as "rivals" and "adversaries." Polite euphemisms for **enemies**! The Pentagon always has "all options on the table" for potential military strikes against these major powers, ranging from "strategic actions" to all-out nuclear war. If you doubt this, I fear you are dangerously naive. The level of waste of taxpayer dollars to maintain these overseas facilities, expended in a desperate attempt to maintain global economic hegemony for the US Ruling Class, is simply staggering. In my view, it is more than simply staggering; it is criminal.

Summarizing his view of the American War in Vietnam, Mr. Loory concludes that the undertaking was not a cause, but a symptom of, how the military came to be misused in the "holy crusade" against Communism. But we must tear away the layers of propaganda that argued the USA was the defender of freedom and democracy, which Loory desperately wants himself and us to believe, and examine the real motives. The motives are clearer, to those with vision unobstructed by "patriotic" fairy tales, than ever: the US Ruling Class is in a desperate struggle to maintain its domination of the world, especially in opposition to China's rise in prominence, and postures as **"the Exceptional Nation."** This Ruling Class, as heartless as any that has existed since Man started to exploit Man, is quite prepared to lay waste to a whole planet in pursuit of its objectives. Did the US agree to drastically reduce its nuclear arsenal after the collapse of "the Evil Empire," the Soviet Union? Hell no! The concern now, we are told, is that the US needs desperately to <u>modernize</u> its nuclear arsenal! "A strong, well-motivated, properly controlled, reasonably proportioned military machine, dedicated to the preservation of American Democracy but not the extension of a Pax Americana, would help stabilize world peace . . ." (pg. 386). World public opinion polls have shown that, outside the bubble reality of "American Exceptionalism," people understand that it is none other than the USA that is the major **<u>threat</u>** to peace on our planet.

Essentially, our nation has followed the exact opposite path from Mr. Loory's recommendations. The Military Machine, despite its reduced personnel rolls since the Vietnam Era, devours ever greater, ever more obscene amounts of resources. Technological developments now empower military personnel sitting in air-conditioned offices on US soil to rain death, by armed drones, on targets anywhere in the world. Occasionally, one of these drone operators discovers a conscience—something the military doesn't "issue"—and calls it quits. The Machine goes its merry way regardless. But it still cannot defeat **People's War!**

APPENDIX 7

A Dirty Little Secret

The good-hearted everyday people whom, in my Dedications, I designated real heroes of the struggle to end the Vietnam War may have occasionally puzzled over why there were two major umbrella organizations sponsoring anti-war activities in the United States. Why not a genuinely unified movement, which could mobilize the most people, forcefully demanding "End the war now!"? What could be more urgent than to halt the mass killing and maiming of civilians in Vietnam, Cambodia and Laos, and the further sacrifice of lives and limbs of American military personnel?

Why not a truly unified movement? The answer lies in a mere three words: **Stalin versus Trotsky**. What does this mean? Whole books have been written on this subject. I will attempt to concoct an "Executive Summary": After the 1924 death of V.I. Lenin, leader of the Russian Communist movement, a struggle erupted for control of the party. Leon Trotsky, despite some earlier disagreements with Lenin, had helped lead the insurrection to seize power in Petrograd (Saint Petersburg) in November 1917. This event, popularly called The Bolshevik Revolution, dealt the final blow to the reformist interim regime in place since Czar Nicholas II fell earlier that year. Prior to these events, the revolutionary movement in Russia had become split between Lenin and his followers, and less-militant elements—reformists, if you will. At a conference held in 1903, Lenin's group constituted a majority of delegates and became known as the Bolsheviks (from *bolshoi*, meaning large or great). The smaller faction became known as the Mensheviks, or "minority." Prior to the developments in 1917, Leon Trotsky was considered sympathetic to the Mensheviks.

Despite a lack of any formal military training, Trotsky forged the Soviet Red Army that defended the young revolution against all attempts to overthrow it. This required defeating not just internal enemies—those still supporting Czarist rule, called "White Russians"—but expeditionary forces sent from 19 other nations, including the United States. Trotsky set his brilliant, comprehensive mind to trying to solve numerous organizational and economic problems. It was a brave new world, trying to instill Socialist ideals in a backwards, predominantly agrarian society. All the while, Josef Stalin, future General Secretary of the party, was maneuvering to accumulate influence and power within the government apparatus.

Ultimately, Stalin would liquidate those who opposed his rise to power in the infamous "show trials" of the 1930s. Trotsky, meanwhile, had been forcibly expelled from the USSR (Union of Soviet Socialist Republics) in 1928. Stalin rewarded his loyal lackeys with privileges, leading George Orwell to pen his famous phrase " . . . but some of us are more equal than others" in <u>Animal Farm</u>. All the propaganda firepower of Russia was unleashed to vilify Trotsky, painting him as the enemy of the revolution, and linking any internal opposition to Stalin as orchestrated from abroad by the exiled former leader. No country on Earth save Mexico (others had caved to pressure from the US, Britain, France, etc.) would grant Trotsky asylum, and he was assassinated there in 1940. We can bet the champagne flowed generously at Stalin's quarters that day.

Stalin and his minions held the reins of power until the former's death in 1953. Successive Soviet leaders gradually admitted to his severe abuses of power, and a period of loosening of controls began. Trotsky's adherents abroad, primarily the Socialist Workers Party (SWP) in the United States and associated groups elsewhere, presented themselves as the inheritors of Lenin's militant legacy. They accused Stalin of conservatism and actually holding back the tide of world revolution. All the mainline, official Communist parties in the world that had gained state power—in eastern Europe after World War II, in China's birth as the People's Republic in 1949, and in the parts of Korea and Vietnam not occupied by foreign troops—adhered to the ideological line that Stalin was a hero and Trotsky the greatest of villains. Even after China rejected Soviet guidance to try to carve out new paths of development—exemplified by the "Great Leap Forward" campaign for self-dependence launched in 1958—the stale Stalinist legacy lingered.

Absurd as it may seem . . .

The ripples of the Stalin versus Trotsky schism in world Communist circles were still lapping the shores of leftwing politics in the US when my opposition to the Vietnam War made me a participant in that scene in the 1960s. One of the major national anti-war umbrella organizations, the National Mobilization Committee to End the War in Vietnam, was under the influence of the Communist Party-USA. It should be understood that by the 1960s, the CP-USA was a bad joke to young militants. We viewed that organization as no threat to the Establishment whatsoever. The rival grouping, NPAC (National Peace Action Coalition), was under the sway of the Socialist Workers Party. Workers World Party was founded by disgruntled SWP members in 1959, precisely because the SWP, too, appeared by then quite conservative and toothless. An interesting historical footnote: in the photograph doctored by the FBI to try to paint Lee Harvey Oswald, alleged assassin of President Kennedy, as a dangerous fanatic, he is seen holding a rifle in one hand and in the other a copy of . . . The Militant, party organ of the SWP! Spectacular irony!

And so, Workers World Party was treated as a virtual enemy by the CP-USA and all the "Maoist" sects, and didn't exactly have a friend in the SWP. The "Maoists" in the US felt compelled to side with China in any ideological dispute with the USSR. But somehow the CPers and the "Maoists" found it in their hearts to unite in their hostility toward WWP. So the "taint" of Trotskyism and the hostility it engendered trickled down to the American Servicemen's Union—ah, we finally come to the nub of the matter!—because we were supported/guided by WWP.

Now, along came the coffeehouse movement. This was an approach, founded by anti-war civilians, to encouraging dissent within the armed services by establishing locations in the community, as close to military installations as feasible, where GIs could congregate and be propagandized. A name was coined: Movement for a Democratic Military, or MDM. In the Monterey area, and probably predominantly on a nationwide basis, this movement was run by "Maoists." Andy Stapp, Chairman of the ASU, referred to this movement derisively as "the *kaffee-klatsch*." As I explained in **CHAPTER X**, it was Jane Fonda's association with this crowd, with their bias against the ASU, that caused me to pass up the opportunity to socialize with her.

Critique: <u>Turning The Guns Around—Notes On The G.I. Movement</u>

When I got to read the book written by Larry Waterhouse and Mariann Vizard, I was taken aback. The authors criticized the trade union model of the ASU and argued that a civilian-led approach, i.e. the coffeehouse movement, was superior to organizing from directly within the ranks of the military. They claimed that this movement's ally, the aforementioned Movement for a Democratic Military, bested the ASU on the issue of racism; this despite the fact that from its beginning, the latter made combatting racism a main plank of its program. We clearly labeled the war in Southeast Asia itself as **racist** in its nature.

The program of the ASU was simple: oppose the Brass and their criminal war on a daily basis by any means we could muster. Had we gained sufficient influence, would we have called for a kind of general strike against the war from within the ranks? Most assuredly!

I worked with the coffeehouse activists on a weekly basis in the Monterey area for well over a year, but I am not aware of any great organizing successes they had among active-duty GIs. Adding a final insult, on pages 137-138 of <u>Turning The Guns Around</u> (original hardcover edition), the authors list the official demands of MDM and conveniently fail to notice that they were **blatantly** modeled on those of the ASU. My thanks for all the discussions I'd had with Larry back at Ft. Ord was this stab in the back. Well, what else should one expect from a damned Stalinist?! When word of all this reached Chairman Stapp back in New York, he simply observed: "Well, you know, Praeger [which had commissioned and issued the book] is the CIA's favorite publishing house."

Concerning the Burns-Novick "The Vietnam War"

The first article below was written in response to a New York Times Op-Ed piece by Ken Burns and Lynn Novick in late May 2017. This was the first confirmation I received that the PBS series was to be a reality. My open letter was published in July 2017 on the website "The Contrary Perspective." The editor of that site chose the title.

Vietnam Redux: An Open Letter to Ken Burns

Dear Mr. Burns:

I only learned relatively recently that you had undertaken a documentary project on the Vietnam War, running about 18 hours total, due to air on PBS television in September of this year. I'm sure you are aware that the Federal Government launched a multi-year Vietnam War 50th [Anniversary] Commemoration program during the Obama administration, scheduled to run well into next decade. Its website states that 9,852 events are being held under its aegis. That website has a Timeline which infamously downgraded the 1968 My Lai Massacre of hundreds of unarmed Vietnamese civilians by US troops to the My Lai "incident." We who opposed this criminal war while it transpired, and oppose historical revision of it, cannot but suspect that the government effort's intent is to whitewash this utter waste of lives and resources as something somehow "noble" and "well intentioned." And I am concerned that your upcoming series may have the same effect, if not intent.

In the official online preview material for the series (where it's proclaimed "the television event of the year"), you state that a complex issue needs 20 to 30 years' perspective to be fully understood and fairly evaluated. Yet you go on to state that, "This film is not an answer, but a set of questions about what happened." It appears that you will give a lot of attention to the issue of "Vietnamese versus Vietnamese." If you are attempting to paint this war as a civil war among Vietnamese, you will start right off by perpetuating the foundational lie of the mountain of lies stacked up by the US government to try to justify the carnage. Vietnam is one nation that was artificially divided by an imaginary border at the behest of President Eisenhower, who later admitted that had the election scheduled for 1956 been allowed to take place, Ho Chi Minh would have been elected president. How does a nation commit "aggression" against itself, Mr. Burns? There was only one aggressor in this war, and it wore a flag with 13 stripes and 50 stars on its uniform. The southern "Army of the Republic of Viet Nam" (ARVN) largely consisted of conscripted, poor, frightened young men who hated being put in a position of being puppets for an invading foreign force, not believers in the need to "stop another Communist domino from falling."

To put it succinctly, there was no "noble cause" for which more than 58,000 US personnel and an unfathomable number of Southeast Asian civilians (some in Cambodia and Laos) had their lives snuffed out. Was the war a "well intentioned mistake"? With close to 600,000 US personnel (counting Naval units off the coast) deployed at the peak, that's one massive "mistake"! Veterans For Peace, of which I am a member, launched the Vietnam Full Disclosure initiative to try to counter the government's distortions in trying to rewrite the history of this thoroughly sordid episode of our country's 20th Century history. I understand that you have characterized your series as an attempt to finally heal the wounds of divisiveness over this war. In my opinion, these wounds can never be healed without a full admission by the US government of its crimes in Southeast Asia, an official apology to its victims—which include American veterans, of course—and the payment of adequate reparations to the Southeast Asian nations affected. What is truly sad to observe is that the course of US military adventures since 1975 reflects a remarkable ability to learn nothing from past experience!

If there is to be any roundtable discussion of your Vietnam War project at its conclusion, as part of the series itself, on "The Charlie Rose Show" or any other forum, I feel very strongly that a representative of Veterans For Peace's Vietnam Full Disclosure campaign merits a place at the table. That is the best way to ensure that "all sides of the story" are presented.

$$\star \quad \star \quad \star$$

The second article was written immediately after I attended a preview-promotion for the PBS series in Boston, Massachusetts at which the creators of the program were present. The huge disappointment that ensued is painfully detailed below. This article was also published on "The Contrary Perspective," in September 2017.

Ken Burns and Lynn Novick Ripped Me Off! . . . and I Want My Money Back!!

On Wednesday, September 6 I drove roundtrip to Boston, MA to attend a screening of the Preview for the Burns-Novick gargantuan TV series on the Vietnam War, debuting September 17 on PBS affiliates. The event was held in an 1100-seat auditorium and, frankly, I didn't expect it would be a full house. To my amazement, the place was bursting at the seams, I imagine most attendees there to worship "America's Storyteller." Peter Lynch, the former Fidelity Investments (originally headquartered in Boston) "guru," who has his own non-profit foundation now, was sitting about eight feet from me.

Here is the official Program for the evening, verbatim: "6:30pm—Doors open; 7pm—screening begins; 8pm—Audience Q&A with panelists." And here is how things actually unfolded: It was at least 7:10pm before the recorded announcement about emergency exits and turning off cellphones was heard. Finally out came the President of WGBH TV/Radio (this is one of the major public broadcasting operations in the nation). He thanked the corporate underwriters, Bank of America most prominently, and heaped praise on Ken Burns. Next came a senior executive from Bank of America to say how thrilled they are to be a long-time financial supporter of the Burns-Novick documentary machine. Finally the magic little fellow himself was brought to the podium to introduce the actual video. It was clear from these remarks that Burns actually believes there once was a legitimate, sovereign entity called "South Vietnam." Next, the Preview played, as the clock ticked away.

The Preview concluded, the clock on the wall read about 8:30pm. Time to squeeze in a few questions from the audience, perhaps? Wrong!! Next, Dr. Harris, a Boston educator and combat Marine in the war who's featured in the series, was introduced. This African-American gentleman told how, having landed at Logan Airport in Boston, returning from the war, in uniform, he was snubbed by multiple taxi drivers. That was real, as we say, and he comes off in the film as very real, speaking of becoming accustomed to killing: "We're Marines and it's war. It's what we do." Okay, well and good. Now may the audience ask some questions of Burns and Novick (Ms. Novick has joined Burns on stage by now), please? No!! Two radio journalists from WGBH are now trotted out and **they** put questions, between bouts of additional adulation-heaping on Mr. Burns. The latter reiterates that his objective in his work is to "tell a good story." Note that this is not the same as boiling matters down to essential truths. "There is no single truth in war" is the promotional tagline for this series, let the record reflect. And suddenly, as if by magic, it's 9pm and the evening is over. Not one single question taken from the audience!

By this time several members of the Boston Chapter of Veterans For Peace and I had positioned ourselves at the exits to distribute a 28-page document explaining the VFP Full Disclosure Campaign that was launched to try to counter the Pentagon's 13-year effort (2012-2025, at taxpayer expense) to whitewash this most shameful and criminal episode in our history. I handed a copy to Peter Lynch, calling him by name to get his attention. (His facial features and "shock" of pure white hair are unmistakable.) When there was but one copy of our handout remaining, I went back inside the auditorium on the slim chance I might be able to hand it directly to Mr. Burns, in an attempt to educate him. But Ken had already vanished. I shook Dr. Harris's hand, thanked him for being real, and left the handout with him. I explained why I felt I was entitled to a refund, and he took it well (obviously he wasn't to blame for the misrepresentation of what was to transpire that evening). I suggested he might pass the handout on to Mr. Burns when he's done with it.

You must understand that for over a week, leading up to this event, I was unable to sleep soundly because I was fretting over how compactly, how concisely, I could phrase a question for the panel . . . assuming I could even get to the microphone. And admittedly, from a practical standpoint, audience Q&A would have been a madhouse. Nevertheless, I paid $16.28 for admission to this Preview in hope of getting to speak. To say nothing of $21 for parking, tolls and gasoline and three hours roundtrip driving. And what was I going to say, you ask? Up to the time of Burns's introduction of the video, I was going to say: "For me and like-minded veterans, there is one overarching fundamental truth: this war was utterly unjustified." But I decided I would say instead: "Mr. Burns, I am mortified that you are perpetuating the myth of 'South' Vietnam, a puppet state only created when the USA maneuvered to cancel the 1956 election which would have seated Ho Chi Minh as president of a unified nation."

Without a doubt, this series has assembled never before seen material, including interviews in Vietnam with combat veterans from "the other side." However, my personal decision now is to not invest any of my time watching it. And I shall always remember Burns and Novick as **"The folks who required 18 hours to offer no answers!"** And furthermore, Mr. Burns and Ms. Novick, I want my money back!!

*[Post-script: It should be noted that the Burns/Novick series was definitely **not** the first documentary to include interviews with combat veterans of the Vietnamese Liberation Forces and Vietnamese civilians caught in the crosshairs of the US's war. The producers filmed new material, but did <u>not</u> score a first in this regard.]*

"Letter to the Wall" May 2015

Introduction: The Vietnam Full Disclosure campaign was initiated by Veterans For Peace (VFP) to counter the Vietnam War sanitization effort launched by the Pentagon during Barack Obama's presidency. As part of this undertaking, VFP encouraged people—veterans of any time period, relatives and loved ones of deceased military personnel, civilians with no connection to military service—to write letters to the US military members who'd been directly killed in the American War in Vietnam, their names displayed on the official Vietnam War Memorial in the nation's capital. The letters could be addressed to someone specific, known personally by the letter writer, or addressed to these 58,000+ people collectively. [As I publish this book, it is believed that at least as many veterans have died by suicide, Agent Orange after-effects, etc. as died in Vietnam itself.] Representatives of VFP would personally place these letters at the monument on Memorial Day and invite the general public to read them. This practice was intended to be an ongoing annual exercise. VFP published the first collection of these letters, from 2015 and 2016, in the latter year. My own letter appears on page 27 and is reproduced below.

* * *

MEMORIAL DAY 2015

To Those Whose Names are Here Memorialized:

You came from small towns and big cities; you came from different socio-economic backgrounds (though tilted, of course, toward the lower end of the income spectrum); you came from different ethnic and religious heritages. Some of you enlisted enthusiastically, believing you were saving "The Free World" from a communist menace; many of you, like myself, enlisted in order to "beat the draft"; but undoubtedly the majority of you were conscripted: "Take this rifle, son, or . . . meet your cellmates for the next few years in this Federal Penitentiary." A few of you were women, serving in a medical or perhaps clerical setting. Death, the Great Leveler, has here united you all.

But Death is not the only thing that binds you together. You were all victims of a national sickness, a belief that the United States of America has a God-given mandate to rule the entire globe, to its own economic benefit. You were all victims of a chain of monstrous lies which led to your deployment to a strange land that most Americans didn't know existed prior to the 1960s. The first of these was the fiction that there was a separate, sovereign nation called "The Republic of South Vietnam" that needed you to defend it against "aggression from the north." Democrat, Republican, it mattered not: our national leaders lied to us again and again and perpetuated one of the most criminal wars of modern times. Not a single one of you should have been deployed to Vietnam in the first place. Not a single one! And thus, as surely as the uncounted millions of inhabitants of the region killed by US weaponry, each and every one of you is a victim of US military aggression. And no one in the leadership of the war machinery, at any level, has ever been prosecuted for their roles in this criminal undertaking. Not a single solitary one.

If resurrected from the realm of the dead you could be, what would you make of the state of the world today? Sure, the advances in technology would wow you at first. Such wizardry! Hey, what became of the USSR? And is that a black man in the White House?!? That would be a shocker, no doubt. But after examining what is recent history for us in this present era, I hope you would be alarmed and ultimately outraged that American troops are still deployed all over the world in the effort to maintain economic hegemony, and that they kill and occasionally get killed or maimed . . . for what, exactly? To "defend freedom"? While our own dwindling freedom here at home is in mortal peril of being extinguished, in the name of "our own protection"! While the streets of our cities and towns are patrolled by cops wearing full combat gear, generously donated by the Pentagon. And that very Pentagon is spending millions of taxpayer dollars on a campaign to persuade the generations following ours that the war that took your lives was far, far from the monstrous crime that it was. I hope you would be sufficiently appalled that the USA learned not a damned thing from its defeat in Vietnam and that you would be moved to actively resist current government policies. But that is a struggle we, the still living, will have to pursue. Continue to rest in peace, brothers and sisters. Your fighting days are over.

GREG LAXER
Spec. 4, Medic
US Army
May 1967-July 1971

Acknowledgments

I will always be grateful that my parents, both long deceased, raised me in an environment almost entirely free of racial, ethnic or religious prejudices and biases. This allowed me to develop my own sense of what constituted, and what violated, the idea of social justice as I grew up in a society that only gave lip service to such a concept. The United States of America presented itself as The Light of the World, while darkness of the soul lurked everywhere.

Though, as indicated in the Preface, I had toyed for some time with the idea of writing the story of my war against the US Army from within its ranks, one person must be credited with encouraging me to the point of actually undertaking the project. This is Litsa Binder, a peace and social justice advocate I "met" via the Internet when she responded passionately to a group email in support of Palestinian human rights. At time of publication of this book, she and I have yet to meet in person, a situation I hope to rectify. Litsa was also the first person to read the early draft of this memoir in its entirety. I also am grateful to Dee Knight—author of the memoir From Resister to Revolutionary—and Terry Klug for being ensuing early readers. Jim "Frandsen" read **CHAPTER X** and refreshed my memory on some details of our time together at Fort Ord and other areas in California.

Special thanks go to Tom Paxton and 'Country Joe' McDonald for permission to reproduce some of their song lyrics free of charge. I'm grateful to Mike Hastie, US Army medic who was deployed to Vietnam, for use of his photo of the helicopter on the back cover of this book. I hope Mike succeeds in getting a book of his own published. Thanks also go to Fyr Drak Fabrications for setting up the graphics for the covers of this book.

Due to my own financial condition, this book would not have come into physical existence without the help of the backers of my fundraising campaign on the Kickstarter website. I am extremely grateful to all of you, especially you who went "above and beyond the call of duty" on the book's behalf.

Notes on Quoting Song Lyrics

The "received wisdom" in the author community is that one should not directly quote even a single line of song lyrics without seeking permission from the copyright owner of said lyrics. My real-world efforts to follow this advice led largely to disappointment and frustration in the extreme.

The Internet is practically awash in websites that offer full sets of lyrics to popular, and even not very popular, songs. Aside from lyrics often being misquoted, the larger issue is that I very rarely find a statement that these lyrics are reproduced with anyone's official permission. Another layer to the situation is that, once upon a time, in the age of the LP record, song lyrics were sometimes printed on the back of the cardboard record jacket for all the world to see. Yes, the sacred words could be read in a retail shop, even by someone not planning to purchase the product. Even some of Bob Dylan's song lyrics were displayed this way early in his career. Further, a music lover could jot down the lyrics in the privacy of her own kitchen, after repeat listenings to a song over radio airwaves. So how did song lyrics become so privileged that the threat of a lawsuit could be wielded by record companies against someone publicly reproducing the words in print?

Federal Law, 17USC107 specifically, addresses the rights of copyright owners to protect their intellectual property. The law does, it so happens, allow for limited direct quoting of copyrighted works—this is called the Fair Use Doctrine—for purposes of offering critical reviews of the works in question, or incorporation in scholarly studies of a given subject. This is how knowledge is advanced, after all, building on the work of our predecessors. The wording is somewhat vague, it's true, allowing for legal wrangling in the courts. But Federal statutes do **not** explicitly exempt song lyrics from being subject to direct quotation; what they decline to spell out is where exactly the line is to be drawn on how much of a song's lyrics may legally be reproduced.

In my due diligence efforts to gain permission to reproduce lyrics in this book, I encountered the following problems: 1.) that wonderful source of all knowledge on all subjects, the Internet, cannot be relied on to indicate the actual, current ownership of some sets of lyrics. Furthermore, ownership changes hands not infrequently in corporate mergers; 2.) amazingly, in this day and age, some copyright owners that are listed do not offer online inquiry options. I had to "snail-mail" a half-dozen or more inquiries to music publishing companies, none of which provided the courtesy of a reply. I don't feel that the fact that this was occurring during the Covid-19 virus pandemic adequately explains the situation. Shouldn't <u>someone</u> have been "minding the shop"?; 3.) in most cases where I <u>was</u> able to communicate with copyright owners, the prices asked for use of lyrics were beyond my budget. The late Phil Ochs wrote some of the hardest hitting songs of social commentary of the 1960s/1970s. But a $300 fee (minimum) to quote from any given song? No way! For this reason, though this memoir mentions Phil frequently, I was unable to quote significantly from his work. This applies to other songwriters from whom I really wanted to quote as well.

It is hardly news among musicians that the Music Industry has a sordid history of cheating songwriters and recording artists of royalties that should have been due them. Though the situation has improved over the decades, we may say that **Greed** has ruled that industry from the time that recorded music became technologically able to be made available to the masses. In every instance in this book that I have quoted from, or referenced the work of, a songwriter, it is with admiration for their work, and the hope that readers will make an effort to explore for themselves the work of these musicians. Maybe the copyright owners should be paying me! Where I have quoted actual lyrics without official permission, I assert that this is my right under Fair Use principles. This author respects the intellectual property rights of others, and hopes my own will be likewise respected. Should any entity wish to pursue legal action against me, I vow to fight that entity all the way to the Supreme Court of the United States if necessary.

More About The Author

GREGORY LAXER leads a reclusive life in retirement, and states he is perfectly content with that arrangement. Notwithstanding his severe grievances against the human race, he occasionally tolerates individual people. His keen loves, other than reading and learning about the greater Universe, are movies and music. The author ran two marathons in each of the years 1978 and 1979. For three decades he was a volunteer at noncommercial radio stations, broadcasting Jazz and/or working behind the scenes, and helped produce a dozen Jazz CDs in the 1990s. His ideal automobile to own would be an Emerald Green 1933/34 Ford coupe finished with 27 hand-rubbed coats of lacquer, retrofitted to be an electric vehicle.

While putting the finishing touches on this memoir, Mr. Laxer started writing two novels and reports he finds working in the realm of fiction quite enjoyable. He anticipates the first novel completed will be a savage satire of the Music Industry. Laxer says, with completely straight face, that he harbors a secret desire to sing bass parts in a sea chanty and/or Doo-Wop group. Failing that, he says he will settle for an end to militarism and the unjustified wars to which it gives birth.

* * *

At time of publication of this book, the author's commentary on current events, as well as a wide range of other topics, may be found at *www.gregorylaxer.com*